HUMAN RIGHTS AND LEGAL JUDGMENTS

Human rights can be defined as the basic fundamental rights inherent to all human beings in any society. How these rights are made available and protected in individual countries is an area of much study and debate. Focusing on the significance of human rights in American law and politics, this book seeks to understand when, where, and how American law recognizes and responds to claims made in the name of human rights. How are they used by social movements as they advance rights claims? When are human rights claims accommodated and resisted? Do particular kinds of human rights claims have greater resonance domestically than others? What cultural and psychological factors impede the development of a human rights culture in the United States? This is an exciting and engaging volume that will appeal to a broad range of scholars, practitioners, and students interested in the study of human rights.

Austin Sarat is William Nelson Cromwell professor of Jurisprudence and Political Science at Amherst College. He is author or editor of over ninety books in the fields of law and political science. His book *When Government Breaks the Law: Prosecuting the Bush Administration* (2010) was named one of the best books of 2010 by the *Huffington Post*.

Human Rights and Legal Judgments

THE AMERICAN STORY

Edited by

AUSTIN SARAT

Amherst College

CAMBRIDGE
UNIVERSITY PRESS

University Printing House, Cambridge CB2 8BS, United Kingdom

One Liberty Plaza, 20th Floor, New York, NY 10006, USA

477 Williamstown Road, Port Melbourne, VIC 3207, Australia

4843/24, 2nd Floor, Ansari Road, Daryaganj, Delhi - 110002, India

79 Anson Road, #06-04/06, Singapore 079906

Cambridge University Press is part of the University of Cambridge.

It furthers the University's mission by disseminating knowledge in the pursuit of education, learning and research at the highest international levels of excellence.

www.cambridge.org
Information on this title: www.cambridge.org/9781107198302
DOI: 10.1017/9781108182287

© Cambridge University Press 2017

This publication is in copyright. Subject to statutory exception and to the provisions of relevant collective licensing agreements, no reproduction of any part may take place without the written permission of Cambridge University Press.

First published 2017

Printed in the United States of America by Sheridan Books, Inc.

A catalogue record for this publication is available from the British Library

ISBN 978-1-107-19830-2 Hardback

Cambridge University Press has no responsibility for the persistence or accuracy of URLs for external or third-party internet websites referred to in this publication, and does not guarantee that any content on such websites is, or will remain, accurate or appropriate.

To Ben, with love

Contents

List of Contributors		*page* ix
Acknowledgments		xi
	Introduction: Human Rights in American Law and Politics Austin Sarat	1
1	Human Rights, Solitary Confinement, and Youth Justice in the United States Cynthia Soohoo	12
2	The Story of Environmental Justice and Race in the United States: International Human Rights and Equal Environmental Protection Erika R. George	46
3	Incorporation, Federalism, and International Human Rights David Sloss	76
4	Why Do International Human Rights Matter in American Decision Making? Stephen A. Simon	100
	Afterword: Instrumental Human Rights William S. Brewbaker III	131
Index		139

Contributors

William S. Brewbaker III is William Alfred Rose Professor of Law, University of Alabama.

Erika R. George is Professor, College of Law, University of Utah.

Austin Sarat is Associate Dean of the Faculty and William Nelson Cromwell Professor of Jurisprudence and Political Science, Amherst College, and Hugo L. Black Visiting Senior Scholar, University of Alabama School of Law.

Stephen A. Simon is Associate Professor of Political Science and Philosophy, Politics, Economics, and Law, University of Richmond.

David Sloss is Professor, University of Santa Clara School of Law.

Cynthia Soohoo is Director of the Human Rights and Gender Justice (HRGJ) Clinic, CUNY Law School, and Board Chair of the US Human Rights Network (USHRN). Through the HRGJ Clinic and the USHRN, she has been involved in human rights advocacy efforts to challenge the criminalization of youth in the United States.

Acknowledgments

This volume is the product of a symposium held at the University of Alabama School of Law on September 23, 2016. I want to thank the colleagues, students, and staff who helped make it such a successful event. I am grateful for the financial support of the University of Alabama Law School Foundation and for the able research assistance of John Malague, Steven Reynolds, and David Yang.

Introduction: Human Rights in American Law and Politics

Austin Sarat

We respect the religious, social, and cultural characteristics that make each country unique. But we cannot let cultural relativism become the last refuge of repression.
  – Warren Christopher, former secretary of state, 1993 address to the World Conference on Human Rights

In 2008, just before his inauguration as president, Barack Obama issued a clarion call in which he urged this nation to fully embrace what he saw as its human rights heritage.[1] "The United States," Obama said, "was founded on the idea that all people are endowed with inalienable rights, and that principle has allowed us to work to perfect our union at home while standing as a beacon of hope to the world. Today," he went on, "that principle is embodied in agreements Americans helped forge – the Universal Declaration of Human Rights, the Geneva Conventions, and treaties against torture and genocide – and it unites us with people from every country and culture."[2]

"When the United States stands up for human rights," Obama continued,

> by example at home and by effort abroad, we align ourselves with men and women around the world who struggle for the right to speak their minds, to choose their leaders, and to be treated with dignity and respect. We also strengthen our security and well-being, because the abuse of human rights can feed many of the global dangers that we confront – from armed conflict and humanitarian crises, to corruption and the spread of ideologies that promote hatred and violence.[3]

---

[1] "Obama Marks Human Rights Day," *Washington Post* (December 10, 2008), http://voices.washingtonpost.com/44/2008/12/obama-marks-human-rights-day.html, accessed November 10, 2016.
[2] Id.   [3] Id.

Statements aligning the United States with the project of strengthening human rights are a rather familiar part of American political rhetoric.[4] To offer one other example, former president Clinton invoked America's commitment to human rights during a trip to the People's Republic of China in 1998.[5] "I believe and the American people believe," President Clinton declared, "that freedom of speech, association and religion are, as recognized by the United Nations Charter, the right of people everywhere and should be protected by their governments."[6]

The next day, speaking to another audience in China, Clinton repeated his embrace of human rights.[7] "We are convinced that certain rights are universal," he said. "I believe that everywhere people aspire to be treated with dignity, to give voice to their opinions, to choose their own leaders, to associate with whom they wish, to worship how, when, and where they want. These are not American rights or European rights or developed-world rights. They are the birthrights of people everywhere."[8]

While American politicians and officials, like President Clinton, frequently treat human rights as a foreign policy tool, *Human Rights and Legal Judgments: The American Story* takes up the domestic life of human rights, following President Obama in asking whether America offers "an example at home" in the realm of human rights.[9] This book focuses on the significance of human rights in American law and politics. It recognizes that just as controversy has surrounded the appropriateness of using foreign law in constitutional adjudication, so too has it accompanied the use of human rights in domestic law. Thus, dissenting from a 1988 Supreme Court decision, Justice Scalia contended that "reliance upon Amnesty International's account of what it pronounces to be civilized standards of decency in other countries is totally inappropriate as a means of establishing the fundamental beliefs of this nation."[10]

Human Rights and Legal Judgments: The American Story seeks to understand when, where, and how American law recognizes and responds to claims made in the name of human rights. How are they used by social movements as they advance rights claims? When are human rights claims accommodated and resisted? Do particular kinds of human rights claims that have greater resonance domestically than others? What cultural and psychological factors impede the development of a human rights culture in the United States?

---

[4] Much of what follows is taken from "The Unsettled Status of Human Rights: An Introduction," in *Human Rights: Concepts, Contests, Contingencies*, ed. Austin Sarat and Thomas R. Kearns (Ann Arbor: University of Michigan Press, 2001).
[5] *New York Times*, June 28, 1998, 9.   [6] Id.
[7] President Clinton's Beijing University Speech, 1998, USC-US China Institute (June 29, 1998), http://voices.washingtonpost.com/44/2008/12/obama-marks-human-rights-day.html, accessed November 10, 2016.
[8] Id.
[9] See Michael Ignatieff, ed., *American Exceptionalism and Human Rights* (Princeton, NJ: Princeton University Press, 2005).
[10] See Thompson v. Oklahoma, 487 US 815, 868 n. 4.

Today the language of human rights, if not human rights themselves, is nearly universal.[11] Governments everywhere claim to believe in and respect the dignity of their citizens, even if they do not endorse the brand of human rights to which President Clinton would have them adhere.[12] This is not to say that everyone agrees on the meaning of human rights or what they entail. This is surely not the case.[13] And it is surely not the case in the United States.

Here our legal and constitutional traditions substitute for a robust human rights culture. All too often, we think about legal rights for ourselves and human rights for others. Generally we recognize human rights only insofar as they have been codified in binding legal agreements.[14] As Morton Horowitz puts it, "few legal writers have believed that it was appropriate for higher law directly to trump positive law, and the Constitution has been more or less consistently understood as a form of super-positive law enacted by the sovereign people."[15]

Throughout recent American history our embrace of human rights has been variable and contingent. Conflict within the United States about the relevance of human rights to domestic racial, economic, and other injustices was particularly exacerbated by the mid-twentieth-century politics of the Cold War.[16] Thus the Truman administration insisted on breaking the Covenant on Human Rights in two, separating political and civil rights from economic and social rights which were

---

[11] "International human rights," David Weissbrodt claims, "is the world's first universal ideology." See "Human Rights: An Historical Perspective," in *Human Rights*, ed. P. Davies (London: Routledge, 1988). For a different perspective, see Rhoda Howard, "Dignity, Community, and Human Rights," in *Human Rights in Cross-Cultural Perspectives: A Quest for Consensus*, ed. Abdullahi A. An-Na'im (Philadelphia: University of Pennsylvania Press, 1992). Howard argues that "most known human societies did not and do not have conceptions of human rights" (80).

[12] "We are witnessing an unequivocal process of universalization of the concern for human dignity." Fernando Teson, "International Human Rights and Cultural Relativism," 25 *Virginia Journal of International Law* (1985): 869. "People the world over," Parekh argues, "have frequently appealed to these principles in their struggles against repressive governments. For their part the latter have almost invariably preferred to deny the existence of unacceptable practices rather than seek shelter behind relativism and cultural autonomy. In their own different ways both parties are thus beginning to accept the principles as the basis of good government, conferring on them the moral authority they otherwise cannot have." See Bhiku Parekh, "The Cultural Particularity of Liberal Democracy," in *Prospects for Democracy*, ed. David Held (Stanford, CA: Stanford University Press, 1993), 174. Donnelly contends that while concern for human dignity is central to non-Western cultural traditions, human rights are quite foreign to them. See Jack Donnelly, "Human Rights and Human Dignity: An Analytic Critique of Non-Western Conceptions of Human Rights," *American Political Science Review* 76 (1982): 303. See also Bilhari Kausikan, "Asia's Different Standard," 92 *Foreign Policy* (1993): 24.

[13] For a discussion of this diversity, see Abdullahi A. An-Na'im, "Islamic Law, International Relations, and Human Rights: Challenge and Response," 20 *Cornell International Law Journal* (1987): 335.

[14] Stephen A. Simon, *The US Supreme Court and the Domestic Force of International Human Rights Law* (Boston: Lexington Books, 2016).

[15] Morton Horwitz, *The Transformation of American Law, 1870–1960* (New York: Oxford University Press, 1992), 140.

[16] David L. Cingranelli and David Richards, "Respect for Human Rights after the End of the Cold War," 12 *Journal of Peace Research* (September 1999): 511.

perceived as communistic.[17] It also insisted on inserting a provision which meant that although the federal government might sign and ratify the treaty, no state government in our federal system would be bound by its tenets.[18] Similarly, in the 1950s, Republican senator John W. Bricker of Ohio, fearing that international human rights treaties, particularly the Genocide Convention, would mandate federal government to outlaw and prosecute lynching, proposed a constitutional amendment saying that treaties and executive agreements would not be binding unless they were ratified by state legislatures.[19]

Today, here as elsewhere, disagreements arise over particular human rights claims. And even where there is agreement in principle, human rights may not be respected in practice. No matter how they are defined, human rights are variably realized; indeed, as America's post-9/11 history suggests, they are regularly violated even when governments proclaim their adherence to human rights ideals. Thus, after 9/11, the Bush Justice Department developed novel legal theories to work around America's legal obligations under UN Conventions.[20]

Despite their controversial status in American law and politics, appeals to human rights, as a way of understanding and regulating the behavior of nations toward their people, are as prevalent as they have ever been. "The past few decades," Richard Wilson notes, "have witnessed the inexorable rise of the application of international human rights law as well as the extension of a wider public discourse on human rights, to the point where human rights could be seen as one of the most globalized political values of our times."[21] This development is a result of the convergence of many factors, but perhaps none is more important than the demise of communism and the ascendance of capitalism and liberal democracy throughout the world.

Democracy has replaced Marxism as what Amrita Basu recently called "the hegemonic ideology of social change."[22] With the fall of communism and the spread of democratization in Africa, Asia, and Latin America, human rights have taken on new salience in political struggles both in those places and in the United States. In the years since the end of World War II, Glendon argues,

---

[17] "Human Rights – The UN Declaration of Human Rights and President Harry Truman," in *Encyclopedia of the New American Nation*, www.americanforeignrelations.com/E-N/Human-Rights-The-un-declaration-of-human-rights-and-president-harry-truman.html, accessed November 12, 2016.

[18] Id.

[19] Justin Raimondo, "The Bricker Amendment," www.antiwar.com/essays/bricker.html, accessed November 11, 2016. Also Arthur Dean, "The Bricker Amendment and Authority over Foreign Affairs," 56 *Foreign Affairs* (October 1953), www.foreignaffairs.com/articles/united-states/1953-10-01/bricker-amendment-and-authority-over-foreign-affairs, accessed November 11, 2016.

[20] Frederick A. O. Schwarz Jr. and Aziz Z. Huq, *Unchecked and Unbalanced: Presidential Power in a Time of Terror* (New York: New Press, 2013).

[21] Richard Wilson, "Human Rights, Culture, and Context: An Introduction," in *Human Rights, Culture and Context*, ed. Richard Wilson (London: Pluto Press, 1996), 1.

[22] Amrita Basu, "Social Movements, Globalization, and Human Rights: Perspectives from Asia," typescript, 1997, 8.

rights discourse has spread throughout the world. At the transnational level, human rights were enshrined in a variety of covenants and declarations, notably the United Nations Universal Declaration of Human Rights... At the same time, enumerated rights, backed up by some form of judicial review, were added to several national constitutions... Nor was the rush to rights confined to 'liberal' or 'democratic' societies. American rights talk is now but one dialect in a universal language of rights.[23]

Commentators worry that reliance on human rights in political struggles and by political movements outside the United States invites a kind of legal imperialism, in which Western ideas and institutions take on an unhealthy prominence.[24] At home, critics see the pressure to embrace human rights, over and above legal and constitutional rights, as weakening American sovereignty and as a symptom of an unhealthy embrace of globalization.[25]

The globalization about which they worry is, of course, by no means a new phenomenon; what is new is its pace and intensification.[26] Globalization always involves the redistribution of power "outward" from the state and inward from beyond national boundaries. This is what Anthony Giddens calls the "intensification of worldwide social relations which link distant localities in such a way that local happenings are shaped by events occurring many miles away and vice versa."[27] Both in the United States and abroad, globalization is altering the context in which discussions of human rights occur and is, at the same time, reshaping what it means to talk about those rights. All of these developments transform patterns of power within states, open up new possibilities of influence for forces seeking social change, and bring on new challenges.

Yet, at the very moment when possibilities for realizing human rights seem particularly promising, one encounters questions about the fit between human rights and respect for cultural difference and the integrity of cultural traditions; worries about whether rights are, in truth, culture specific; and doubts about the effectiveness of

---

[23] Mary Ann Glendon, *Rights Talk: The Impoverishment of Political Discourse* (New York: Free Press, 1991), 7.
[24] Adamantia Pollis and Peter Schwab, "Human Rights: A Western Construct with Limited Applicability," in *Human Rights: Cultural and Ideological Perspectives*, ed. Adamantia Pollis and Peter Schwab (New York: Praeger, 1979).
[25] See "Essay: The Human Rights Agenda versus National Sovereignty," Freedom House (2001), https://freedomhouse.org/report/freedom-world-2001/essay-human-rights-agenda-versus-national-sovereignty, accessed November 13, 2016.
[26] As Appadurai notes, "today's world involves interactions of a new order and intensity... With the advent of the steamship, the automobile, the airplane, the camera, the computer and the telephone, we have entered into an altogether new condition of neighborliness, even with those most distant from ourselves." Arjun Appadurai, "Disjuncture and Difference in the Global Cultural Economy," *Public Culture* 2 (1990): 1, 2.
[27] Anthony Giddens, *The Consequences of Modernity* (Stanford, CA: Stanford University Press, 1990), 64.

human rights in restraining the power of nations, like the United States, even when they proclaim their fidelity to human rights norms.[28]

Like all rights, human rights authorize action and yet undermine authority's claims. They are, by definition, mandatory claims, yet they are fecund with interpretive possibilities. They both constitute us as subjects and provide a language through which we can resist that constitution and forge new identities.

For the student of American law and politics, engaging with the theory and practice of human rights is an especially inviting arena. Here with unusual vividness and force, important debates are being played out, debates in epistemology and ethics, in hermeneutics and social theory. One turns to the subject of human rights to learn about the genealogy of law and its association with the production and reproduction of national power, about the meaning of culture and cultural variation as well as its significance for law, about rhetorical practices and political contests and the place of rights in those practices and contests, about globalization and its significance, and about the way legal meanings are made and remade through the increasing, and increasingly unpredictable, play of local–global linkages. Students of American law and politics turn to human rights to understand the practices of social movements and of our judicial and political institutions.

We know that human rights politics may occur as social movements seek change in the policies of domestic regimes. Thus, in 1850, Frederick Douglass invoked the language of human rights in his "Inhumanity of Slavery":

> Slavery is wicked, in that it contravenes the laws of eternal justice, and tramples in the dust all the humane and heavenly precepts of the New Testament... The presence of slavery may be explained by – as it is the explanation of – the mobocratic violence which lately disgraced New York, and which still more recently disgraced the city of Boston. These violent demonstrations, these outrageous invasions of human rights, faintly indicate the presence and power of slavery here.[29]

Almost a century later, in 1947, the NAACP petitioned the United Nations (UN) Commission on Human Rights to investigate conditions under which African Americans lived in the United States.[30]

Today, social movements use human rights claims to mobilize alliances within countries and across national borders.[31] Sometimes those claims are resisted by

---

[28] Richard Falk, "Cultural Foundations for the International Protection of Human Rights," in *Human Rights in Cross-Cultural Perspectives: A Quest for Consensus*, ed. Abdullahi Ahmen An-Na'im (Philadelphia: University of Pennsylvania Press, 1992), 46.

[29] Frederick Douglass, "Inhumanity of Slavery" (1850), http://etc.usf.edu/lit2go/45/my-bondage-and-my-freedom/1515/inhumanity-of-slavery-extract-from-a-lecture-on-slavery-at-rochester-december-8-1850/, accessed November 13, 2016.

[30] Cynthia Soohoo, Catherine Albisa, and Martha Davis, eds., *Bringing Human Rights Home: A History of Human Rights in the United States* (Philadelphia: University of Pennsylvania Press, 2007), Chapter 3.

[31] See Neil Stammers, "Social Movements and the Social Construction of Human Rights," 21 *Human Rights Quarterly* (1999): 980.

coalitions of national governments working in and through international organizations; sometimes movements are able to use those organizations to press their claims.

In this context we need to rethink the traditional vocabularies of human rights: what is the meaning of self-determination? Of human dignity? Of choice for individuals and for cultures? We need to reconfigure the debate about universalism/relativism that has been at its core by moving away from an understanding of human rights which repeatedly juxtaposes the plurality of cultures and the alleged universal validity of moral norms. As Appadurai puts it, "the central feature of global culture today is the politics of the mutual effort of sameness and difference to cannibalize one another and thus to proclaim their successful hijacking of the twin Enlightenment ideas of the triumphantly universal and the resiliently particular."[32]

The contributions to *Human Rights and Legal Judgments: The American Story* illustrate this tension between the universal and the particular in human rights discourse in the United States. They offer case studies to illuminate the way human rights arguments are mobilized by social movements and operate as background norms in some areas of Supreme Court doctrine. They offer arguments about where, when, and how human rights have, and should have, authority in the American political and legal system and offer ideas about what is needed to increase their salience in the United States. Throughout, they help us understand America's ambivalent embrace of human rights.

Chapter 1, by Cynthia Soohoo, explores human rights aspects of the treatment of youth in conflict with the law.[33] She discusses challenges faced by human rights activists and how those challenges relate to efforts to protect youth accused and convicted of crimes. She notes that over the last 15 years, US activists working on a range of domestic issues – from police violence and mass criminalization to reproductive rights to access to water – have incorporated human rights claims into their work. Gone are the days when human rights were thought only to apply to distant countries controlled by brutal despots. Instead, Americans, Soohoo contends, have become increasingly aware of the gap between human rights and the protections offered by our Constitution and legal and political systems.

The United States does not, Soohoo reminds us, have a definitive human rights charter, leaving decisions about rights subject to the fluid dynamics of American politics. Where constitutional protections exist, human rights rhetoric is considered less effective and is rarely invoked. Advocacy for human rights norms becomes necessary when such norms are not protected by a specific constitutional provision.

This is the case with youth rights. The 1989 Convention on the Rights of the Child (CRC) gave momentum to the recognition of youth as rights holders. The United States, however, has not ratified the CRC. As a result, 200,000 youth are tried as adults each year. Treating children like adults in the criminal justice system, using

---

[32] Appadurai, "Disjuncture and Difference in the Global Cultural Economy," 17.
[33] What follows is drawn from material prepared by John Malague for inclusion in this book.

adult jails, adult prison, adult sentencing guidelines, and adult prison disciplinary policy, makes children especially prone to psychological damage, physical abuse, and sexual assault. Soohoo examines how activists have gone about challenging these phenomena.

She outlines four criteria for activism efforts to be successful. There must be (1) general acceptance of the norm and recognition of its relevance to the local context and advocacy target, (2) documentation and publication of the rights violation, (3) passion provoked by the issue, and (4) international standards able to provide concrete bright line rules and relatively direct policy solutions.

While the right of the child to special judicial protection is not included in the Constitution, American law is no stranger to differential treatment of minors. Public policy has long been guided by the presumption of an obligation to care for and protect children. This obligation seems to be suspended in criminal justice. The CRC provisions, along with bans on solitary for juvenile prisoners that exist in other countries, could potentially reverse this trend. To do this would require a recognition of those norms in American law.

Soohoo notes that state and local governments are the primary targets for rights activism designed to protect youth since they control prisons and jails. Corrections officials also have discretion in prison management (e.g., if youth are placed into solitary, where they are housed). There is growing international recognition that more than 15 days of solitary confinement constitutes torture or cruel, inhuman, or degrading treatment and that it should be prohibited for vulnerable populations. American activists have provided information to international bodies, which have expressed concern over American use of solitary.

Efforts to limit solitary confinement for youth have gained some traction. Senate commissions have condemned the use of solitary, and President Obama has announced that federal prisons will no longer use it for juveniles. Obama's announcement implicitly invoked human rights language.

Soohoo concludes that for human rights activism to be successful, it must resonate with the public as a message and inspire the action of state actors.

Chapter 2, by Erika R. George, considers the role of human rights in another social movement, the movement for environmental justice in the United States. It argues that environmental injustice remains a significant problem in the United States and that exposure to environmental contaminants is segregated along lines of race and class. Communities of color in the United States have complained against polluting industries, opposed the permitting of new industry projects, and called for investigations. Yet legal doctrines requiring proof of intentional discrimination render it increasingly difficult to resolve claims of environmental racism in court.

Activism around environmental racism, George argues, was first found in the black faith community. The Universal Church of Christ released a report in 1987 attempting to document the common attributes of those who live in polluted areas.

Poverty, limited mobility, and lack of political clout were among these, but race was the most definitive predictor. Many disagreed with this assessment, claiming instead that the causal factor is economic status and that race is an unfortunate companion to poverty. In contrast, George identifies three things that support claims of environmental racism: disparate siting of hazardous facilities, disparate enforcement of environmental protection under existing laws, and disparate efforts at remediation.

George notes that the international community seems receptive to the message of environmental justice advocates. A growing body of international declarations is providing a foundation for environmental rights. The 1972 Stockholm Declaration on the Human Environment was the first to see a relationship between environmental purity and the protection of human rights. The 1989 Hague Declaration included an obligation of states to protect the environment. Regional institutions have also addressed the issue. The Special Rapporteur on Human Rights and the Environment advocated for an express right to a healthy environment. The Human Rights Council's Independent Expert found that states have obligations to assess the impact of environmental realities on human rights and to provide access to effective remedies.

While the international community has taken a strong stance on behalf of environmental protection, those seeking redress of environmental racism have met seemingly insurmountable obstacles in American jurisprudence. The landmark case *Washington v. Davis* held that a disparate impact alone is insufficient to prove discrimination and that racial motivation must be evident. Although the Court did allow that discriminatory intent can be *inferred* from a totality of relevant facts, environmental justice plaintiffs are often unable to establish a racist aim.

George suggests ways that international norms can be used to energize environmental racism activism in the United States. The United States, she notes, has ratified both the Covenant on Erasing Racial Discrimination (CERD) and the International Covenant on Civil and Political Rights (ICCPR), two treaties with the force of law. American courts have consistently refused to evaluate claims based on the ICCPR, and the United States claims that its domestic laws sufficiently comply with the CERD. That said, a 2016 search of case law found the ICCPR cited 44 times, and the CERD 49.

The Committee on Erasing Racial Discrimination (CERD Committee) has recently taken on environmental justice issues. It has found various things, including the siting of waste facilities, that violate the CERD and recommended measures to ensure the right to health in response to environmental pollution. Given this willingness to recognize and condemn the effects of environmental injustice without regard for provable intent, George concludes that American law's stance on environmental justice is directly at odds with its foreign commitments.

Chapter 3 moves us from a consideration of human rights and social movements to an examination of the significance of human rights in one arena of Supreme Court doctrine, namely, the effort to incorporate the Bill of Rights and apply its provisions to the states. David Sloss proposes what he calls a "human rights" model to explain incorporation and to justify protecting human rights while shifting considerable power from the federal courts to the state governments.

Sloss describes the parallel development of rights protection in both international treaties and federal law. The UN's Universal Declaration of Human Rights was adopted in 1948. Before that, in the United States, the separate states were expected to take responsibility for the protection of rights. By 1971, however, the federal government had begun to enforce many human rights norms against the states by selectively incorporating provisions of the Bill of Rights. Sloss argues that rights were made binding on the states if they are enumerated in the International Covenant on Civil and Political Rights.

By 1972, the list of rights that had been applied to the states via the Fourteenth Amendment closely resembled the civil and political rights enumerated in the Universal Declaration of Human Rights. Moreover, that resemblance is no accident. The Universal Declaration was based on a political morality that resonated deeply with most Americans. While Supreme Court justices did not cite the Declaration explicitly to support their views about which rights qualify as "fundamental," the Court's decisions in the incorporation cases generally conformed to the justices' intuitions as to which rights the American people thought were fundamental. The fact that the Universal Declaration was based on a moral framework that was widely shared among Americans at the time meant that the Court's incorporation decisions effectively brought the civil and political rights enumerated in the Universal Declaration of Human Rights into the Fourteenth Amendment.

Chapter 3 concludes by elaborating a normative argument for employing human rights theory in American law. Using international law, Sloss claims, better protects state sovereignty by freeing the states from uniformity in standards of rights compliance. European human rights courts afford individual nations a "margin of appreciation," which allows them to fashion their own standards for protecting human rights. The human rights theory that Sloss promotes would include a margin of appreciation for American states and would recognize that the Supreme Court does not have a monopoly on wisdom regarding complex policy problems.

Chapter 4, by Stephen A. Simon, takes up Sloss's interest in understanding the relevance of human rights in Supreme Court decision making. Simon argues that "human rights" function as an aspirational ideal, as a form of moral discourse. Moral discourse differs in important respects from legal discourse. Moral discourse operates according to what Simon calls a model of persuasion. Appeals to moral norms seek to influence others' behavior by altering their opinions. For moral norms "to work," Simon argues, we must achieve agreement on substantive principles.

Legal discourse, by contrast, operates according to a model of compliance. Appeals to legal norms seek to influence others' behavior by establishing that they are required to do (or not do) certain things, regardless of whether they agree. Legal norms do not depend on substantive agreement for their operation.

The American view of international norms, Simon contends, revolves around a fundamental tension in American politics, between the nation's ethical commitment to natural rights and its structural dedication to the principle of popular sovereignty. Simon examines judicial decisions concerning the germaneness of international law in American contexts and various ways in which international norms make an appearance in US courts. He asks to what extent justices think human rights declarations are a binding force and what justifications they have given when they ignored them.

In *Sanchez-Llamas v. Oregon*, for example, a foreign national sued to have his murder confession suppressed because he was not given the right to meet with a member of his nation's consulate, a right protected by the Vienna Convention on Consular Relations (VCCR). Writing for a majority of the Supreme Court, Chief Justice Roberts denied the practical power of the convention, insisting that it allows the administration of justice to occur within the confines of local law and requires no remedy in the form of suppression. Justice Breyer disagreed, wishing instead to instruct state courts to analyze the need for suppression as a form of remedy on a case-by-case basis. No justice felt that the Court should treat rulings of the International Court of Justice as conclusive. But, while Justice Roberts flatly rejected their authority in the American legal system, Breyer argued that their rulings could be instructive, since they are well positioned in the international community to promote harmony between nations.

Those opposed to considering international law and human rights norms are what Simon calls "sovereigntists." They want only the opinions of Americans, as expressed through legislative and executive action, to be the basis for American law. Following international law, whether in the sense of complying with the international bill of rights or by enforcing general moral or common law principles, gives political power to unelected judges and members of foreign states.

On the flip side are the "internationalists." They emphasize the importance of comporting with international law and the opportunities for fair treatment that conforming would afford. They fear that failing to enforce international law could weaken the rule of law for which the Constitution stands. Internationalists, perhaps most importantly, do not confine themselves to an all-or-nothing approach in dealing with international law. It can, they believe, be instructive without being conclusive, providing a view of interests that the United States shares with other nations.

This book concludes with an Afterword that draws together and assesses the common and contrasting empirical observations and normative arguments offered in the previous chapters. It elaborates a natural law approach to human rights and warns against what it sees as a dangerous and limiting instrumentalism in the way scholars, activists, and judges think about the applicability of human rights in the American context.

1

Human Rights, Solitary Confinement, and Youth Justice in the United States

Cynthia Soohoo[*]

Over the last 15 years, US activists working on a range of domestic issues – from police violence and mass criminalization to reproductive rights to access to water – have incorporated human rights claims into their work. Gone are the days when human rights were thought only to apply to distant countries controlled by brutal despots. Instead, Americans have become increasingly aware that a significant gap often exists between human rights standards and the protections offered by our Constitution and legal and political systems. But even as it becomes more commonplace to hear activists make human rights claims, the question remains, what impact do the claims have? When are they successful in contributing to changes in attitudes, laws, and policies?

Unlike countries that directly incorporate international law into their domestic legal systems, for the most part, the United States's human rights obligations cannot be directly enforced in US courts. The lack of a legally enforceable human rights charter or text leaves both the substantive rights and the forums and spaces to implement them up for grabs. Indeed, while Americans have a commitment to human rights, we often lack a common understanding of what is encompassed by the term. This can result in disputed and contested meanings. But the fluidity of the term also creates opportunities for social justice activists. US activists often seek to expand the public's understanding of what can be claimed as a right beyond the confines of rights formally recognized under US law. Discussing an issue as a human right can provoke the listener to consider the issue in a different way. Ultimately, if she is convinced that the claimed right has some fundamental character rooted in human dignity that requires universal respect, acceptance of the human rights claim can help drive law and policy reform.

In the United States (as in other countries), successful human rights claims can be leveraged in debates to change public attitudes on issues as long as they are

---

[*] The author is grateful to Katy Naples-Mitchell for her outstanding research and editing assistance.

accepted by American audiences as human rights. These claims may ultimately result in changes in laws, standards, and policies irrespective of whether they create legally binding obligations under international or domestic law. These claims are strengthened and legitimized when the international human rights community recognizes and prioritizes the claims as important human rights issues, but ultimately their success relies upon whether they resonate with Americans as human rights issues and inspire activism for change. Successful human rights advocacy must make violations visible by telling the stories of people whose rights are violated. Often the public is unaware of the nature or extent of rights abuses, and when confronted with the facts, recognition that the issue is a human rights abuse quickly follows. Once an issue is recognized as a human rights abuse, international standards may be helpful in providing principled ways to address rights abuses based on the experience of the international community and human rights experts.

Given strong public commitment to the Constitution, generally, human rights claims are not invoked where strong constitutional protections exist. Instead, human rights claims are made in the United States in areas where we lack sufficient constitutional protections or to encourage more progressive interpretations of recognized constitutional rights. One area where we have seen increased human rights activism is in efforts to reform the criminal justice system. Current US laws and practices concerning the death penalty, extreme and mandatory sentencing, solitary confinement, and treatment of youth in conflict with the law are inconsistent with international human rights standards.[1] There is a long history of US human rights advocacy to end the death penalty,[2] both inside and outside the legal system.[3] Most recently, human rights arguments have supported US Supreme Court decisions prohibiting the juvenile death penalty[4] and significantly limiting the imposition of juvenile life-without-parole sentences.[5]

In addition to influencing judicial decisions, human rights advocacy can profoundly change the way that the public understands an issue outside the courtroom. Two areas where there has been increased human rights advocacy in the United

---

[1] Deborah LaBelle, *Criminal Justice and Human Rights in the United States* (Atlanta, GA: US Human Rights Network, 2013), www.ushrnetwork.org/sites/ushrnetwork.org/files/criminal_justice_framing_paper_-_ushrn.pdf.

[2] Diann Yvonne Rust-Tierney, "The United States Government and the Death Penalty," *American Journal of Criminal Law* 22 (1994): 260; Warren Allmand et al., "Human Rights and Human Wrongs: Is the United States Death Penalty System Inconsistent with International Human Rights Law?," *Fordham Law Review* 67 (1999): 2793; Richard C. Dieter, *The Death Penalty and Human Rights: US Death Penalty and International Law* (Washington, DC: Death Penalty Information Center, 2002), www.deathpenaltyinfo.org/files/pdf/Oxfordpaper.pdf.

[3] Sandra Babcock, "Human Rights Advocacy in United States Capital Cases," in *Bringing Human Rights Home*, vol. III, ed. Cynthia Soohoo, Catherine Albisa, and Martha F. Davis (London: Praeger, 2008), 91–120.

[4] Roper v. Simmons, 543 US 551, 576–78 (2005).

[5] Graham v. Florida, 560 US 48 (2010); Miller v. Alabama, 132 S. Ct. 2455 (2012); Montgomery v. Louisiana, 136 S. Ct. 718 (2016).

States are in challenges to the use of solitary confinement and to the practice of trying and incarcerating youth (individuals under age 18 years) in the adult criminal justice system. In New York and in many other states, work around the second issue is known as "raise the age." This chapter examines advocacy efforts around these two issues, with a particular focus on reform efforts in New York City and New York State, and considers the ways in which human rights activism and popular understandings of rights influence law and policy making.

While there has been considerable progress on both issues, human rights claims have had more impact on efforts to reform solitary confinement. This article considers the factors influencing when issues are accepted as human rights issues in the United States and whether human rights acceptance impacts law and policy. It also analyzes the roles that activists and officials at different levels of government can play in the process. Part I discusses theories of successful human rights advocacy in the United States. It considers the factors that influence whether an issue will be accepted as a human right in the United States and result in changes in law and policies. It also looks at the roles that activists and government officials play and the impact of federalism. Part II describes human rights advocacy around solitary confinement in the United States, which has enjoyed considerable success, especially around the prohibition of solitary confinement of youth. Part III looks at reform efforts around raise the age. These efforts have also enjoyed success. However, advocates did not embrace or widely use human rights claims.

I. THEORIES ON SUCCESSFUL HUMAN RIGHTS ADVOCACY IN THE UNITED STATES

Around the world, and especially in countries like the United States, where there is weak formal incorporation of human rights obligations into domestic law, human rights compliance relies upon the work of committed activists to push for recognition and prioritization of human rights issues. Over time, successful human rights advocacy can lead to societal acceptance of human rights norms that result in changes in law and policy.[6] In the United States and other countries, activists may work in concert with government officials who share a common commitment to human rights. Sometimes these officials may have the power to bring about significant changes in law and policy. Other times, they, like activists, must convince their colleagues in government to recognize and prioritize issues as human rights. For instance, a state legislator who favors legislation to prohibit solitary confinement of youth because it violates human rights must convince a majority of his peers in order to pass the

---

[6] Thomas Risse, Stephen C. Ropp, and Kathryn Sikkink, *The Power of Human Rights: International Norms and Domestic Change* (Cambridge: Cambridge University Press, 1999); Judith Resnik, "Law's Migration: American Exceptionalism, Silent Dialogues, and Federalism's Multiple Ports of Entry," *Yale Law Journal* 115 (2006): 1564.

law. Similarly, an official at the federal Office of Juvenile Justice and Delinquency Prevention may recognize that trying youth as adults violates human rights standards and is bad policy but must influence state government officials in order to change state laws. This section considers the factors that influence successful human rights claims and advocacy in the United States. It then examines the different actors involved and the impact of federalism.

A. *Factors That Influence Successful Human Rights Advocacy*

Anthropologist Sally Merry writes, "If human rights ideas are to have an impact, they need to become part of the consciousness of ordinary people around the world."[7] In examining the impact of human rights, political scientists have articulated "constructivist theories," which examine the role that norms and principled ideas have on international behavior. According to Hans Peter Schmitz and Kathryn Sikkink, human rights norms gain support because they "resonate with basic ideas of human dignity shared in many cultures around the world."[8] While all successful human rights claims must have a universal normative core, constructivist theories recognize the role that norm entrepreneurs play in disseminating human rights ideas and the role that international organizations play in validating and promoting compliance with international human rights norms.[9]

Building on constructivist theories that look at how human rights norms are developed at the international and global level and Professor Merry's work analyzing how human rights ideas become part of local social movements and legal consciousness, this chapter considers the factors that influence US audiences to recognize an issue as a human right and for that recognition to influence law and policy. In order for a human rights claim to have impact in the United States, there must be (1) widespread local acceptance of the human rights norm and (2) recognition of the norm's application and relevance to the local context and issue, and (3) the issue must inspire the public or key decision makers to push for change. While each of these factors is influenced by preexisting local attitudes toward an issue, activists and government officials can play important roles in changing attitudes and mobilizing for change. I analyze these three factors in turn.

---

[7] Sally Engle Merry, *Human Rights and Gender Violence: Translating International Law into Local Justice* (Chicago: University of Chicago Press, 2006), 3.
[8] Hans Peter Schmitz and Kathryn Sikkink, "International Human Rights," in *Handbook of International Relations*, ed. Walter Carlsnaes, Thomas Risse, and Beth A. Simmons (London: Sage, 2013).
[9] Scholars have recognized that major human rights nongovernmental organizations (NGOs) can both play the role of norm entrepreneur and human rights gatekeeper along with international organizations. Clifford Bobb, "Introduction: Fighting for New Rights," in *The International Struggle for New Human Rights*, ed. Clifford Bobb (Philadelphia: University of Pennsylvania Press, 2009); Catherine Powell, "Lifting Our Veil of Ignorance: Culture, Constitutionalism, and Women's Human Rights in Post–September 11 America," *Hastings Law Journal* 57 (2005): 377–78.

In order for a human rights claim to be successful in the United States, it must be viewed as a legitimate human rights issue and must have some connection to broader values held by local communities. To have an impact, human rights advocacy must walk a fine line. Activists seek to use human rights to provoke a change in attitudes around an issue, but they will not be successful if their claim does not have some inherent resonance with their communities. As Professor Merry states, "rights need to be presented in local cultural terms in order to be persuasive, but they must challenge existing relations of power in order to be effective."[10] For example, US human rights advocacy around solitary confinement sought to build public recognition that, under some conditions, solitary confinement can constitute torture. Although there is debate in the United States about the specific practices that constitute torture, there is general acceptance of torture as a human rights violation.[11] As discussed below, this may have made human rights acceptance easier than advocacy around raising the age because there is no general acceptance that all youth have an unwaivable right to special protection or treatment.

In addition to strong acceptance of human rights norms, there must be an understanding that the recognized human right applies to the issue that is the subject of the advocacy campaign. Human rights are often expressed in vague, generalized terms. For instance, while there is almost universal agreement that torture is prohibited, there is often substantial disagreement as to what behavior rises to the level of torture. International human rights bodies and experts can play an important authoritative role by building recognition that certain behaviors constitute violations of the norm – in our example, that under certain circumstances, solitary confinement is torture.

Even if human rights experts opine that a certain behavior violates human rights, the expert opinion must "ring true" to the public. In order to gain acceptance that a certain treatment of individuals violates human rights, telling the stories of victims is crucial. Indeed, sharing personal accounts explaining what it is like to be in solitary confinement and the effect that it has on people has been one of the most effective methods of convincing the public that solitary confinement can constitute torture.

Public recognition that an issue is a human rights violation alone will not necessarily lead to changes in law and policy. Indeed, human rights violations continue to occur around the world, but not every violation captures the public's attention or is prioritized. Although, as I discuss below, activists can play an important role

---

[10] Merry, *Human Rights and Gender Violence*, 5.
[11] Loren Siegel, Kate Stewart, and Nora Ferrell, *Human Rights in the US: Opinion Research with Advocates, Journalists, and the General Public* (Washington, DC: The Opportunity Agenda, 2007), 3, https://opportunityagenda.org/pdfs/HUMAN%20RIGHTS%20REPORT.PDF (finding in a national survey that 83% of Americans believe "freedom from torture or abuse by law enforcement" is a human right that should be upheld). But see Bruce Drake, "Americans' Views on Use of Torture in Fighting Terrorism Have Been Mixed," *PEW Research Center Fact Tank* (blog), December 9, 2014, www.pewresearch.org/fact-tank/2014/12/09/americans-views-on-use-of-torture-in-fighting-terrorism-have-been-mixed/ (finding that only 47% of those surveyed said torture could rarely or never be justified).

in actively articulating, publicizing, and promoting human rights claims,[12] certain types of claims are more successful in bringing about change. Margaret Keck and Kathryn Sikkink posit that successful human rights advocacy campaigns typically focus on issues involving bodily harm to vulnerable individuals – especially where there is a clear causal chain between the victim and the perpetrator. For instance, in the women's rights area, scholars have noted that violence against women was a more easily accepted and successful advocacy frame than a discrimination against women or women in development frame in part because the right to dignity, including the right to bodily integrity and protection from physical abuse, is a deeply held, transcultural value.[13] As a result, in the 1990s, violence against women emerged as the dominant frame for global recognition that women's rights are human rights. Alice Miller writes that the violence against women frame "succeeded primarily by following the form of the mainstream human rights paradigm of the time: a focus on bodily suffering from acts committed by the state" and also reinforced existing societal attitudes about women as vulnerable members of society in need of protection.[14] Miller notes that torture is the most recognized human rights violation, making it easier for the public to conceive of violence as a human rights issue, but that activists' focus on bodily harm reinforced a lack of attention to structural or systemic rights violations, remedies, and enabling conditions.[15]

Scholars have also suggested that human rights claims are more effective when there is an identifiable bad actor and a clear causal chain. It is more difficult to activate the public when a rights violation is the result of societal and structural inequalities.[16] In addition to the appeal of a simple narrative, addressing structural rights violations typically requires a more complex remedy, making it more difficult for activists to articulate and rally behind a demand.

B. *The Role of Activists and Government Officials in Translating Human Rights to the US Context*

Human rights ideas must be "translated into local terms and situated within local contexts of power and meaning" in order to resonate.[17] In the United States, activists, and often government officials, can play important roles in building acceptance of human rights norms, encouraging recognition that norms apply to local issues and building public attention and prioritization of these human right issues. It is also important to recognize that their influence flows in two directions. Activists and

---

[12] Margaret E. Keck and Kathryn Sikkink, *Activists beyond Borders: Advocacy Networks in International Politics* (Ithaca, NY: Cornell University Press, 1998), 174.
[13] Id. at 195.
[14] Alice M. Miller, "Sexuality, Violence against Women, and Human Rights: Women Make Demands and Ladies Get Protection," *Health and Human Rights* 7, no. 2 (2004): 21, 23.
[15] Id. at 27.   [16] Keck and Sikkink, *Activists beyond Borders*, 184.
[17] Merry, *Human Rights and Gender Violence*, 1.

government officials (usually federal, but increasingly state and city as well) serve as intermediaries between the local and international by importing international human rights standards into local contexts and helping to build and reshape global dialogue and understandings of rights based on their specific contexts.[18] US actors (as well as local actors around the world) play an important and necessary role by ensuring that human rights standards develop to reflect and respond to actual struggles faced by communities rather than reflecting abstract legal principles devoid of content.

Both US activists and government officials are increasingly helping to develop human rights standards in international forums. The US State Department has always been actively involved in developing international human rights standards. Recent scholarship documents the role that officials at all levels of government can play in disseminating human rights norms and promoting government compliance.[19] Increasingly, state and local officials have built their own formal and informal networks with counterparts in other countries. Many of these networks are active sites for educating government officials about human rights and sharing best practices to promote human rights.[20] This involvement (1) ensures that resulting international human rights standards reflect US experiences and (2) builds government and civil society familiarity with international standards.

US activists are also increasingly taking their issues to international forums, influencing the development of international standards, and encouraging United Nations (UN) human rights bodies and experts to scrutinize and criticize the United States for human rights violations. National civil rights organizations like the American Civil Liberties Union (ACLU), the Center for Constitutional Rights, the Center for Reproductive Rights, and the National Law Center for Homelessness and Poverty have incorporated human rights advocacy in their work for many years, but a growing number of local grassroots groups and campaigns have also begun advocating in international forums, including two New York–based coalitions, the Raise the Age Campaign and the Campaign for Alternatives to Isolated Confinement. The ability of local organizations and coalitions to participate in international human rights advocacy has been facilitated by the US Human Rights Network. The Network provides technical assistance and support for grassroots groups to raise issues before UN human rights bodies.[21] In addition to building international pressure around

---

[18] Id. at 3; Joann Kamuf Ward, "From Principles to Practice: The Role of US Mayors in Advancing Human Rights," in *Global Urban Justice: The Rise of Human Rights Cities*, ed. Barbara Oomen, Martha F. Davis, and Michele Grigolo (Cambridge: Cambridge University Press, 2016), 81.

[19] Resnik, "Law's Migration," 1567.

[20] Cynthia Soohoo, "Human Rights Cities: Challenges and Possibilities," in *Global Urban Justice: The Rise of Human Rights Cities*, ed. Barbara Oomen, Martha F. Davis, and Michele Grigolo (Cambridge: Cambridge University Press, 2016), 257.

[21] For instance, in 2008, the US Human Rights Network coordinated the efforts of more than 130 national, state, and local organizations to provide input around the UN review of US compliance with the International Convention on the Elimination of All Forms of Racial Discrimination. "Our Work," US Human Rights Network, www.ushrnetwork.org/our-work.

their issues, groups can use UN forums to educate and engage with federal government officials who may become allies in addressing local rights violations. Finally, engagement of US groups in these processes allows them to translate international human rights advocacy directly into their work on the ground.

US activists also play an important role in building local recognition of human rights issues through effective education, advocacy, and organizing. Activists make the public aware of human rights violations by documenting abuses – telling the stories of individuals whose rights have been violated, providing statistics and information illustrating how widespread the problem is, and analyzing it using human rights standards. Effective human rights documentation must provoke recognition that current practices violate human rights and must also inspire passion and action. This is done, in part, by referring to international human rights standards and the opinions of human rights experts, but perhaps more importantly, documentation must emphasize the humanity and experience of individuals who have suffered the violation. These stories are often the most effective way to get the public to understand that the experience the individuals suffered violated basic core understandings of human dignity. Activists also try to encourage public attention to issues as human rights issues by engaging international human rights bodies to provoke international scrutiny and criticism of US policies and practices.

If these efforts are successful, others outside of the advocacy community, such as government officials and the press, will begin to pay attention to the issue and incorporate human rights standards as part of their discussion and understanding of the issue.

C. *The Interaction of Different Levels of Government in the United States*

In the United States, federalism makes human rights advocacy more complex because each level of government is responsible for different issues, creating distinct, and sometimes multiple, advocacy targets. While federalism makes advocacy more complex, it also creates additional sites for advocacy and influence and the opportunity to leverage different government entities to make change.

For instance, because criminal justice issues are mostly within the purview of state authorities, advocacy around solitary confinement and raising the age must target state governments. Furthermore, while state correctional authorities run state prisons, jails – where individuals accused of crimes are detained pretrial – are typically run by county or city authorities. Thus, comprehensive change in solitary confinement policies and treatment of youth in the adult criminal justice system also requires change at the local level, making local governments an additional advocacy target. Finally, as discussed below, although the federal government only has direct control over individuals tried in the federal criminal justice system, it can play an important role in encouraging state and local governments to reform their practices.

Federalism also impacts human rights advocacy in another way. Under international law, the national government is responsible for ensuring compliance with international human rights obligations. In the United States, it is the federal government, in particular the State Department, that must engage with the international community and respond to or explain violations of human rights obligations. This includes rights violations that occur at the state or local level. Because state and local governments do not directly interact with international human rights bodies, they are somewhat insulated from international pressure to remedy rights violations. It is the federal government that feels international pressure, but it often lacks the direct ability to remedy rights violations.

For human rights claims to impact state and local governments, successful claims often are made from the ground up – from local activists who have adopted human rights claims – or from the top down: not from the international community, but from the federal government that may either be seeking to ensure that state and local governments comply with human rights obligations or may have independently internalized the importance of the human rights norm. In the United States, there are multiple ways the federal government can encourage state and local governments to comply with human rights obligations. Often egregious human rights violations also constitute constitutional violations or violations of federal law. In such cases, the federal government can launch investigations and institute civil rights litigation. If actions or policies do not violate existing laws but raise serious human rights concerns, the federal government can consider developing legislation and plans of action to create new domestic obligations to promote local compliance with human rights. It also can articulate national standards that comply with human rights obligations. These standards can be encouraged through political and moral pressure and reinforced through technical assistance, training, and funding incentives.

II. SOLITARY CONFINEMENT

This section considers the impact that human rights advocacy has had on reform of solitary confinement policies in the United States, with a focus on reforms in New York City and New York State.

A. *A History of Solitary Confinement in the United States*

At the beginning of the twentieth century, the use of solitary confinement was rare in the United States.[22] In the 1800s, several states adopted solitary confinement, only to abandon its use. In 1890, the Supreme Court surveyed the history of solitary confinement in the United States, finding that "there were serious objections to it" and that it was "found to be too severe." In particular, the Court noted that

---

[22] New York Civil Liberties Union (NYCLU), *Boxed In: The True Cost of Extreme Isolation in New York's Prisons* (New York: New York Civil Liberties Union, 2012), 11, www.nyclu.org/files/publications/nyclu_boxedin_FINAL.pdf.

[a] considerable number of the prisoners fell, after even a short confinement, into a semi-fatuous condition, from which it was next to impossible to arouse them, and others became violently insane; others still, committed suicide; while those who stood the ordeal better were not generally reformed, and in most cases did not recover sufficient mental activity to be of any subsequent service to the community.[23]

Although the experience of state correctional officials and the opinion of the Supreme Court suggested that the use of solitary confinement had been soundly rejected because of its inhumane impact, beginning in the 1980s and 1990s, prison overcrowding and a new punitive climate in corrections led correctional officials to forget the lessons learned in the 1800s. Between 1973 and 1993, the prison population in the United States increased by 346%, causing correctional officials to struggle with prison overcrowding and management issues. Starting in the 1980s, correctional officials sharply increased the use of solitary confinement as a disciplinary and prison management tool.[24] A recent estimate calculates that on any given day in 2014, US jails and prisons were holding between 89,000 and 120,000 individuals in solitary confinement.[25]

Like other states, New York also faced the pressures of overcrowding from a skyrocketing prison population. In 2014, on any given day, there were an estimated 4,500 individuals held in extreme isolation in New York state prisons.[26] The number of individuals held in solitary confinement in pretrial facilities, like Rikers Island Jail in New York, also ballooned. In 2013, Rikers Island had 998 solitary confinement beds, and 7.5% of the population was held in punitive segregation.[27]

As the population of youth and persons with mental illness in the adult criminal justice system has grown in the United States, solitary confinement has been used as way to manage them.[28] Researchers estimate that at least 30% of prisoners in solitary confinement suffer from mental illness.[29] In 2013, 140 adolescent inmates at Rikers Island were in solitary confinement, and 102 (or 74%) of those adolescents

---

[23] *In re* Medley, 134 US 160, 168 (1890). [24] NYCLU, *Boxed In*, 11–12.
[25] Marie Gottschalk, "Staying Alive: Reforming Solitary Confinement in US Jails and Prisons," *Yale Law Journal Forum* 125 (2016): 253, www.yalelawjournal.org/forum/reforming-solitary-confinement-in-us-prisons-and-jails.
[26] NYCLU, *Boxed In*, 1 (roughly half of the 4,500 were housed in solitary confinement; the other half were locked in isolation cells with another prisoner).
[27] James Gilligan and Bandy Lee, *Report to the New York City Board of Correction* (September 5, 2013), 3, http://solitarywatch.com/wp-content/uploads/2013/11/Gilligan-Report.-Final.pdf.
[28] Id. at 2; American Civil Liberties Union (ACLU) and Human Rights Watch (HRW), *Growing Up Locked Down: Youth in Solitary Confinement in Jails and Prisons across the United States* (New York: Human Rights Watch, 2012), 21, www.aclu.org/files/assets/us1012webwcover.pdf.
[29] American Civil Liberties Union, *Briefing Paper: The Dangerous Overuse of Solitary Confinement in the United States* (New York: ACLU Foundation, 2014), 8, www.aclu.org/sites/default/files/field_document/stop_solitary_briefing_paper_updated_august_2014.pdf.

were diagnosed as seriously or moderately mentally ill.[30] Over 40% of the inmates in punitive segregation at Rikers were mentally ill.[31]

Since 1890, there have been some legal challenges to the use of solitary confinement in the United States. Lower court cases have recognized that solitary confinement of adults with serious mental illness is unconstitutional.[32] Activists and scholars have also argued that the Supreme Court's recent holdings recognizing differences between youth and adults support a constitutional challenge to the solitary confinement of youth.[33] Although the Supreme Court has yet to rule on the issue, federal, state, and local governments have begun to adopt reforms that limit the use of solitary confinement. Human rights standards have been an important part of these advocacy efforts.

B. *The Development of International Human Rights Standards on Solitary Confinement*

The international community has long recognized that under certain circumstances, solitary confinement can violate human rights law prohibiting torture and cruel, inhuman, and degrading treatment (CIDT) and has recommended efforts to restrict solitary confinement to exceptional circumstances. However, human rights treaties do not categorically prohibit solitary confinement and determination of whether a specific use of solitary confinement crossed the line was deemed dependent on the circumstances. In the 1990s, the international community began paying greater attention to solitary confinement and articulating the situations in which its use could violate human rights. In 1992, the UN Human Rights Committee, which oversees compliance with the International Covenant on Civil and Political Rights (ICCPR), noted that "prolonged solitary confinement" may constitute torture or CIDT.[34] There was also recognition that solitary confinement of individuals under 18 should be prohibited. In 1990, the UN Rules for the Protection of Juveniles Deprived of Their Liberty categorized solitary confinement of juveniles as impermissible cruel, inhuman, and degrading treatment.[35] In 1994, the UN Committee on the Rights of the Child, which oversees compliance with the Convention on the Rights of the Child (CRC), stated that solitary confinement was inconsistent with the "inherent dignity of the juvenile and the fundamental objectives of institutional care" and that,

---

[30] Gilligan and Lee, *Report*, 3.   [31] Id.
[32] NYCLU, *Boxed In*, 15.   [33] ACLU and HRW, *Growing Up Locked Down*, 78–80.
[34] Human Rights Committee, General Comment No. 20: Article 7 (Prohibition of Torture or Other Cruel, Inhuman or Degrading Treatment or Punishment), UN Doc. HRI/GEN/1/Rev.1 (March 10, 1992), 31, para. 6.
[35] UN Rules for the Protection of Juveniles Deprived of Their Liberty, UN Doc. A/RES/45/113 (December 14, 1990), para. 67.

because it constituted torture and cruel, inhuman, and degrading treatment, it must be strictly forbidden.[36]

When Juan Méndez, a human rights expert and survivor of torture under Argentina's military dictatorship, became UN Special Rapporteur on Torture in 2010, he recognized the need to bring greater clarity to human rights standards around solitary confinement. In addition to the skyrocketing use of solitary in the United States, complaints received from countries around the world indicated global overuse and misuse of solitary confinement and growing evidence of the devastating impact the practice had on inmates and detainees.[37] Special Rapporteurs play a unique role in the UN human rights system. Independent experts appointed by the UN Human Rights Council, Special Rapporteurs are charged with monitoring and reporting on human rights violations on thematic issues. Their expertise on the issue and knowledge about conditions around the world enable them to develop or clarify human rights norms.[38]

In 2011, Méndez issued a groundbreaking report on solitary confinement. Based on medical and psychiatric studies that showed that solitary confinement produces adverse impacts on individuals within days and that after 15 days, harmful psychological effects may become irreversible,[39] Méndez defined prolonged solitary confinement as any period exceeding 15 days, concluding that confinement longer than 15 days must be prohibited as cruel and inhuman treatment or even torture. Méndez did not abandon a case-by-case analysis, noting that solitary confinement for less than 15 days could also violate human rights depending on the circumstances, including the purpose and conditions of confinement.[40] However, the 15-day rule provided much-needed specificity to international standards.

Méndez also articulated bright-line rules for vulnerable populations. The 2011 report stated that subjecting children and persons with mental disabilities to solitary confinement for any length of time constituted cruel and inhuman treatment in violation of the ICCPR and the Convention against Torture (CAT).[41] Méndez

---

[36] Committee on the Rights of the Child, General Comment No. 10 (2007): Children's Rights in Juvenile Justice, UN Doc. CRC/C/GC/10 (April 25, 2007), para. 89.

[37] Juan E. Méndez et al., *Seeing into Solitary: A Review of the Laws and Policies of Certain Nations Regarding Solitary Confinement of Detainees* (New York: Weil, 2016), 2–3, www.weil.com/~/media/files/pdfs/2016/un_special_report_solitary_confinement.pdf.

[38] Columbia Law School Human Rights Institute, *Engaging UN Special Procedures to Advance Human Rights at Home: A Guide for US Advocates* (New York: Columbia Law School Human Rights Institute, 2015), 3, https://web.law.columbia.edu/sites/default/files/microsites/human-rights-institute/files/special_rapporteurs_report_final.pdf.

[39] Istanbul Statement on the Use and Effects of Solitary Confinement (adopted at the International Psychological Trauma Symposium, Istanbul, Turkey, December 9, 2007), http://solitaryconfinement.org/uploads/Istanbul_expert_statement_on_sc.pdf.

[40] Juan Méndez, Interim Report of the Special Rapporteur on Torture and Other Cruel, Inhuman or Degrading Treatment or Punishment, UN Doc. A/66/268 (August 5, 2011), paras. 26, 62–63, 71, 76.

[41] Id. at paras. 26, 61, 77.

reiterated the absolute prohibition on solitary confinement of children in a 2015 report on juveniles deprived of liberty.[42] The most recent UN Standard Minimum Rules for the Treatment of Prisoners (known as the Mandela Rules) adopt these evolving limitations on the use of solitary confinement, including the 15-day limit and a prohibition on solitary for children and persons with mental or physical disabilities if their conditions would be exacerbated by solitary confinement.[43] The rules also emphasize that solitary "shall be used only in exceptional cases as a last resort for as short a time as possible and subject to independent review."[44] While not legally binding, the rules are recognized as reflecting international best practices.

The involvement of US civil society and government officials in the development of international standards on solitary confinement ensured both that the international standards were informed by, and relevant to, the US context and that US audiences were educated about the standards. This enabled US actors to integrate the standards into their domestic work. US activists played an important role in pushing for the development and articulation of human rights standards on solitary confinement. Like NGOs around the world, the ACLU contributed cases and other information to the Special Rapporteur on Torture for his 2011 report. After the report was issued, the ACLU helped to organize events to publicize the Special Rapporteur's report and solitary conditions in the United States.[45] At a 2013 hearing on solitary confinement at the Inter-American Commission on Human Rights, the ACLU provided information about solitary confinement in the United States, and other activists discussed practices in other countries. Special Rapporteur Méndez also testified, presenting the findings of his 2011 report. Following the hearing, the Inter-American Commission adopted recommendations consistent with the Special Rapporteur's report, including a ban on solitary confinement for youth and people with disabilities and a ban on prolonged solitary confinement defined as more than 15 consecutive days.[46]

US correctional officials also were involved in drafting the Mandela Rules. During negotiations around the rules, corrections directors from Washington and Colorado, two states that have pioneered reform of solitary confinement in the United States,

---

[42] Juan Méndez, Report of the Special Rapporteur on Torture and Other Cruel, Inhuman or Degrading Treatment or Punishment, UN Doc. A/HRC/28/68 (March 5, 2015), para. 44.

[43] The prior version of the rules was published in 1955, and the revisions bring the rules up to date to reflect the Special Rapporteur on Torture's 2011 report, which concluded that "periods of solitary confinement exceeding 15 days constitute torture, and also recommended that juveniles and the mentally disabled be exempt from solitary confinement altogether." Aylin Manduric, "UN's 'Mandela Rules' to Set New International Limits on Solitary Confinement," Solitary Watch, July 17, 2015, http://solitarywatch.com/2015/07/17/uns-mandela-rules-to-set-new-international-standards-for-treatment-of-prisoners-including-limits-on-solitary-confinement.

[44] UN Standard Minimum Rules for the Treatment of Prisoners ("The Mandela Rules"), G.A. Res. 70/175, UN Doc. A/RES/70/175 (December 17, 2015), rule 45.1.

[45] Kayyali et al., Engaging UN Special Procedures, 41. [46] Id.

participated in Expert Group meetings to revise the rules and became part of the official US delegation.[47] The participation of the correctional officials reinforced the State Department's confidence that the Mandela Rules articulated workable standards and made it possible for the United States to become a leading advocate for the rules. In addition to ensuring that the standards were relevant to, and workable in, the US context, the involvement of state correctional officials helped to build knowledge and visibility of the rules among US correctional officials and bridge the federalism divide described above.

C. US Advocacy to Recognize Solitary Confinement as a Human Rights Issue

Reports Documenting Solitary Confinement as a Human Rights Issue

After Juan Méndez's 2011 report recognizing a 15-day limit on solitary confinement and encouraging the prohibition of solitary for youth and the mentally disabled, US activists issued reports documenting the extensive use of solitary confinement in the United States as a human rights issue. They also successfully framed solitary as a form of torture by emphasizing the physical and psychological impact of locking someone into a small cell for 23 hours a day. In 2012, the New York Civil Liberties Union (NYCLU) released *Boxed In*, which focused on the excessive use of solitary confinement in New York prisons.[48] That same year, the ACLU and Human Rights Watch (HRW) issued a joint report, *Growing Up Locked Down*, on youth in solitary confinement in jails and prisons in the United States.[49]

These reports put a human face on the individuals in solitary confinement. Taylor Pendergrass of NYCLU emphasized the importance of making the public aware of the experience of individuals in solitary confinement:

> the fact that New York's use of solitary confinement was unhidden was hardly the same thing as saying that its use and human toll were well known to most policymakers and the public... New York's solitary practices continued to largely persist in a "shadow world," and the voices of the men and women confined for months or years in extreme isolation were rarely heard.[50]

---

[47] David Fathi, "Victory! UN Crime Commission Approves Mandela Rules on Treatment of Prisoners," *ACLU Speak Freely* (blog), May 27, 2015, www.aclu.org/blog/speak-freely/victory-un-crime-commission-approves-mandela-rules-treatment-prisoners.

[48] NYCLU, *Boxed In*.

[49] ACLU and Human Rights Watch, *Growing Up Locked Down: Youth in Solitary Confinement in Jails and Prisons Across the US* (New York: Human Rights Watch, 2012), www.aclu.org/files/assets/us1012webwcover.pdf; Eric Ferkenhoff, "ACLU, Human Rights Watch Press for End to Juvenile Solitary Confinement," *Juvenile Justice Information Exchange*, October 10, 2012, http://jjie.org/aclu-human-rights-watch-press-for-end-juvenile-solitary-confinement/96014.

[50] Taylor Pendergrass, "Human Rights Fact-Finding in the Shadows of America's Solitary Confinement Prisons," in *The Transformation of Human Rights Fact-Finding*, ed. Philip Alston and Sarah Knuckey (Oxford: Oxford University Press, 2016), 308.

The reports educated the public about the vast numbers of people in solitary confinement, the excessively long periods and harsh conditions they endured, and the lack of proper procedures and standards around the use of solitary. Using individual stories and scientific evidence, they described the severe emotional and psychological harm caused by solitary confinement and framed solitary as torture and cruel, inhuman, and degrading treatment. Both reports cite to human rights standards requiring that solitary confinement only be employed as an exceptional measure, as a last resort for as brief a period as possible, and prohibited for youth and individuals with mental disabilities. *Growing Up Locked Down* also emphasizes that while human rights law requires that all prisoners be protected from mistreatment, children and persons with mental disabilities must be afforded heightened protections.

Advocacy before International Human Rights Bodies and Experts

In addition to issuing reports incorporating a human rights frame, activists have also raised US solitary confinement practices in international forums to encourage international and domestic recognition of the issue as a human rights violation. This work reinforced the frame of solitary confinement as torture or CIDT and increased the visibility of the issue in the United States.

The United States has ratified three international human rights treaties: the International Covenant on Civil and Political Rights, the Convention against Torture, and the Convention on the Elimination of All Forms of Racial Discrimination (CERD). Although the treaties generally cannot be enforced through private rights of action in US courts,[51] by ratifying the treaties, the United States has agreed to undergo periodic reviews of its treaty compliance before committees of UN human rights experts. Prior to the UN's review of the United States's compliance with the ICCPR and CAT in 2014, US organizations such as the ACLU,[52] the National Religious Campaign against Torture (NRCAT),[53] and the New York Campaign for Alternatives to Isolated Confinement (NY CAIC) submitted reports[54] documenting solitary confinement practices in the United States as a violation of its treaty obligations to prevent torture and cruel, inhuman, and degrading treatment.

Based upon information provided by US activists and the US government in 2014, following its review of the United States's compliance with the ICCPR, the UN Human Rights Committee expressed concern about the use of solitary confinement

---

[51] Medellín v. Texas, 552 US 491, 505–6, 506 n. 3 (2008).
[52] American Civil Liberties Union, *United States' Compliance with the International Covenant on Civil and Political Rights: American Civil Liberties Union Shadow Report for the Fourth Periodic Report of the United States*, September 13, 2013, http://tbinternet.ohchr.org/Treaties/CCPR/Shared%20Documents/USA/INT_CCPR_NGO_USA_15191_E.pdf.
[53] National Religious Campaign against Torture, *Torture in US Prisons: Interfaith Religious Coalition Calls for End to Widespread Use of Prolonged Solitary Confinement*, September 2014, www.nrcat.org/storage/documents/nrcat-cat-shadow-report-2014.pdf.
[54] New York Campaign for Alternatives to Isolated Confinement, *United States' Widespread and Systematic Practices of Torture by the Use of Abusive, Long Term Solitary Confinement*, 2014, http://tbinternet.ohchr.org/Treaties/CAT/Shared%20Documents/USA/INT_CAT_CSS_USA_18547_E.pdf.

and recommended that the United States comply with the UN Standard Minimum Rules for the Treatment of Prisoners, impose strict limits on the use of solitary, and abolish solitary for juveniles and persons with serious mental illness.[55] Later that year, the UN Committee against Torture recommended that the United States use solitary confinement "as a measure of last resort, for as short a time as possible, under strict supervision and with possibility of judicial review." It also recommended that the United States prohibit solitary for juveniles and persons with "intellectual or psychosocial disabilities."[56]

US activists have also successfully engaged with Juan Méndez to publicize solitary confinement as a form of torture and to educate government officials and courts about human rights standards limiting the use of solitary. Following his appointment, Méndez repeatedly sought an invitation to visit the United States to investigate conditions in federal and state prisons. Because UN Special Rapporteurs cannot conduct official visits to a country without a formal government invitation, Méndez's visit had to be approved and sanctioned by the federal government. The United States repeatedly declined to issue an invitation upon terms that Méndez could accept.

Without a formal visit, activists rallied around the pending request as an advocacy opportunity. In February 2013, more than three dozen human rights, civil rights, mental health, and faith-based organizations publicly submitted a letter to Méndez requesting an investigation into the use of solitary confinement in New York State prisons, alleging that New York's use of extreme isolation violated "the right to be protected from torture and other forms of cruel, inhuman, or degrading treatment or punishment" and "the right to be free from discrimination."[57] When Méndez renewed his request in May 2013,[58] 50 civil and human rights groups called on the United States to issue an invitation.[59] Méndez's lack of access to the United States became such an issue that Amnesty International launched a petition to Secretary of

---

[55] UN Human Rights Committee, Concluding Observations on the Fourth Periodic Report of the United States of America, UN Doc. CCPR/C/USA/CO/4 (April 23, 2014), www.un.org/ga/search/view_doc.asp?symbol=CCPR/C/USA/CO/4, para. 20.

[56] UN Committee against Torture, Concluding Observations on the Combined Third to Fifth Periodic Report of the United States of America, UN Doc. CAT/C/USA/CO/3–5 (December 19, 2014), www.un.org/ga/search/view_doc.asp?symbol=CAT/C/USA/CO/3--5, para. 20.

[57] "Human Rights, Mental Health and Faith-Based Organizations Ask UN to Investigate Solitary Confinement in New York Prisons," New York Civil Liberties Union, February 5, 2013, www.nyclu.org/news/human-rights-mental-health-and-faith-based-organizations-ask-un-investigate-solitary-confinement; Letter to Special Rapporteur Juan Méndez from Civil and Human Rights Organizations, New York Civil Liberties Union, February 5, 2013, www.nyclu.org/files/releases/ExtremeIsolation_UNletter_2.5.13.pdf.

[58] Juan Méndez, Interim Report of the Special Rapporteur of the Human Rights Council on Torture and Other Cruel, Inhuman or Degrading Treatment or Punishment, UN Doc. A/68/295 (August 9, 2013), https://documents-dds-ny.un.org/doc/UNDOC/GEN/N13/422/85/PDF/N1342285.pdf?OpenElement, para. 8.

[59] Jamil Dakwar and Ian Kysel, "Rights Groups to Government: Allow UN Torture Expert to Examine US Use of Solitary Confinement," ACLU (blog), June 20, 2013, www.aclu.org/blog/rights-groups-government-allow-un-torture-expert-examine-us-use-solitary-confinement.

State John Kerry urging that Méndez "be invited" to carry out a fact-finding mission in the United States.[60]

Méndez has been able to weigh in on solitary confinement in the United States in other ways. As discussed below, in February 2015, Méndez testified to a Congressional subcommittee on solitary confinement practices in the United States. In March 2015, Méndez submitted an expert report in litigation challenging the constitutionality of the use of prolonged solitary confinement in California's Pelican Bay State Prison where more than 400 prisoners were held in solitary confinement for more than a decade.[61] The report summarized international standards on solitary confinement and concluded that the use of solitary at Pelican Bay amounted to torture or CIDT.[62] The case was settled in 2016.

D. Federal Acceptance of Solitary Confinement as a Human Rights Issue

Federal government officials have also accepted that solitary confinement is a human rights issue, resulting in changes in federal policies and federal pressure to reform state and local solitary practices. In hearings in June 2012 and February 2013, the Senate Subcommittee on the Constitution, Civil Rights, and Human Rights emphasized that human rights organizations and the international community have condemned US practices around solitary confinement.[63] The Committee's second hearing explicitly focused on solitary confinement as a human rights issue. Juan Méndez submitted testimony for the hearing, stating that the United States's wide use of solitary confinement for prolonged periods of time raises "significant concerns regarding the compliance ... with the United States' obligations under the International Covenant for Civil and Political Rights (ICCPR), and the Convention Against Torture and other Cruel, Inhuman or Degrading Treatment or Punishment (CAT)." Méndez added that "solitary confinement of any duration may never be

---

[60] "Solitary Confinement: US Government Must End This Cruel and Inhumane Practice," Amnesty International, October 4, 2014, http://act.amnestyusa.org/ea-action/action?ea.client.id=1839&ea.campaign.id=32299.

[61] "California Jails: 'Solitary Confinement Can Amount to Cruel Punishment, Even Torture' – UN Rights Expert," Office of the United Nations High Commissioner for Human Rights, August 23, 2013, www.ohchr.org/EN/NewsEvents/Pages/DisplayNews.aspx?NewsID=13655&LangID=E.

[62] Expert Report of Juan Méndez in Ashker v. Governor of the State of California, Case No.: 4:09-cv-05796-CW (March 6, 2015), https://ccrjustice.org/sites/default/files/attach/2015/07/Mendez%20Expert%20Report.pdf.

[63] Erica Goode, "Senators Start a Review of Solitary Confinement," *New York Times*, June 19, 2012, www.nytimes.com/2012/06/20/us/senators-start-a-review-of-solitary-confinement.html; Senator Dick Durbin's (D-IL) posthearing statement declared that "[t]he United States holds more prisoners in solitary confinement than any other democratic nation in the world and the dramatic expansion of solitary confinement is a human rights issue we can't ignore." "Durbin Statement on Federal Bureau of Prisons Assessment of Its Solitary Confinement Practices," February 4, 2013, www.durbin.senate.gov/newsroom/press-releases/durbin-statement-on-federal-bureau-of-prisons-assessment-of-its-solitary-confinement-practices; "US Bureau of Prisons to Review Solitary Confinement," Reuters, February 4, 2014, www.reuters.com/article/us-usa-prisons-solitary-idUSBRE91404L20130205.

imposed on juveniles under the age of 18, or persons with mental disabilities."[64] At the hearing Senate leaders echoed the call to ban solitary confinement for juveniles and persons with mental disabilities.[65]

In January 2016, President Obama announced that the federal government would cease the use of solitary on juveniles in federal prisons and impose other reforms on solitary including prohibiting solitary confinement for "low level infractions" and limiting solitary confinement to 60 days for the first infraction.[66] The attorney general also issued a national review of solitary practices that set forth 50 guiding principles for solitary reform.[67] Obama authored an op-ed in the *Washington Post* announcing the federal changes.[68] Although Obama did not refer to US human rights obligations, the op-ed quoted Pope Francis for the proposition that "every human person is endowed with an inalienable dignity" and made references to "our common humanity." These references made a moral claim for solitary confinement reform based on respect for human dignity, which is the core of human rights claims.

The majority of prisoners in the United States are in state custody, and only a handful of the thousands of youth in jails and prisons are in federal custody. However, the president's statement and the attorney general's guiding principles provide both moral authority and a best practice model that can encourage and inspire change at the state and local level. In addition, as discussed below, the Department of Justice has played an important role in reforming the treatment of detained youth in New York City, including the excessive and improper use of solitary confinement at Rikers Island Jail. The DOJ investigation and report are discussed in more detail below.

E. Acceptance of Solitary Confinement as a Human Rights Issue in New York

The acceptance of solitary confinement as a human rights issue in New York was illustrated by the embrace of human rights language beyond human rights experts and NGOs. The NY CAIC coalition incorporated human rights language in its

---

[64] Juan E. Méndez, "Special Rapporteur on Torture's Written Submission to Second Congressional Hearing on Solitary Confinement," February 24, 2014, http://antitorture.org/wp-content/uploads/2014/02/Special-Rapporteur-on-Torture-Submission-to-Second-Congressional-Hearing-on-Solitary-Confinement.pdf.

[65] Kevin Johnson, "Panel: No Solitary Confinement for Minors, Mentally Ill," *USA Today*, February 25, 2014, www.usatoday.com/story/news/nation/2014/02/25/judiciary-prison-ban-juvenile-solitary-confinement/5817559/.

[66] Juliet Eilperin, "Obama Bans Solitary Confinement for Juveniles in Federal Prisons," *Washington Post*, January 26, 2016, www.washingtonpost.com/politics/obama-bans-solitary-confinement-for-juveniles-in-federal-prisons/2016/01/25/056e14b2-c3a2-11e5-9693-933a4d31bcc8_story.html.

[67] US Department of Justice, *Report and Recommendations Concerning the Use of Restrictive Housing: Guiding Principles* (Washington, DC: US Department of Justice, 2016), www.justice.gov/dag/file/815556/download.

[68] Barack Obama, "Why We Must Rethink Solitary Confinement," *Washington Post*, January 25, 2016, www.washingtonpost.com/opinions/barack-obama-why-we-must-rethink-solitary-confinement/2016/01/25/29a361f2-c384-11e5-8965-0607e0e265ce_story.html.

advocacy and legislative demands. Other national and local coalitions invoked human rights standards to urge a 15-day limit on solitary confinement[69] and to prohibit solitary for youth under 18. Activists incorporated a videotaped statement from Juan Méndez underscoring international standards in a state lobby day.[70] Statements from legislators and activists characterized the use of solitary confinement in New York as "torture" and a "human rights crisis" in support of legislative reform proposals.[71] City council members have also recognized solitary confinement as a human rights issue in oversight hearings on the solitary confinement of youth at Rikers.[72]

Traditional civil rights groups incorporated human rights standards into reports and reform proposals. In 2014, the New York Advisory Committee to the US Commission on Civil Rights recommended the elimination of solitary confinement for youth, noting that New York's solitary confinement regime violated international human rights standards.[73] That same year, a committee of the New York City Bar Association supported a 15-day limit on solitary, citing Juan Méndez's report and noting that the 15-day limit is more in line with other countries.[74] At the City level, activists outside of the human rights community have similarly embraced human rights arguments.[75]

---

[69] Testimony of Laura Markle Downton, Director of US Prisons Policy and Program, National Religious Campaign against Torture, New York City Board of Corrections Hearing, December 19, 2014, http://nrcat.org/storage/documents/nrcat_testimony_nyc_boc_hearing.pdf; Testimony of Lisa Schreibersdorf, Executive Director, Brooklyn Defender Services, New York City Board of Corrections Hearing, October 16, 2015, http://bds.org/bds-testifies-at-boc-to-save-jail-visiting-fight-the-rollback-of-solitary-reforms-and-more/.

[70] "Lawmakers, Advocates, and Survivors of Solitary Confinement Back Legislation Limiting Use of Isolation in New York's Prisons and Jails," Correctional Association of New York, April 12, 2016, www.correctionalassociation.org/news/lawmakers-advocates-and-survivors-of-solitary-confinement-back-legislation-limiting-use-of-isolation-in-new-yorks-prisons-and-jails.

[71] Id.

[72] Christopher Mathias, "Lawmakers Calls Use of Solitary Confinement for Teen on Rikers Island 'Torture,'" Huffington Post, October 9, 2014, www.huffingtonpost.com/2014/10/09/rikers-island-teen-inmates_n_5959230.html.

[73] New York Advisory Committee to the US Commission on Civil Rights, The Solitary Confinement of Youth in New York: A Civil Rights Violation (New York: US Commission on Civil Rights, 2014), 47–48, www.usccr.gov/pubs/NY-SAC-Solitary-Confinement-Report-without-Cover.pdf; Samar Khurshid, "Report: Solitary Confinement Violating Human Rights of Youth," Gotham Gazette, December 18, 2014, www.gothamgazette.com/index.php/government/5481-report-solitary-confinement-violating-human-rights-of-youth.

[74] New York City Bar Association, Report on Legislation by the Corrections and Community Reentry Committee and International Human Rights Committee, 2014, www2.nycbar.org/pdf/report/uploads/20072748-HALTSolitaryConfinementReport.pdf.

[75] Mary E. Buser, "Solitary Confinement's Mockery of Human Rights," Washington Post, April 4, 2014, www.washingtonpost.com/opinions/solitary-confinements-mockery-of-human-rights/2014/04/04/537f32b4-b9c5-11e3-9a05-c739f29ccb08_story.html; Johnny Perez, Letter to the Editor, New York Times, April 7, 2016, www.nytimes.com/2016/04/08/opinion/prison-isolation-torture.html (citing to international standards that prohibit solitary confinement beyond 15 days because the practice constitutes torture).

Because human rights claims were actively incorporated into debates and demands to reform solitary confinement, the standards proposed in pending legislation and ultimately incorporated into litigation settlements reflected human rights norms. For instance, a bill introduced by New York State senator Danny O'Donnell in 2015 proposed limiting the use of solitary confinement as a measure of last resort and for the minimum period necessary and banning solitary for youth under 21 and for the developmentally disabled and mentally ill.[76] A separate bill proposed excluding vulnerable populations from solitary and limiting its use to 15 days as recommended by international law.[77] O'Donnell and other state senators have repeatedly stated that reform is necessary to comply with the Committee against Torture's recommendations.[78]

Ultimately, lawsuits brought by the NYCLU and Prisoners Legal Services led to settlements that have reformed state correctional policies on solitary. Although the lawsuits were brought based on constitutional standards, the negotiated settlements arguably go beyond minimum constitutional requirements and reflect human rights standards.

Indeed, press accounts reflect a popular understanding that the settlements vindicated important human rights. In February 2014, the *New York Times* editorial board praised an interim settlement in the NYCLU state case, noting that agreed-upon guidelines on the maximum length of solitary and steps to curb the use of solitary for inmates under 18 would "come as no surprise to most other advanced nations, where solitary confinement is used sparingly, if at all." The editorial specifically referenced Méndez's 2011 report calling "for the banning of the practice in all but extraordinary circumstances, and even then only for a maximum of 15 days."[79]

The final state settlement agreement eliminates solitary confinement for youth and other vulnerable populations and also imposes significant limitations on the use of solitary confinement for other populations.[80] The state also agreed

---

[76] "O'Donnell, Rozic Bills to Comply with Committee against Torture's Recommendations Pass Correction Committee," February 3, 2015, http://assembly.state.ny.us/mem/Daniel-J-O'Donnell/story/61139.

[77] "Lawmakers, Advocates, and Survivors of Solitary Confinement Back Legislation Limiting Use of Isolation in New York's Prisons and Jails," Correctional Association of New York, April 12, 2016, www.correctionalassociation.org/news/lawmakers-advocates-and-survivors-of-solitary-confinement-back-legislation-limiting-use-of-isolation-in-new-yorks-prisons-and-jails.

[78] For instance, Senator Rozic has stated that "the findings of the United Nations Committee against Torture clearly indicate that we need to re-evaluate the disciplinary practices used in facilities across New York and consider humane alternatives." "O'Donnell and Rozic Introduce Bills to Reform Solitary Confinement, Bring New York into Compliance with International Human Rights Standards," January 14, 2015, http://assembly.state.ny.us/mem/Daniel-J-O'Donnell/story/60760/.

[79] Editorial, "New York Rethinks Solitary Confinement," *New York Times*, February 20, 2014, www.nytimes.com/2014/02/21/opinion/new-york-rethinks-solitary-confinement.html.

[80] The agreements move youth out of traditional solitary confinement to less isolated housing and cap the time that youth can be confined in their cells to 18 hours five days a week and 22 hours the other two days. They also require that age be considered as a mitigating factor in disciplinary proceedings when a youth has been accused of misconduct.

to prohibit the imposition of solitary confinement for inmates of all ages for minor violations and to set a maximum term of 30 days for first-time nonviolent offenses.[81]

Efforts to reform solitary confinement in New York City had a similar trajectory, reflecting the influence of successful human rights advocacy and pressure from threatened federal litigation. Following an investigation of conditions at the youth facility on Rikers Island, the DOJ issued a report finding extremely high incidence of violence and excessive use of solitary confinement. City officials agreed to make changes at Rikers (described in more detail below), including moving youth out of solitary. Advocates also pushed for other reforms of solitary confinement, including a ban on the placement of young people aged from 18 to 21 years in solitary confinement.[82] In January 2015, the Board of Corrections formally adopted regulations prohibiting the use of solitary for youth under 18 and set January 2016 as the date to end solitary confinement of 18- to 21-year-olds.[83] The Department of Correction has also created a clinical alternative to punitive segregation for detainees who are mentally ill.[84]

III. YOUTH IN CONFLICT WITH THE LAW

This section considers the impact that human rights advocacy has had on challenges to the practice of treating youth as adults in the criminal justice system, with a focus on the raise the age campaign in New York.

---

[81] Margo Schlanger and Amy Fettig, "Class-Action Suit Brings Sweeping Changes to Solitary Confinement in New York," American Prospect, December 23, 2015, http://prospect.org/article/class-action-suit-brings-sweeping-changes-solitary-confinement-new-york; "Cookhorne v. Fischer Settlement Provides Beneficial Reforms for Youth in Solitary Confinement," Campaign for Youth Justice, October 28, 2014, www.campaignforyouthjustice.org/news/blog/item/cookhorne-v-fischer-settlement-provides-beneficial-reforms-for-youth-in-solitary-confinement.

[82] Glenn Martin and Riley Doyle Evans, Op-Ed, "End Solitary Confinement of Young Adults on Rikers Island Now," Slant, July 27, 2016, http://nyslant.com/article/opinion/end-solitary-confinement-of-young-adults-on-rikers-island-now.html.

[83] Brian Sonenstein, "New Rules for Solitary Confinement on Rikers Island Attempt to Fix What Must Be Replaced," Shadowproof, January 22, 2015, https://shadowproof.com/2015/01/22/new-rules-for-solitary-confinement-on-rikers-island-attempt-to-fix-what-must-be-replaced. Implementation of the prohibition on solitary for 18- to 21-year-olds has been put off repeatedly. Human rights continues to be part of the debate. In July 2016, Councilmember Dromm criticized the city's Department of Corrections for dragging its feet and stated that the city's continued use of prolonged solitary confinement for young people was "deeply troubling since the United Nations considers any period over 15 days torture." Miranda Katz, "Rikers Won't End Solitary Confinement of Young Adults Just Yet," Gothamist, July 13, 2016, http://gothamist.com/2016/07/13/solitary_confiement_rikers.php.

[84] Jillian Jorgensen, "Correction Department Touts Drop in Solitary Confinement at Rikers Island," *Observer*, May 8, 2015, http://observer.com/2015/05/correction-department-touts-drop-in-solitary-confinement-at-rikers-island.

A. History of Youth in the Adult Criminal Justice System

Recognition of distinctions between youth and adults is embedded throughout the US legal system. Individuals under 18 cannot vote, enter into contracts, or serve on juries. Because youth are deemed less capable of making decisions, US laws limit their ability to make personal choices about marriage, abortion, and drinking. States also regulate their behavior to protect them and to promote their development by requiring school attendance, imposing curfews, and proscribing child labor. Historically, recognition of the difference between youth and adults also applied to the criminal context. All 50 states and the District of Columbia have separate juvenile justice systems to adjudicate crimes committed by youth. These systems are premised at least in part on the idea that youth are less culpable than adults and that the state has a duty to protect them from harm and to support their rehabilitation and growth.

Yet although all 50 states and DC have separate juvenile justice systems, many youth under 18 are excluded from the juvenile justice system and tried as adults. In the 1990s, in response to increased rates of violent crimes committed by youth, there was a push to criminally prosecute youth and impose "adult time for adult crime."[85] In response, all but five states passed laws making it easier for youth to be transferred to the adult criminal justice system. Many of the laws passed allowed transfer to occur without any individualized determination by giving prosecutors the unfettered authority to decide whether to try youth as adults or by automatically requiring youth to be tried as adults if charged with certain crimes.[86] In addition, several states exclude all 17-year-olds from juvenile court jurisdiction, requiring that they be tried as adults without any consideration of the nature of the crime charged or their individual circumstances. As of 2016, two states, New York and North Carolina, also excluded 16-year-olds from juvenile court jurisdiction, automatically trying them as adults no matter what the alleged crime or circumstances.

Each year, an estimated 200,000 youth are tried in adult criminal courts. Once an individual is tried as an adult, unless the state has passed special protections for youth in the adult system, he or she is deemed an adult, subject to adult criminal penalties. As a result, youth are detained in adult jails and prisons and are subject to the same rules and procedures governing behavior in adult facilities. Placing youth in adult facilities creates unique risks for them, including an increased risk of physical and sexual violence. Moreover, youth in adult facilities are more likely to be subjected

---

[85] ACLU and HRW, *Growing Up Locked Down*, 11.
[86] Howard N. Snyder and Melissa Sickmund, *Juvenile Offenders and Victims: 1999 National Report* (Washington, DC: US Department of Justice, 1999), 89, www.ncjrs.gov/html/ojjdp/nationalreport99/toc.html; Patrick Griffin et al., *Trying Juveniles as Adults: An Analysis of State Transfer Laws and Reporting* (Washington, DC: US Department of Justice, 2011), www.ncjrs.gov/pdffiles1/ojjdp/232434.pdf.

to "protective" solitary confinement to separate them from adult inmates to protect them from physical or sexual abuse.[87]

In 2015, 27,000 16- and 17-year-olds were arrested in New York State, the vast majority of the arrests for misdemeanor offenses. More than 2,000 of them were sentenced to serve sentences in adult facilities. Indeed, on any given day, approximately 800 16- and 17-year-olds are in adult jails and prisons.[88]

Challenges to state laws that push youth into the adult criminal justice system have consistently failed in state and lower federal courts. The Supreme Court has never considered whether trying youth as adults without any individualized consideration of their age or circumstances violates the Constitution. However, recently, the Supreme Court has held that differences between individuals under 18 and adults require a different constitutional standard when states seek to impose extreme adult criminal sentences. In *Roper v. Simmons*, the Supreme Court held that the Eighth Amendment's prohibition on cruel and unusual punishment prohibits imposition of the death penalty for crimes committed by individuals under 18 years of age. In *Graham v. Florida* and *Miller v. Alabama*, the Supreme Court held that the Eighth Amendment limits the imposition of life without parole sentences for crimes committed by youth. In reaching its holdings on juvenile death and life without parole sentences, the Supreme Court considered international and comparative law to find that the sentences violate evolving standards of decency and constitute cruel and unusual punishment under the Eighth Amendment.[89]

Elsewhere, I have argued that the Supreme Court's recent holdings recognizing that youth are less culpable than adults, more vulnerable to harm, and more capable of growth and rehabilitation support recognition of a substantive constitutional right to juvenile treatment for youth in conflict with the law under the Fourteenth Amendment to the US Constitution. Although a substantive right to juvenile treatment for youth in conflict with the law has yet to be recognized in the United States, it is consistent with the Supreme Court's historic recognition that "children cannot be viewed simply as miniature adults" and is supported by universal understandings of differences between youth and adults reflected in international law and the legal systems around the world.[90]

Although US courts have not held that trying youth as adults is a constitutional violation, the Supreme Court cases recognizing differences between youth and adults and scientific evidence about differences between adult and adolescent brains have

---

[87] ACLU and HRW, *Growing Up Locked Down*, 48, 53–54.
[88] Mark Hays, "Why Is New York Still Prosecuting 16-Year-Olds as Adults?," Gothamist, November 3, 2016, http://gothamist.com/2016/11/03/new_york_raise_the_age.php.
[89] Roper v. Simmons, 543 US 551, 575, 578 (2005); Graham v. Florida, 560 US 48, 81 (2010) (noting that "the overwhelming weight of international opinion against" life without parole for nonhomicide offenses committed by juveniles "provide[s] respected and significant confirmation of our own conclusions").
[90] J.D.B. v. North Carolina, 564 US 261, 274 (2011).

encouraged state governments to adopt reforms. Some states have raised the age;[91] others have imposed protections for youth in the adult system by decreasing criminal sentences.[92] Human rights standards were invoked in some of these advocacy efforts but did not have not the same impact as human rights claims had in the solitary confinement context.

B. *The Development of International Human Rights Standards on Youth in Conflict with the Law*

Under international human rights law, protections for children in conflict with the law apply to all individuals under 18.[93] Thus, in the following discussion of human rights law, I use the terms "child" and "children" rather than "youth."

The right of the child to special protection and treatment is reflected in foundational human rights documents, including the Universal Declaration of Human Rights and the ICCPR.[94] International recognition of the rights of the child vastly expanded with the adoption of the Convention on the Rights of the Child (CRC) in 1989. Many countries around the world have either incorporated children's rights provisions into their constitutions or amended their law to comply with the CRC, including by requiring that individuals who are accused of committing crimes under the age of 18 are tried in a separate specialized juvenile justice system and are held

---

[91] Conn. Gen. Stat. § 46b-127 (2015) (requiring review of children's treatment in juvenile court prior to transfer to adult criminal docket, raising the age for transfer to 15, and raising the legal age of a child to 18); 705 Ill. Comp. Stat. 405/6-12 (2016) (raising age of automatic transfer from 15 to 16, allowing transfer only for most severe crimes, requiring demographic reporting on transferred youth, and enumerating specific criteria for transfer decision); N.H. Rev. State. Ann. § 169-B:4 (2015) (raising the age of minority for juvenile delinquency proceedings from 17 to 18 years of age); N.J. Stat. Ann. § 2A:4A-26.1 (2016) (raising minimum age of adult prosecution from 14 to 15, limiting transfer to most serious and violent crimes, and requiring prosecutors to submit written analysis of reason for transfer to judge). State courts that have rejected challenges to transfer statutes have encouraged their state legislatures to review the statutes in view of current evidence about the differences between adults and youth. People v. Patterson, 25 N.E.3d 526, 553 (Ill. 2014); State v. Houston-Sconiers, 365 P.3d 177, 181 ¶ 16 (Wash. Ct. App. 2015).

[92] Colo. Rev. Stat. § 19-2-908 (2013) (limiting mandatory minimum sentences for juveniles); N.M. Stat. Ann. § 31-18-13(B) (2014) (allowing juvenile offenders to be sentenced to less than the mandatory minimum); Or. Rev. Stat. § 161.620 (2003) (limiting applicability of mandatory minimum sentences for juveniles tried as adults to aggravated murder or felonies committed with a firearm); Wash. Rev. Code § 9.94A.540(3)(a) (2010) (limiting applicability of mandatory minimum sentences for juveniles to aggravated first-degree murder).

[93] The Committee on the Rights of the Child requires that "every person under the age of 18 at the time of the alleged commission of an offense must be treated in accordance with the rules of juvenile justice." Committee on the Rights of the Child, General Comment 10, para. 37.

[94] Article 25(2) of the Universal Declaration of Human Rights (1948) states that "motherhood and childhood are entitled to special care and assistance." Universal Declaration of Human Rights Art. 25(2), G.A. Res. 217 (III) A, UN Doc. A/RES/217(III) (December 10, 1948). Article 24 of the International Covenant on Civil and Political Rights (1966) provides that "every child shall have... the right to such measures of protection as are required by his status as a minor." International Covenant on Civil and Political Rights (ICCPR) Art. 24, opened for signature December 16, 1966, 999 UNTS 171.

in separate juvenile facilities if detention or incarceration is required. The United States is the only country that has not ratified the CRC.

The child's right to special protection is both a "stand alone" right and an interpretive principle for what other fundamental rights – like the right to be free from torture and cruel, inhuman, and degrading treatment and the right to a fair trial – require when a child is involved. This "specialization" requirement recognizes that different systems and protections are necessary for youth given their cognitive development, unique vulnerabilities, and capacity to grow and develop. Both the ICCPR and CRC require that youth in conflict with the law be subject to specialized procedures tailored to youth (like a juvenile justice system) and that they be separated from adults who are accused or convicted of crimes.[95] The international community has developed detailed rules concerning the treatment of youth in conflict with the law, including rules on the Administration of Juvenile Justice and Protection of Juveniles Deprived of Their Liberty (adopted in 1985 and 1990, respectively). These rules articulate minimum standards and underscore that, because of differences between youth and adults, youth who are charged with criminal offenses are entitled to greater protections.

International law also recognizes that prevention of torture and CIDT requires different standards for youth. Juan Méndez summarized international standards in a 2015 report on children deprived of their liberty. The report states that "[c]hildren deprived of their liberty are at a heightened risk of violence, abuse and acts of torture or cruel, inhuman or degrading treatment." He notes that children deprived of liberty have "higher rates of suicide and self-harm, mental disorder and developmental problems."[96] Because of their heightened vulnerability, children deprived of liberty require "higher standards and broader safeguards for the prevention of torture and ill-treatment." These include separation from adults and modified and specialized standards concerning the organization and administration of facilities, disciplinary sanctions, rehabilitation opportunities, staff training, family visits and supports, alternative measures to detention, and monitoring and oversight.[97]

While many legal systems have long recognized differences between youth and adults by creating and maintaining separate juvenile justice systems, Article 40(3) of the CRC specifically requires that ratifying nations undertake comprehensive reforms to ensure specialized treatment of youth in conflict with the law, and many countries have passed reforms to comply with this provision of the CRC. Today, the majority of countries treat youth facing judicial proceedings for alleged violation of criminal laws differently than adults.[98]

---

[95] ICCPR, Art. 10(2)(b), 10(3) (requiring separation of juveniles and adults), 10(2), 14(4) (requiring age appropriate treatment); Convention on the Rights of the Child (CRC) Art. 37(b)-(c), 40(1), (3), opened for signature November 20, 1989, 1577 UNTS 3 (requiring separation, specialized procedures and personnel).
[96] Méndez, Report of the Special Rapporteur 2015, para. 16.   [97] Id. at para. 17.
[98] Cynthia Soohoo, "You Have the Right to Remain a Child," *Columbia Human Rights Law Review* 48, no. 3(2017): note 55.

Perhaps because the United States has not ratified the CRC, there is less awareness of human rights standards protecting youth in conflict with the law in the United States, and US activists have not been actively involved in pushing the international community to develop standards relevant to issues in the United States.

C. US Advocacy to Recognize Raise the Age as a Human Rights Issue

Reports Documenting the Criminal Prosecution of Youth as a Human Rights Issue

The 2012 HRW/ACLU report *Growing Up Locked Down* on youth in solitary confinement in jails and prisons also provided an in-depth analysis of state laws that result in youth being tried as adults and cited international standards that require that children in conflict with the law be treated in a manner that is appropriate to their age and development. In 2014, HRW issued *Branded for Life*, which documented the impact of Florida's direct file statute, which allows prosecutors to decide whether to try youth as adults.[99] The report found that more than 12,000 youth were transferred to adult court within a five-year period and that 60% of the youth transferred were charged with nonviolent crimes. The report emphasized the child's right to special protection under international human rights law and detailed the human rights violations that flow from granting prosecutors unreviewable discretion to try youth as adults; from subjecting youth to adult criminal procedures that fail to take into account their special status, best interests, and ability to meaningfully participate; and from incarcerating them in adult facilities that fail to take into account their special needs and impose unique physical and psychological dangers.

Advocacy before International Human Rights Bodies and Experts

Over the last several years, activists have raised the issue of youth in the adult criminal justice system before the UN and the Inter-American human rights system. In March 2013, the Inter-American Commission conducted a hearing on the human rights situation of youth detained in adult prisons in the state of Michigan, which included statistical information and testimony from youth who had been physically abused and sexually assaulted in prison. Although Michigan officials did not attend, federal officials present supported removing youth from the adult criminal justice system. Following the hearing, in 2014, the Commission undertook a visit to the United States, meeting with government officials, NGOs, local activists, and formerly incarcerated youth and visiting detention facilities in New York, Colorado, and Washington, DC.[100] A final report has not been issued.

---

[99] Human Rights Watch, *Branded for Life: Florida's Prosecution of Children as Adults under Its "Direct File" Statute* (New York: Human Rights Watch, 2014), www.hrw.org/report/2014/04/10/branded-life/floridas-prosecution-children-adults-under-its-direct-file-statute.

[100] "IACHR Conducted a Visit to New York, United States," Inter-American Commission on Human Rights, April 24, 2014, www.oas.org/en/iachr/media_center/PReleases/2014/044.asp; "IACHR Conducts Visit to Colorado, United States," Inter-American Commission on Human Rights, November 14, 2014, www.oas.org/en/iachr/media_center/PReleases/2014/134.asp.

Activists also raised the criminalization of youth in the United States during UN reviews of US compliance with the ICCPR, CERD, and CAT. Joint reports were submitted to the UN for each review by a coalition of national and state groups,[101] including the Correctional Association of New York, which is one of the leaders of New York's Raise the Age Campaign.

Each of the UN treaty bodies criticized US policies criminalizing youth. They emphasized that youth should not be transferred to adult criminal proceedings and should be separated from adults during pretrial detention and after sentencing. In addition to recommending the abolition of solitary confinement for youth, they also emphasized that life without parole sentences for youth should be prohibited. The CERD Committee also expressed concern about racial disparities at all levels of the juvenile justice system and the disproportionate rate at which minority youth are referred to the criminal justice system, prosecuted as adults, incarcerated in adult prisons, and sentenced to life without parole.

D. *Federal Involvement in Raise the Age Reform*

Although not as high profile as efforts to end solitary confinement of youth, the federal government has been supportive of efforts to move youth out of the adult criminal justice system. In addition, federal legislation has addressed the separation of youth and adults in jails and prisons. However, for the most part, these efforts have not adopted human rights language or standards, instead approaching the issue from an antiviolence or crime reduction perspective.

In 2012, the Attorney General's National Task Force on Children Exposed to Violence issued a report recommending that no juvenile offender should be treated as an adult: "Laws and regulations prosecuting them as adults in adult courts, incarcerating them as adults, and sentencing them to harsh punishments that ignore and diminish their capacity to grow must be replaced or abandoned."[102] As discussed above, at the March 2013 hearing at the Inter-American Commission, a representative of the Office of Juvenile Justice and Delinquency Prevention (OJJDP) took the position that youth should not be tried as adults. Melodee Hanes of the Department of Justice's OJJDP stated, "We have learned that kids who go into the adult system have a higher rate of recidivism. Children [at] all costs should not be sent into

---

[101] Reports were submitted by CUNY Law School's International Women's Human Rights Clinic, the ACLU of Michigan/Juvenile Life without Parole Initiative, the Campaign for Youth Justice, the Project on Addressing Prison Rape, American University, Washington College of Law, the University of Miami Human Rights Clinic, and the Correctional Association of New York. "Youth Justice Project," CUNY School of Law Human Rights and Gender Justice Clinic, www.law.cuny.edu/academics/clinics/hrgj/projects/youth-justice-project.html, accessed August 24, 2016.

[102] Robert L. Listenbee Jr. et al., *Report of the Attorney General's National Task Force on Children Exposed to Violence* (Washington, DC: National Task Force on Children Exposed to Violence, 2012), www.justice.gov/defendingchildhood/cev-rpt-full.pdf, 23.

the adult system."[103] At the hearing, the Commission expressed "deep concern" and urged the United States "to identify and urgently implement a federal mechanism to identify anyone under the age of 18 as a child, to keep them from being tried as adults or incarcerated alongside adults."[104] The OJJDP works with federal, state, and local agencies to prevent and combat juvenile delinquency and victimization and has also issued reports recommending that the minimum age of criminal court be raised to 21 or 24 based on studies showing that transferring youth to the adult criminal justice system increased violent crime rates and studies showing that because of youth's developing cognitive ability, they are less culpable and able to fully understand and exercise their rights in adult courts.[105]

The federal government has also taken steps to protect youth in adult jails and prisons by encouraging separation of youth and adults and by investigating and commencing litigation where the level of physical violence has risen to a potential constitutional violation. Federal regulations adopted to implement the federal Prison Rape Elimination Act (PREA) in 2012 require that any person under 18 under adult court supervision must be housed separately from adults in jails and prisons. State and local officials are not required to comply with PREA regulations, but the regulations articulate best practices in correctional policies, and states that do not comply stand to lose federal funding. As discussed below, the DOJ conducted a multiyear investigation of abusive conditions and the unnecessary use of force against youth at Rikers Island. On December 18, 2014, the DOJ sued New York City over unconstitutional conditions for youth on Rikers.[106]

E. Raise the Age as a Human Rights Issue in New York

In the United States writ large and in New York specifically, some activists have described raise the age as a human rights issue, but the frame has yet to gain broader acceptance. In a 2012 report, the Campaign for Youth Justice (CFYJ), a national organization that works to raise the age, criticized the United States as "an outlier among nations." The report argues that US laws allowing youth to be tried as adults violate human rights standards, including CRC provisions that require separation of

---

[103] Testimony of Melodee Haines, IACHR Hearing: Human Rights Situation of Children Deprived of Liberty with Adults in the United States, March 11, 2013, at 00:39:15–00:39:29, www.youtube.com/watch?v=DtIHjB1m76o&list=PLkh9EPEuEx2st1_l-W6cr0o30H9DxBSDc.

[104] Cassie Fleming and Bianca Cappellini, "International Human Rights Commission Criticizes Abuse of Michigan Youth," *ACLU of Michigan* (blog), April 22, 2013, www.aclumich.org/article/international-human-rights-commission-criticizes-abuse-michigan-youth.

[105] National Institute of Justice and Office of Juvenile Justice and Delinquency Prevention, *Young Offenders: What Happens and What Should Happen* (Washington, DC: US Department of Justice, 2014), www.ncjrs.gov/pdffiles1/nij/242653.pdf.

[106] Jennifer Fermino and Dareh Gregorian, "Department of Justice Sues New York City over Rikers' Treatment of Young Prisoners," *Daily News*, December 18, 2014, www.nydailynews.com/new-york/doj-sues-nyc-rikers-treatment-young-prisoners-article-1.2049658.

youth from adults, limit incarceration to the most serious offenses, and require that youth have access to education and services that meet their needs.[107] In New York, the former executive director of Amnesty International has argued that "as a matter of international law children facing criminal prosecution and detention should not be treated in the same manner as adults" and that raising the age is necessary to secure the human rights of New York's youth.[108] Some non–human rights organizations have also taken up human rights claims. The New York Chapter of the National Association of Social Workers has framed raise the age as "a Matter of Human Rights," arguing that current state laws "violate[] the UN Convention on the Rights of the Child, to which the United States is a signatory."[109] Similarly, Brooklyn Defender Services has also argued that New York is out of line with the CRC.[110]

However, in New York, key reports on youth in the adult criminal justice system have failed to use human rights language. In August 2014, the US Department of Justice issued the findings of its multiyear investigation into the conditions of confinement of male adolescents on Rikers Island. The report found rampant use of unnecessary force by correctional officers and that adolescents are subjected to solitary confinement at "an alarming rate and for excessive periods of time."[111] Focusing on constitutional rather than human rights standards, the Department of Justice report emphasized the City's failure to sufficiently protect adolescent inmates from physical harm and the excessive and inappropriate use of prolonged punitive segregation.

In January 2015, the Governor's Commission on Youth, Public Safety, and Justice issued a report recommending that New York raise the age of juvenile court jurisdiction. The report also did not include a human rights analysis. Instead, it described New York state as an outlier in the nation because at the time only New York and North Carolina tried all 16-year-olds as adults and cited Supreme Court jurisprudence establishing that youth are less culpable and more amenable

---

[107] Liz Ryan, *Youth in the Adult Criminal Justice System* (Washington, DC: Campaign for Youth Justice, 2012), www.campaignforyouthjustice.org/images/policybriefs/policyreform/FR_YACJS_2012.pdf, 10; Brian Evans, "Youth Rights Are Human Rights," *Campaign for Youth Justice* (blog), December, 10, 2015, www.campaignforyouthjustice.org/news/blog/item/youth-rights-are-human-rights.

[108] Steven W. Hawkins, Op-Ed, "Raise the Age and Secure Human Rights for New York's Youth," *The Hill* (blog), May 1, 2015, http://thehill.com/blogs/congress-blog/judicial/240716-raise-the-age-and-secure-human-rights-for-new-yorks-youth.

[109] Sandy Bernabei et al., *It's a Matter of Human Rights: Raise the Age of Criminal Responsibility* (New York: National Association of Social Workers, 2015), https://c.ymcdn.com/sites/naswnyc.site-ym.com/resource/resmgr/Docs/12-09-15_Raise_the_Age_State.pdf.

[110] Wesley Caines, "Getting It Right: Raising the Age and Justice System Reforms for Adolescents," *Huffington Post*, February 10, 2014, www.huffingtonpost.com/brooklyn-defender-services/getting-it-right-raising-_b_4419370.html.

[111] Preet Bharara, *US Attorney for the Southern District of New York, CRIPA Investigation of the New York City Department of Correction Jails on Rikers Island* (Washington, DC: US Department of Justice, 2014), www.justice.gov/sites/default/files/usao-sdny/legacy/2015/03/25/SDNY%20Rikers%20Report.pdf, 4, 7–8.

to rehabilitation.[112] In general, the report adopted a policy focus rather than a rights focus, emphasizing that raising the age would reduce recidivism and crime. Despite the support of Governor Cuomo, the New York legislature failed to adopt the Commission's recommendations in 2015, which led to lengthy negotiations over the next two years.

F. Raise the Age Reform in New York

As New York activists waited to see if raise the age legislation would pass, advocacy efforts and federal pressure resulted in improvements in the treatment of youth detained in adult facilities. In 2015, New York State created separate housing units for youth aged 17 and under in prisons, including "specialized programming and education along with additional recreation time," to comply with PREA requirements.[113]

On June 22, 2015, the DOJ settled its lawsuit with New York City over the treatment of youth on Rikers Island. The 63-page agreement includes changes to City policies on the use of force by correctional officials, enhanced video surveillance, improved training and supervision of correctional officials, and a prohibition on the punitive use of solitary confinement. The agreement also requires that the City attempt to identify alternatives to housing youth on Rikers Island.[114] In July 2016, the City announced plans to move youth out of Rikers and into juvenile detention centers.[115]

New York State and City policies providing segregated housing for youth in prisons and moving youth off of Rikers Island are significant developments in the treatment of youth. However, these changes only addressed the most visceral physical harm inflicted on youth by reducing the risk that youth will be assaulted by adult prisoners and moving youth off of Rikers Island, which the Manhattan US attorney characterized as "a broken institution" with a "deep-seated culture of violence."[116]

After failing to raise the age in 2015 and 2016, the New York legislature finally passed a law raising the age in 2017. In addition to the negotiations and political

---

[112] *Final Report of the Governor's Commission on Youth, Public Safety and Justice: Recommendations for Juvenile Justice Reform in New York State* (New York: Commission on Youth, Public Safety and Justice, 2014), www.governor.ny.gov/sites/governor.ny.gov/files/atoms/files/ReportofCommissiononYouthPublicSafetyandJustice_0.pdf.

[113] Daniel J. O'Donnell, *Annual Report 2015* (New York: State Assembly Committee on Correction, 2015), http://assembly.state.ny.us/comm/Correct/2015Annual/index.pdf, 6.

[114] Letter about Settlement Agreement from US Attorney Preet Bharara to Judge Francis, Nunez v. City of New York, 11 Civ. 5845, June 22, 2015, www.justice.gov/usao-sdny/file/479956/download.

[115] Cindy Rodriguez, "Some Rikers Teens Could Be Moved to Bronx Detention Center," WNYC News, July 21, 2016, www.wnyc.org/story/16-and-17-year-olds-rikers-could-be-moving-bronx-detention-center.

[116] "Manhattan US Attorney Finds Pattern and Practice of Excessive Force and Violence at NYC Jails on Rikers Island That Violates the Constitutional Rights of Adolescent Male Inmates," US Attorney's Office for the Southern District of New York, US Department of Justice, August 4, 2014, www.justice.gov/usao-sdny/pr/manhattan-us-attorney-finds-pattern-and-practice-excessive-force-and-violence-nyc-jails.

compromises that created legislation that would satisfy "tough on crime" legislators, the tragic death of Kalief Browder in the summer of 2015 helped to build awareness and public pressure to pass legislation. Kalief was arrested at age 16 for allegedly stealing a backpack. He was detained on Rikers Island for more than three years without ever going to trial. During his time on Rikers, Kalief was beaten by guards and subjected to extended periods of solitary confinement. Charges against him were eventually dropped, but he could not re-acclimate once he came home and committed suicide. Browder's story was chronicled in-depth in the New Yorker and other news outlets.[117] Kalief and Ben Van Zandt, who was arrested and sent to prison at age 17 where he endured rape and solitary confinement and ultimately committed suicide, became the human faces of the raise the age issue.[118] Indeed, it is difficult to hear their stories without becoming both saddened and enraged. When Governor Cuomo signed the raise the age legislation in April 2017, Kalief's brother Akeem was at his side.

The raise the age law passed in 2017 will result in an estimated 17,000 youth who are charged with misdemeanors being tried as juveniles in Family Court instead of as adults in Criminal Court every year. However, the law reflects political compromises and does not remove all youth from the adult criminal system. Youth charged with violent felonies will remain in adult criminal court to face adult criminal consequences, though in a separate section called the "youth part." (There is a chance that some youth in this category could be moved to Family Court, but the number of youth who are moved is likely to be small.) The new legislation leaves untouched a prior law that requires youth as young as 13 to be tried as adults for certain serious offenses. Furthermore, youth charged with nonviolent felonies may also be tried as adults based on the demonstration of extraordinary circumstances (which is undefined) by a prosecutor.[119]

CONCLUSION

In New York, advocates working to reform solitary confinement policies and in particular to prohibit the solitary confinement of youth successfully integrated human rights claims into their work. Human rights proved to be an effective organizing frame because there is general acceptance that torture should be prohibited and because activists were able to define solitary confinement as a form of torture. Activists were

---

[117] Jennifer Gonnerman, "Three Years on Rikers without Trial," *The New Yorker*, October 6, 2014, www.newyorker.com/magazine/2014/10/06/before-the-law; Jennifer Gonnerman, "Kalief Browder 1993-2015," *The New Yorker*, June 17, 2015, www.newyorker.com/news/news-desk/kalief-browder-1993–2015.

[118] Karen Savage, "Activists Hopeful 'Torture' If NY Teens Ends with Passage of Raise the Age Legislation This Year," *Juvenile Justice Information Exchange*, March 30, 2017, http://jjie.org/2017/03/30/activists-hopeful-torture-of-ny-teens-ends-with-passage-of-raise-the-age-legislation-this-year.

[119] Eli Hager, "The Fine Print of New York's Raise the Age Law," *The Marshall Project*, April 14, 2017, www.themarshallproject.org/2017/04/14/the-fine-print-in-new-york-s-raise-the-age-law#.WQ2VFQoIJ.

then able to document and publicize New York solitary practices as a human rights violation, which became part of the public's understanding of the issue. In particular, youth solitary confinement, which involves bodily harm to vulnerable individuals, was able to generate significant public outrage and pressure for change. As a result, New York State and City officials agreed to end solitary confinement of youth and impose limits on the use of solitary for the general adult population.

US activists effectively worked with international human rights bodies and experts to recognize solitary confinement as torture or CIDT and to develop concrete standards to limit its use. They also used international human rights bodies as credible, respected experts to reinforce the message that current US policies violate human rights and to make recommendations for change. Civil and human rights organizations documented solitary practices in the United States and cited relevant human rights standards to support claims that US solitary practices violate international prohibitions on torture and CIDT. The human rights frame became an accepted part of the public's understanding of the issue, with government officials at the federal, state, and local levels repeatedly invoking statements from UN human rights bodies and experts to validate claims that use of solitary confinement in many US jurisdictions constituted torture.

Raise the age legislation eventually passed in New York, but human rights claims were less successful in influencing and supporting reform efforts. Although some non–human rights organizations adopted human rights arguments, including the national Campaign for Youth Justice and some local activists, unlike advocacy around solitary confinement, human rights did not become part of the main framing or the public's understanding of the issue. The Governor's Commission Report which provided the initial blueprint for reform failed to mention human rights. Although the public was moved by the stories of Kalief Browder and Ben Van Zandt, public outrage was not coupled with an understanding that youth have a right to juvenile treatment. As a result, the legislation that ultimately passed did not raise the age for all youth and instead distinguished between youth who are deemed more sympathetic – those accused of misdemeanors – and those accused of felonies.

There are several possible reasons why the human rights frame was less successful. First, although there is a long history of recognizing differences between youth and adults in US law, the concept that children have a right to special protection and treatment does not have the same local acceptance and resonance as the right to be free from torture. Although activists engaged with UN and regional human rights bodies, which criticized the practice of criminally prosecuting youth as adults, their statements were not widely publicized or adopted by local activists.

Second, it may be that the public is likely to perceive youth in solitary confinement as more vulnerable and sympathetic than youth who are tried as adults. Although both issues involve youth who have been accused of committing a crime, activists seeking to raise the age are more likely to be confronted with opposition arguments that public safety and retribution require criminally punishing youth as adults.

These arguments rely on the counternarrative of youth as "super-predators." This counternarrative preys on fear (and often racism) to undercut the public's ability to view youth as vulnerable and deserving of protection. Perhaps in response to this counternarrative, advocacy around raise the age focused more on the policy implications of reform – whether or not trying youth as adults increases or decreases crime and recidivism – rather than on the impact on youth as rights holders. The raise the age legislation that eventually passed reflected the legislature's attempt to balance relief for sympathetic youth (those accused of misdemeanors) and youth perceived as dangerous (those accused of felonies).

Third, raising the age requires more complex structural reform than ending solitary confinement of youth. In the case of solitary confinement, human rights standards provided clear and attainable objectives for activists to rally around – no solitary confinement for youth and the mentally disabled and a 15-day limit for adults. Prohibiting solitary confinement of youth in New York City and New York State initially could be accomplished through unilateral policy changes from the city and state Departments of Correction, although the changes were later made legally binding through city Board of Corrections regulations and state settlement agreements.

Although human rights standards provided a bright-line rule that individuals under 18 should not be tried by or held in the adult criminal justice system, the standard is actually much more complex to implement than the prohibition on youth solitary, requiring changes to the Family and Criminal Courts and countless statutory amendments. The final law adopted by the New York legislature was over 25,000 words long and reflected intense negotiation and compromise – hallmarks of a legislative process rather than the bright line rules favored by rights claims. For all these reasons, human rights claims had less impact in changing laws and policies around the criminalization of youth than in ending the solitary confinement of youth in New York.

To address these issues, activists who continue to work on raise the age in New York and other states should consider whether more can be done to build public acceptance of the right of youth to special protection and treatment. While there is no historic recognition of such right in the United States, there is a long tradition of recognizing that youth are different than adults, and of treating them differently, in a variety of legal contexts. Furthermore, there is increasing scientific support recognizing differences between youth and adults based on studies showing that the brain, including the prefrontal cortex, the part of the brain associated with planning, problem solving, and calibration of risks, does not fully form until the mid-twenties.[120]

---

[120] "Young Adult Development Project," Massachusetts Institute of Technology, http://hrweb.mit.edu/worklife/youngadult/brain.html, accessed November 12, 2016.

Alternatively, activists could try to make a stronger case that trying youth as adults is closely linked to physical harm stemming from incarcerating youth in adult facilities that are not set up to keep them safe. New York reforms seeking to protect youth from violence, including by moving them out of adult detention facilities, have had significant traction. And ultimately, the stories of harm suffered by Kalief Browder and Ben Van Zandt helped garner the support needed to pass New York's raise the age legislation. If activists can succeed in convincing the public that all youth have a right to be free from violence and mental and physical harm inherent in subjecting them to the adult criminal justice system, a human rights frame could support raising the age for all youth.

Unlike countries where human rights obligations are incorporated into the domestic legal system, in the United States, the success of human rights claims relies on the extent to which key decision makers and the American public understand an issue as a human rights issue and feel urgency to address the rights violation. Advocates and government officials can play important roles in encouraging and building the public's acceptance of human right issues and understanding of human rights violations both by engaging with international human rights mechanisms and bodies and by promoting local awareness of the experience of victims.

Interestingly, local use and acceptance of human rights claims do not appear to depend on whether they correspond to binding US obligations under international law. For instance, US activists involved in the Raise the Age Campaign repeatedly rely on the CRC – a treaty the United States has not ratified – to make human rights arguments. Similarly, activists and government officials who describe human rights standards on solitary confinement are more likely to rely on reports from the Special Rapporteur on Torture and the Mandela Rules – nonbinding, soft law – rather than US obligations under international treaties it has ratified. This underscores that while international standards and human rights experts can play an important role in supporting and legitimizing human rights claims, the key factor in successful human rights claims is how persuasive the claim is to the American people and not the source of the right. While this may be unsatisfying for human right activists who would like to see greater US compliance with its international treaty obligations, this form of human rights change is responsive to critiques that compliance with human rights standards somehow erodes US sovereignty or is antidemocratic. Indeed, human rights claims will only be successful in the United States if the American audience accepts them as human rights with inherent normative value, ultimately leaving it to the American people to decide what constitutes a human right in the US context.

2

The Story of Environmental Justice and Race in the United States

International Human Rights and Equal Environmental Protection

Erika R. George*

Environmental injustice remains a significant problem in the United States. In Louisiana, communities of color are concentrated in an industrial corridor between New Orleans and Baton Rouge. Petrochemical processing plants line this corridore. Called "Cancer Alley" for the prevalence of disease and premature death among local residents, the corridor hosts hundreds of processing facilities, including one of the world's largest oil refineries. Exposure to environmental contaminants is segregated along lines of race and class. Communities of color in the United States have complained against polluting industries, opposed the permitting of new industry projects, and called for investigations and interventions. Victims of rights violations associated with environmental pollution presently have little recourse as avenues to seek remedy in US courts have narrowed. Legal doctrines that require intentional discrimination to recognize an abuse render it increasingly difficult to resolve claims of environmental racism in court. This chapter seeks to demonstrate that international human rights instruments can be instructive and that developments in international policy on business responsibility and human rights could hold promise for communities of color in the United States seeking environmental justice. Activists and affected communities could find other avenues more receptive to recognizing the reality of environmental racism.

Part I of the chapter defines environmental justice and deconstructs public debates on environmental racism and environmental justice in the United States. It discusses the emergence of claims of environmental racism and the evolution of the environmental justice movement. It presents evidence of the disproportionate

---

* The author thanks Austin Sarat and William Brewbaker for their constructive comments and Carmen Gonzalez, Rebecca Bratspies, Sara Seck, Hari Osofsky, and Robin Craig for their helpful insights. David Fergeson, Ryan Moser, Pablo Hapsel, Matthew Grow, and Michelle Louise Kfoury provided valuable research assistance.

impact that pollution has had and that climate change is expected to have on communities of color in the United States. It also offers a critical examination of the consequences of moving public discourse away from environmental racism toward environmental justice. Part II of the chapter provides an overview of the international human rights legal framework and efforts to define human rights obligations relating to the enjoyment of a safe, clean, healthy, and sustainable environment as relevant to realizing environmental justice in the United States. Part III of the chapter provides an overview of the domestic civil rights legal framework relevant to the formulation of environmental justice claims. After a discussion of how international human rights treaties are treated by US courts, it surveys environmental racism litigation. The impact of the intent requirement on equal protection and disparate impact claims of racial discrimination related to environmental protection is also examined. Next, it examines the efficacy of initiatives by other branches of government to address environmental injustice from the perspective of people involved in the creation and implementation of programs developed to address adverse impacts of environmental harms on people of color communities. Specifically, executive orders and administrative agency actions are reviewed for content informed by international norms. Part IV presents representations the US government has made to international human rights institutions with respect to environmental justice. It also presents how communities affected by environmental injustice have relied on international institutions for recognition of rights claims. The chapter concludes with a caution that race-neutral, color-blind approaches to disparity in environmental protection are inconsistent with international norms and do little to advance environmental justice. It calls for a more inclusive environmental justice movement to embrace concerns of racial justice and to look to further define the obligations of a range of actors beyond the state to respect environmental human rights, including business enterprises.

INTRODUCTION

In a lawsuit brought in federal court in the United States, Nigerian nationals who once resided in the oil-rich Niger Delta alleged that their international human rights were violated when they suffered harmful health effects due to environmental pollution associated with extractive industry activities. They reported that their livelihoods have been impeded by pollution and that their ability to fish and farm had been compromised due to contamination caused by the actions and omissions of oil companies operating in their region. Affected communities argued that the failure of firms overseeing operations in the area to repair damage done or remedy harm suffered was unfair, unjust, and unacceptable. On the other side of the world, residents of a stretch of land in the Mississippi Delta have similar complaints concerning environmental contamination by commercial activity and the human right to a clean and healthy environment. Environmental degradation along "Cancer Alley" in Louisiana, the corridor between New Orleans and Baton Rouge, has allegedly cost lives while providing livelihoods. As Wilma Subra, an environmental scientist and MacArthur "Genus Grant" award winner, has explained, many residents of the region living near industrial facilities in Cancer Alley "don't have the money to leave, [while] the workers won't leave because of the money they can make."[1] More than 150 industrial facilities line Cancer Alley, and nearly one-quarter of the petrochemicals used in the United States are produced in the area. Common to both the Mississippi Delta region and the Niger Delta, despite distance, are private, commercial enterprises that allegedly have had an adverse impact on the enjoyment of the right to a clean, healthy, and safe environment. Industrial actors are engaged in modes of production that release pollutants into the air and water that most residents of both regions rely on for sustenance and survival.

While communities are making their claims in terms of environmental human rights and racial justice, US law continues to refuse to recognize and respond to claims made in the name of human rights, despite demonstrated racial disparities. Allegations of human rights abuses originating in the United States associated with environmental deterioration are being accommodated by international human rights–monitoring bodies.

I. NAMING AND FRAMING THE HARM: FROM ENVIRONMENTAL RACISM TO ENVIRONMENTAL JUSTICE

Members of the faith community were the first to frame and name the harm of "environmental racism" in the United States. Reverend Benjamin Chavis Jr. of the United Church of Christ Commission for Racial Justice used the term to describe a reality he had observed – that of persistent discrimination in environmental policy making and in the enforcement of environmental regulations and laws to deliberately disadvantage communities of color.[2] In 1987, the United Church of Christ released an influential national report finding that the disproportionate impact on communities of color for the disposal of hazardous waste and development of industries that produce pollution "was not the result of mere coincidence."[3] Environmental

---

[1] Julie Cart, "A Strong Voice in Louisiana's Cancer Alley," *Los Angeles Times*, August 27, 2013.
[2] Benjamin Chavis, foreword to *Confronting Environmental Racism: Voices from the Grassroots*, ed. Robert Bullard (Boston: South End Press, 1993), 3.
[3] United Church of Christ Commission for Racial Justice, *Toxic Wastes and Race: A National Report on the Racial and Socio-Economic Characteristics of Communities with Hazardous Waste Sites* (1987), 9–10. The terms "minorities" and "people of color" are used interchangeably to refer to individuals who self-identify as nonwhite or Hispanic on the US Census. The term "people of color communities" or "minority communities" is used to refer to geographic regions with high concentrations of residents who self-identify as nonwhite.

racism emerged as the term to describe and to draw attention to the disproportionate harmful impacts environmental degradation causes people of color.[4]

The United Church of Christ study identified various factors that contribute to the vulnerability of communities of color, including poverty, inhabiting relatively inexpensive land, and limited mobility or ability to leave land due to discriminatory real estate practices.[5] Lack of the political and economic influence to sustain opposition to business enterprises polluting property also left communities predominantly composed of people of color vulnerable to unsafe environments.[6] The report concluded that above all other factors, the race of the surrounding residents was the single best determinant of the location of a commercial hazardous waste facility.[7]

Understanding environmental challenges through the lens of race revealed how the environmental experiences of people of color differed from those of whites in America. Owing to their differences, communities of color placed different priorities on the environmental activism agenda. Many whites in the United States had more opportunity to appropriate and accumulate land, to enjoy access to resources, and to enjoy freedom of movement and the ability to choose where to reside without discrimination based on race.[8] The dominant early environmental discourse was developed primarily by free, white males with relative influence or wealth or access to it.[9] Far fewer people of color in the United States enjoyed such opportunities. As a result, for communities of color engaged in environmental justice struggles, issues of autonomy, self-determination, civil rights, and human rights came to feature more prominently as priorities.[10] These equity issues were seen as less salient concerns as dominant environmental discourses addressed issues around resource management and environmental degradation.[11] The early environmental activism of people of color opposed residential segregation and exclusion from access to public parks and beaches.[12] Worker health and safety on farms where pesticide contamination presented risks and locating polluting facilities in communities dominated by people of color were also on their environmental agenda.[13] People of color linked their experience of racism with exposure to hazardous environments and exclusion from healthy environments.[14] Early environmental racism activists complained about the "deliberate targeting" of communities of color.[15] In addition to intentional

---

[4] Tara Ulezalka, "Race and Waste: The Question for Environmental Justice," *Temple Journal of Society Technology and the Environment* 27 (2007): 51, 52.
[5] UCC Report at 13.
[6] See Paul Mohai and Bunyan Brant, "Environmental Injustice: Weighing Race and Class as Factors in the Distribution of Environmental Hazards," *University of Colorado Law Review* 62 (1992): 921, 922.
[7] UCC Report at 15–16.
[8] Dorceta E. Taylor, "The Rise of the Environmental Justice Paradigm: Injustice Framing and the Social Construction of Environmental Discourses," *American Behavioral Scientist* 43, no. 4 (2000): 508, 534.
[9] Id. at 534.   [10] Id.   [11] Id.   [12] Id. at 535.   [13] Id.   [14] Id.
[15] Paul Mohai, David Pellow, and J. Timmons Roberts, "Environmental Justice," *Annual Review of Environmental Resources* 34 (2009): 405, 407.

discrimination, allegations of discriminatory impacts on communities of color came to figure prominently in lawsuits brought against polluting industries by minority plaintiffs.

The term "environmental racism" was not without detractors.[16] Commentators and policy makers contested charges that the conditions observed by researchers and the circumstances experienced by communities of color were due to the color of their skin or racism.[17] Commentators critical of "environmental racism" have offered economic class as the primary explanation for the disparate exposure to unhealthy environmental conditions and reference the few studies that suggest that minorities are not unfairly burdened by environmental discrimination.[18] Some scholars have argued that environmentalists who attribute existing environmental injustices to racial discrimination fail to appreciate market forces and economic imperatives.[19] Economic forces and low income attract the poor and people of color to those areas where the environment may be more compromised it is argued.[20]

Still, there is significant empirical evidence justifying reference to racism and requiring environmental justice. For instance, as early as 1982, the US Office of General Accounting investigated complaints originating from Warren County, North Carolina, that hazardous waste sites were disproportionately sited in African American communities.[21] The General Accounting Office investigation found that three of four hazardous waste sites were placed in majority minority communities.[22] While the fourth site was not directly in a majority minority community, it was within a few miles of a predominantly African American community.[23] Subsequent studies have found patterns of disproportionate distribution of environmental health hazards by race and income. For example, in Los Angeles County, the area with the highest level of chemical discharge was 59% African American.[24] A study of three counties bordering Detroit found that people of color were four times more likely

---

[16] David Friedman, "The 'Environmental Racism' Hoax," American Enterprise Institute for Public Policy Research (2008).

[17] See Musa Keenheel, "The Need for New Legislation and Liberalization of Current Laws to Combat Environmental Racism," *Temple Environmental Law Journal* 20 (2001): 105, 108.

[18] See, e.g., Douglas Anderton and Andy B. Anderson et al., "Hazardous Waste Facilities: 'Environmental Equity' Issues in Metropolitan Areas," *Evaluation Review* 18 (April 1994): 2, 123; Brett Baden and Don Coursey, "The Locality of Waste Sites Within the City of Chicago: A Demographic, Social and Economic Analysis," *Hazardous Waste News*, May 19, 1997.

[19] See Lynn E. Blais, "Environmental Racism Reconsidered," *North Carolina Law Review* 75 (1996): 75, 81.

[20] Id.   [21] Keenheel, "Need for New Legislation," 105.

[22] US General Accounting Office (GAO), "Siting of Hazardous Waste Landfills and Their Correlation with Racial and Economic Status of Surrounding Communities," June 1, 1983, www.gao.gov.

[23] Id.

[24] Keenheel, "Need for New Legislation," 1050 (citing Vicki Been, "What's Fairness Got to Do with It? Environmental Justice and the Siting of Locally Undesirable Land Uses," *Cornell Law Review* 71 (1993): 1001); see also Richard J. Lazarus, "Pursuing 'Environmental Justice': The Distributional Effects of Environmental Protection," *Northwestern University Law Review* 87 (1993): 787.

than whites to live within a one-mile radius of a waste facility.[25] A study of incinerator facilities located in Baton Rouge, Louisiana, found that white areas averaged just one facility per 31,000 residents, whereas majority minority areas had on average one facility for every 7,000 residents.[26] More waste facilities are located in middle-class communities of color than in poor white communities in the United States.[27] Since the United Church of Christ national report, several regional and local studies have suggested that race, not poverty, influences the impact of environmental hazards and informs the distribution of environmental risks in the United States.

The distribution of risks of environmental harms varies vastly between people of color and whites across a range of different contexts, at home, at work, and in general.[28] People of color disproportionately work in occupations and live in places that present hazardous risks to health.[29] The homes people of color inhabit are more likely to be located in close proximity to a hazardous waste facility. People of color relative to whites disproportionately live in homes in older urban areas and

---

[25] Mohai and Bryant, "Environmental Racism," 163, 172.
[26] Harvey L. White, "Hazardous Waste Incineration and Minority Communities," in *Race and the Incidence of Environmental Hazards: A Time for Discourse*, ed. Bunyan Bryant and Paul Mohai (Boulder, CO: Westview Press, 1992).
[27] Tara Ulezalka, "Race and Waste: The Question for Environmental Justice," *Temple Journal of Society Technology and the Environment* 27 (2007): 51, 57 (citing Mike Ewall, *Environmental Racism in Chester* (1999), www.ejnet.org/chester/ewall_article.html).
[28] Lara P. Clark et al., "National Patterns in Environmental Injustice and Inequality: Outdoor NO_2 Air Pollution in the United States," *PLOS ONE* 9 (2014): 1, http://journals.plos.org/plosone/article?id=10.1371/journal.pone.0094431 (study describing "spatial patterns in environmental injustice and inequality for residential outdoor nitrogen dioxide (NO_2) concentrations in the contiguous United States." It finds that NO_2 concentrations nationally "are 4.6 ppb (38%, p<0.01) higher for nonwhites than for whites." It states that the health implications of this disparity are "compelling" in that "reducing nonwhites' NO_2 concentrations to levels experienced by whites would reduce Ischemic Heart Disease (IHD) mortality by ~7,000 deaths per year." NO_2, which is one of the six EPA criteria pollutants, is also linked to asthma, decreased lung function in children, and low birth weights); Daniel R. Faber and Eric J. Krieg, "Unequal Exposure to Ecological Hazards 2005: Environmental Injustices in the Commonwealth of Massachusetts," www.northeastern.edu/nejrc/wp-content/uploads/Final-Unequal-Exposure-Report-2005-10-12-05.pdf (an extensive study that looks at unequal exposure in terms of racial and poverty to hazardous waste sites, landfills, transfer stations, incinerators, polluting industrial facilities, and power plants within communities in Massachusetts and finds that "communities of color average well over seven-and-a-half times as many hazardous waste sites per town as low minority communities." The authors explain: "In short, if you live in a community of color, you are thirty-nine times more likely to live in one of the most environmentally hazardous communities in Massachusetts"); Rachel Massey, "Environmental Justice: Income, Race, and Health," Global Development and Environment Institute, Tufts University (2004), www.ase.tufts.edu/gdae/education_materials/modules/Environmental_Justice.pdf (study reviews environmental conditions around Los Angeles public schools, finding that minority children suffered exposure to air pollution while at school and the schools ranked in the bottom fifth for air quality had a 92% minority student population).
[29] David R. Williams and Chiquita Collins, "US Socioeconomic and Racial Differences in Health: Patterns and Explanations," *Annual Review of Sociology* 21 (1995): 349 ("employed blacks are more likely than their white peers to be exposed to occupational hazards and carcinogens, even after adjusting for job experience and education").

risk exposure to lead paint.[30] Aging and inadequate infrastructure poses a danger of unsafe exposure to contaminants in urban areas where people of color are more likely to reside.[31] For example, in 2015, residents of Flint, Michigan, a majority minority city, learned their water was not safe to drink due to lead pollution after a series of government policy decisions put the community's water supply at risk.[32] The government's slow response to the pollution problem has raised questions about environmental racism, with residents wondering whether a predominately white community would have confronted similar challenges.[33] In 2016, the Standing Rock Sioux of North Dakota began protests to protect their water supply which was placed at risk by a government decision to approve a fast-track permit for a private company's pipeline to be rerouted away from the majority white city of Bismarck and through the tribe's sacred lands.[34]

Eventually reference to environmental racism was largely erased from public debates concerning the disproportionate burden borne by people of color residing

---

[30] Jasmine Bell, "5 Things to Know about Communities of Color and Environmental Justice," Center for American Progress, April 25, 2016, www.americanprogress.org/issues/race/news/2016/04/25/136361/5-things-to-know-about-communities-of-color-and-environmental-justice/. The article reviews major environmental justice issues that communities of color face, citing recent studies. It states:
   a Communities of color have higher exposure rates to air pollution than their white, non-Hispanic counterparts.
   b Landfills, hazardous waste sites, and other industrial facilities are most often located in communities of color.
   c Lead poisoning disproportionately affects children of color.
   d Climate change disproportionately affects low-income communities and communities of color.
   e Water contamination plagues low-income areas and communities of color across the nation.

[31] Juliet Christian-Smith et al., *A Twenty-First Century US Water Policy* (Oxford: Oxford University Press, 2012), 65 ("The combination of discriminatory land-use patterns and the impacts of urbanization means that water issues in a low-income community or community of color may be easily overlooked. Whereas many of the water-related impacts of urbanization are related to local planning and permitting decisions, it is also local-level planning that has influenced the concentration of low-income communities and communities of color into marginal urban geographies"); see also EPA Infrastructure Task Force Access Subgroup, "Meeting the Access Goal: Strategies for Increasing Access to Safe Drinking Water and Wastewater Treatment to American Indian and Alaska Native Homes" (2008), www.epa.gov/sites/production/files/2015-07/documents/meeting-the-access-goal-strategies-for-increasing-access-to-safe-drinking-water-and-wastewater-treatment-american-indian-alaska-native-villages.pdf ("According to 2007 data from the Indian Health Service (IHS) approximately 13% of American Indian/Alaska Native (AI/AN) homes do not have safe water and/or wastewater disposal facilities... compared with the 0.6% of non-native homes in the United States that lack such infrastructure as measured in 2005 by the US Census." The report also found that 61% of Native American reservations reported health and safety code violations, compared with 27% of public systems throughout the rest of the country").

[32] Julie Bosman, "Flint Water Crisis Inquiry Finds State Ignored Warning Signs," *New York Times*, March 23, 2016, www.nytimes.com/2016/03/24/us/flint-water-crisis.html.

[33] John Eligon, "A Question of Environmental Racism," *New York Times*, January 21, 2016, www.nytimes.com/2016/01/22/us/a-question-of-environmental-racism-in-flint.html?_r=1.

[34] Jeni Monnet, "For Native 'Water Protectors,' Standing Rock Protest Has Become Fight for Religious Freedom, Human Rights," November 3, 2016, www.pbs.org/newshour/rundown/military-force-criticized-dakota-access-pipeline-protests/.

in communities with environments compromised by harmful industrial pollution. "Environmental justice" advanced as the favored term to capture the demands from communities for equal enforcement of environmental regulations and remedying the range of injuries associated with environmental degradation. The Environmental Protection Agency offers the following definition of environmental justice:

> Environmental Justice is the fair treatment and meaningful involvement of all people regardless of race, color, national origin, or income, with respect to the development, implementation, and enforcement of environmental laws, regulations, and policies.[35]

Environmental justice today is understood as a convergence of movements for environmental protection and racial justice. On the other hand, failure to look at environmental issues through the lens of race in considering the conditions under which communities of color were living risked erasure of recognition of racism as responsible for creating adverse conditions.

Under the view that policy makers and market forces must select somewhere to site hazardous industrial waste, intentional discrimination on the part of policy makers or the market is difficult to prove. Environmental racism in the United States may not be intentional but rather result from indifference toward a vulnerable population group that has simply not been seen as important.

References to environmental racism confronted criticism from commentators questioning claims that polluters were intentionally targeting minorities, instead of simply making decisions based on economic expedience. Reference to racism was perceived as implicating intent. Whether or not the actions that led to adverse impacts were intentional, they often appear to be the result of indifference to the plight of precisely those populations most impacted by decisions and least likely to be in a position to influence decision makers.

The environmental justice movement brings together racial inequality and environmental degradation. Racism is real in three ways: (1) disparate siting and permitting of hazardous facilities, (2) disparate enforcement of environmental protections all are entitled to under existing laws, and (3) disparate remediation efforts. Environmental justice advocates and academics attribute environmental injustice to disproportionate exposure to environmental hazards and insufficient access to healthy environments.

The environmental justice movement has struggled to find an effective legal strategy in courts in the United States. In the international policy arena, environmental justice advocates may find a more receptive audience for evolving legal standards to reach the types of claims raised by people of color communities. Part II traces the evolving understanding of environmental human rights.

---

[35] US Environmental Protection Agency, "Learn about Environmental Justice," www.epa.gov/environmentaljustice/learn-about-environmental-justice.

II. ENVIRONMENTAL JUSTICE AND INTERNATIONAL HUMAN RIGHTS

This section describes the emerging recognition of a relationship between human rights and environmental protection due to an increasing convergence between the environmental movement and the human rights movement at the international level. Specifically, this section offers an assessment of the evolution of a human right to a clean and healthy environment through a review of relevant international environmental legal instruments and international human rights law. It then outlines the developing consensus regarding the procedural and substantive aspects of environmental human rights.

A. *International Environmental Human Rights*

The instruments that make up the International Bill of Human Rights, including the Universal Declaration of Human Rights (UDHR), the International Covenant on Civil and Political Rights (ICCPR), and the International Covenant of Economic Social and Cultural Rights (ICESCR), do not contain express reference to a clean and healthy environment. Nevertheless, several of the rights that are guaranteed in these fundamental human rights instruments require a clean and healthy environment in order to be enjoyed. For example, human rights advocates have documented the ways in which the rights to life, health, food, and water have been seriously compromised by pollution, environmental degradation, and climate change.

While the human right to a clean and healthy environment was not expressly enumerated in early human rights instruments, a growing body of international declarations and soft law standards is providing a foundation for recognition of environmental human rights. Although a central feature of environmental law is a focus on the natural environment,[36] early international environmental legal norms did recognize relationship between environmental quality and human dignity in rights terms.

The visionary Stockholm Declaration on the Human Environment,[37] the outcome document of the influential 1972 United Nations Conference on the Human Environment, sets forth several concepts that continue to influence present debates over the existence of environmental human rights and their content. The Stockholm Declaration laid the foundation for an appreciation of the relationship between preservation and enhancement of the environment and the enjoyment of basic human rights. Although a soft law instrument, the 1972 Stockholm Declaration in its preamble provides a strong statement of the imperative of environmental protection. The preamble to the Declaration proclaims:

---

[36] Rebecca Bratspies, "Do We Need a Human Right to a Healthy Environment?," *Santa Clara Journal of International Law* 13 (2015): 31, 38.
[37] Stockholm Declaration on the Human Environment, June 16, 1972.

> Man is both creature and moulder of his environment, which gives him physical sustenance and affords him the opportunity for intellectual, moral, social and spiritual growth. In the long and tortuous evolution of the human race on this planet a stage has been reached when, through the rapid acceleration of science and technology, man has acquired the power to transform his environment in countless ways and on an unprecedented scale. Both aspects of man's environment, the natural and the man-made, are essential to his well-being and to the enjoyment of basic human rights the right to life itself.[38]

The Stockholm Preamble recognizes humanity's power to alter the environment and entreats humanity to exercise its power responsibly to ensure the continued well-being of humanity. Some international environmental legal scholars have cautioned against a framing of environmental rights that is overly anthropocentric, valuing environmental protection only to promote human interests and emphasize the importance of an ecocentric approach.[39]

Principle 1 of the Stockholm Declaration directly links basic rights, including equality, to environmental protection:

> Man has the fundamental right to freedom, equality and adequate conditions of life, in an environment of a quality that permits a life of dignity and well-being, and he bears a solemn responsibility to protect and improve the environment for present and future generations. In this respect, policies promoting or perpetuating apartheid, racial segregation, discrimination, colonial and other forms of oppression and foreign domination stand condemned and must be eliminated.[40]

Stockholm represents the relationship between the environment and human rights as inseparable, interrelated, and interconnected.

Subsequent to the Stockholm Declaration, in 1989, the Hague Declaration on the Environment also recognized a connection between the enjoyment of human rights and a clean environment by pointing to the potential consequences of failure

---

[38] Id.
[39] Because human rights law is anthropocentric, some scholars caution that a human rights approach to environmental protection would do little to disrupt unsustainable development models that are based on the exploitation and domination of nature. These scholars point to the risks of regarding the environment in solely instrumental terms and highlight other more ecocentric approaches consistent with indigenous knowledge systems as potentially more constructive. See Carmen G. Gonzalez, "Environmental Justice, Human Rights and the Global South," *Santa Clara Journal of International Law* 13 (2015): 151, 185–86 (explaining that indigenous legal systems could "provide the foundation for a more robust conception of human rights that acknowledges the interdependence of humans and nature and promotes intergenerational equity"); Carmen G. Gonzalez, "Bridging the North-South Divide: International Environmental Law in the Anthropocene," *Pace Environmental Law Review* 32 (2015): 407, 407–8; Alex Geisinger, "Sustainable Development and the Domination of Nature: Spreading the Seed of the Western Ideology of Nature," *British Colombia Environmental Affairs Law Review* 27 (1999): 43, 52–58.
[40] Stockholm Declaration on the Human Environment, June 16, 1972.

to address environmental challenges. In pertinent part, the Hague Declaration preamble states:

> The right to live is the right from which all other rights stem. Guaranteeing this right is the paramount duty of those in charge of all States throughout the world. Today, the very conditions of life on our planet are threatened by the severe attacks to which the earth's atmosphere is subjected.[41]

Significantly, the Hague Declaration emphasizes the obligations of States to address threats to the environment.

In addition to the statements contained in international environmental instruments, the decisions of international institutions have recognized the importance of the interrelationship between human rights and environmental degradation. For example, Justice Weeramantry, former vice president of the International Court of Justice, writing in a separate opinion in the 1997 case concerning the Gabcikovo–Nagymaros Project, explained:

> The protection of the environment is likewise a vital part of contemporary human rights doctrine, for it is a sine qua non for numerous human rights such as the right to health and the right to life itself. It is scarcely necessary to elaborate on this, as damage to the environment can impair and undermine all the human rights spoken of in the Universal Declaration and other human rights instruments.[42]

Beyond international judicial bodies, other organizations have elevated the importance of environmental conditions as an antecedent to the enjoyment of fundamental human rights. For example, a 1990 United Nations General Assembly resolution endorsed the position that "all individuals are entitled to live in an environment adequate for their health and well-being."[43] The General Assembly resolution also underscored the rights of everyone to an adequate standard of living for his or her own health and well-being as enshrined in the UDHR and the ICESCR, explaining that "a better and healthier environment can help contribute to the full enjoyment of human rights by all."[44] Moreover, it emphasizes that "environmental degradation can endanger the very basis of life."[45]

Regional human rights institutions have also addressed the importance of environmental conditions to the realization of rights. To date, two regional human rights instruments provide express recognition of an entitlement to a clean environment in human rights terms. The African Charter on Human and Peoples' Rights and the Protocol of San Salvador, an additional Protocol to the American Convention on Human Rights, both contain references to environmental rights in and of themselves.

---

[41] Hague Declaration on the Environment, March 11, 1989, 28 I.L.M. 1308.
[42] See Gabcikovo–Nagymaros Project (Hung v. Slouk), 1997 I.C.S. 7 (September 25) reprinted in 37 I.L.M. 168, 206–7.
[43] G.A. Res.45/94, UN GAOR, 45th Sess., at 2 UN Doc. A/RES/45/94 (1991). [44] Id. [45] Id.

For example, Article 24 of the African Charter provides that "[a]ll peoples shall have the right to a general satisfactory environment favourable to their development."[46] Article 11 of the San Salvador Protocol provides:

1. Everyone shall have the right to live in a healthy environment and to have access to basic public services.
2. The States Parties shall promote the protection, preservation and improvement of the environment. In addition, the Protocol contains a provision on the right to health: "Everyone shall have the right to health, understood to mean the enjoyment of the highest level of physical, mental and social well-being."[47]

Interpreting the San Salvador Protocol, the Inter-American Commission on Human Rights and the Inter-American Court of Human Rights have stated that the American Convention on Human Rights requires States to provide access to judicial recourse for claims alleging the violation of their rights as a result of environmental harm.[48]

Although issues of environmental damage are relevant to human rights and can place the enjoyment of certain rights at risk, the extent to which international environmental law informs human rights doctrine was not explored in detail until the appointment of a Special Rapporteur on Human Rights and the Environment in 1990 by the United Nations Sub-Commission on the Prevention of Discrimination and Protection of Minorities.[49] The inaugural Special Rapporteur, Fatma Zohra Ksentini, advocated in favor of express recognition of a right to a healthy environment through a legal framework, explaining in her final report that

> [i]nternational environmental regulations, which emerged from a worldwide movement and a collective realization of the dangers threatening our planet and the future of mankind, were initially sectoral and essentially envisaged within the traditional framework of inter-State relations; they have finally attained a global dimension, which has made possible the shift from environmental law to the right to a healthy and decent environment.[50]

Ksentini convened a group of experts, including civil society organizations, as part of her mandate to prepare a set of Draft Principles on Human Rights and the Environment. The relationship between development, human rights violations, and environmental degradation was recognized by the expert panel and articulated in the draft principles.[51] The expert panel set forth the following principles pertaining to environmental human rights:

---

[46] African Charter on Human and Peoples Rights, Art. 24.
[47] Additional Protocol to the American Convention on Human Rights in the Area of Economic, Social and Cultural Rights, November 14, 1988, 28 IL.M 156, 165.
[48] UN Doc. E/CN.4/Sub.2/1990/9 (1994), para. 42.
[49] Sara Seck, "Human Rights and Extractive Industries: Environmental Law and Standards," Rock Mountain Minerals Law Foundation Institute Paper 2 (2016): 13.
[50] UN Doc. E/CN.4/Sub.2/1990/9 (1994). [51] Seck, "Human Rights and Extractive Industries," 13.

1. Human rights, an ecologically sound environment, sustainable development and peace are interdependent and indivisible.
2. All persons have the right to a secure, healthy and ecologically sound environment. This right and other human rights, including civil, cultural, economic, political and social rights, are universal, interdependent and indivisible.
3. All persons shall be free from any form of discrimination in regard to actions and decisions that affect the environment.
4. All persons have the right to an environment adequate to meet equitably the needs of present generations and that does not impair the rights of future generations to meet equitably their needs.[52]

In its resolution 19/10, the Human Rights Council, the successor entity to the Commission that appointed the Special Rapporteur, appointed an Independent Expert on Human Rights and the Environment and tasked him to study "human rights obligations, including non-discrimination, relating to the enjoyment of a safe, clean, healthy and sustainable environment."[53] Independent Expert John Knox conducted an initial analysis mapping statements made by important sources on human rights obligations related to the environment, including international human rights treaty monitoring bodies, institutions and special procedure mandate holders of the United Nations, regional human rights systems, and international environmental instruments. In his final analysis, Knox noted, "Despite the diversity of the sources from which they arise, ... the statements are remarkably coherent. Taken together, they provide strong evidence of converging trends towards greater uniformity and certainty in the human rights obligations relating to the environment. These trends are further supported by State practice reflected in the universal periodic review process and international environmental instruments."[54]

Based on the sources reviewed, Knox identified evidence of emerging human rights obligations related to environmental issues. For example, his research revealed that several countries had already recognized the importance of incorporating human rights considerations into environmental laws. While not all states have formally adopted all of the norms related to environmental protection and human rights identified by the Independent Expert, this convergence of recognition around the relationship between human rights and the environment suggests that *opinio juris* could be forming as to state obligations with respect to promoting environmental justice. In the universal periodic review process before the Human Rights Council, the communications by States indicate a growing consensus that there is a state obligation to protect the environment.[55] Indeed, many States have described the steps they have taken to create institutions and to adopt policies and laws to address environmental protection.[56] Still the practices of several states could stand to be

---

[52] UN Doc. E/CN.4/Sub.2/1994/9 (1994). [53] Id.
[54] Id. at para. 27. [55] Id. at para. 52. [56] Id.

brought into better alignment with environmental justice principles. The Human Rights Council's affirmation in its resolution that "human rights obligations and commitments have the potential to inform and strengthen international, regional and national policy making in the area of environmental protection" also urges States "to take human rights into consideration when developing their environmental policies."[57]

The Independent Expert found that States have procedural obligations to assess environmental impacts on human rights, to make information about impacts available to the public, to facilitate public participation in environmental decision making, and to provide access to remedies for adverse environmental impacts.[58] States also have substantive obligations to enact laws and establish institutional frameworks to ensure protection from adverse environmental impacts that interfere with the enjoyment of human rights. Specifically, States have obligations to protect against environmental harm that interferes with the enjoyment of human rights because environmental harm may threaten a range of human rights. The Independent Expert's mapping report of human rights instruments concluded that "the content of States' specific obligations to protect against environmental harm therefore depends on the content of their duties with respect to the particular rights threatened by the harm" and that such "duties may vary from right to right."[59] When environmental harm threatens or infringes the enjoyment of a right protected by one or more of these agreements, States' general obligations relating to the right (e.g., to respect and ensure it, or to take steps toward its full realization) apply with respect to the environmental threat or infringement. According to the Independent Expert, "in addition to procedural and substantive obligations, states possess obligations to protect members of vulnerable groups and must not engage in discrimination in the application of environmental laws."[60] The Independent Expert found State obligations concerning women, children, and indigenous people were well developed, whereas state obligations toward other groups, such as racial or ethnic minorities, were less clear. Significantly, the Independent Expert found that the State's obligation to guard against human rights abuses associated with environmental deterioration extends to environmental harms caused by private, nonstate actors, including commercial enterprises.[61] Many of the environmental injustices complained about by minority communities in the United States involve industrial pollution associated with various commercial industries.

In sum, although the content of environmental obligations continues to evolve, some core characteristics have become evident. In particular, according to the Independent Expert's analysis, states must (1) "adopt and implement legal frameworks to protect against environmental harm that may infringe on enjoyment of human rights" and (2) "regulate private actors to protect against such environmental harm."

---

[57] Resolution 16/11.   [58] UN Doc. E/CN.4/Sub.2/1994/9 (1994) at para. 79.
[59] Id. at para. 44.   [60] Id. at para. 81.   [61] Id. at para. 80.

The relationship between the international human rights framework developed to address the conduct of state actors and the domestic policy decisions facilitating private economic activities that may have adverse and disproportionate impacts on communities of color remains a pressing challenge. A human right to a clean and healthy environment should come to resonate with courts and regulatory authorities in the United States as a practical matter.[62]

III. US JUDGMENTS AND ENVIRONMENTAL JUSTICE

Plaintiffs seeking redress for environmental racism have largely failed to overcome aspects of equality jurisprudence in the United States that restrict claims heard in courts by requiring evidence of discriminatory intent. Claims alleging violations of constitutional rights require action on the part of the state, agents of the state, or government actors. Claims of racial discrimination may be against private actors for violations of federal civil rights statutes prohibiting discriminatory conduct. In the context of environmental justice litigation in the United States, civil rights laws reach the conduct of private actors that have received federal funding or support. This section discusses standards governing review of environmental justice claims and describes how these standards fall far short of securing equal protection for claimants.

A. *Equal Protection: Disparate Impact and Discriminatory Intent Nonequivalence*

Disparate impact alone is insufficient in US law to establish a claim of racial discrimination. In 1972, the US Supreme Court rejected allegations of racial discrimination "based solely on the statistically disproportionate racial impact" because accepting a constitutional theory recognizing racial discrimination by statistics "would render suspect each difference in treatment...however lacking in racial motivation and however otherwise rational the treatment might be."[63] The significance of drawing a distinction between discriminatory impact and discriminatory intent was further elucidated by the US Supreme Court in *Washington v. Davis*.[64] In *Washington v. Davis*, the plaintiffs, unsuccessful black applicants for positions on the police force, complained that the use of test results as a determinative in hiring unconstitutionally discriminated against them. Evidence in the record supported the fact that a higher percentage of blacks than whites failed the test and that the test had not been empirically shown to reliably measure performance in the police force. The Court explained, "We have difficulty understanding how a law

---

[62] Rebecca Bratspies, "The Intersection of International Human Rights and Domestic Environmental Regulation," *Georgia Journal of International Law* 38 (2010): 649, 656.
[63] Jefferson v. Hackney, 406 US 535, 548 (1972).   [64] Washington v. Davis, 426 US 229 (1976).

establishing a racially neutral qualification for employment is nevertheless racially discriminatory and denies 'any person... equal protection of the laws' simply because a greater proportion of Negroes fail to qualify than members of other racial or ethnic groups."[65] The Court concluded that standing alone, disproportionate impact does not constitute the "invidious racial discrimination forbidden by the Constitution" and does not warrant that racial classification be subjected to greater scrutiny. In the opinion of the Court, to accept a rule subjecting purportedly neutral standards that in practice benefit or burden one race more than another to a higher standard of review would be too "far reaching" and could potentially "raise serious questions about, and perhaps invalidate, a whole range of tax, welfare, public service, regulatory, and licensing statute that may be more burdensome to the poor and to the average black man than the more affluent white."[66] In concurrence, Justice Stevens observed that "the line between discriminatory purpose and discriminatory impact is not nearly as bright, and perhaps not quite as critical, as the reader of the Court's opinion might assume... when the disproportion is dramatic [it] really does not matter whether the standard is phrased in terms of purpose or effect."[67]

The Court in *Washington v. Davis* allowed that "an invidious discriminatory purpose may often be inferred from the totality of relevant facts, including the fact, if true, that the law bears more heavily on one race than another."[68] In *Village of Arlington Heights v. Metropolitan Housing Development Corp.*,[69] the Court acknowledged the challenges claimants confronted in establishing discriminatory intent and advanced standards for inferring the existence of discriminatory intent. Factors assessed to establish the existence of discriminatory intent, aside from discriminatory impact, include the historical background of the decision, the legislative and administrative history, the specific sequences of events leading to the decision, and departures from established procedural sequences for decision making.[70]

The extent to which a plaintiff can establish discriminatory intent determines whether a court in the United States will subject a decision, rule, policy, or standard with adverse impacts on a particular racial group to a more exacting standard of review. The Court's objection to allowing disparate impact alone to be sufficient for supporting a claim of discrimination was rooted in the concern that to do so would render too much of the nation's law and policy to scrutiny, ironically revealing just how far racial inequality reaches. Where a significant amount of discrimination may be manifest in institutional racism or implicit bias, an intent-based standard is insufficient to reach much of the discrimination suffered based on race.[71] There is a disconnect between the manner in which discrimination

---

[65] Id. at 245. [66] Id. at 248.
[67] Washington v. Davis, 426 US 229, 253 (1976) (Stevens J. concurring) [68] Id. at 242.
[69] Village of Arlington Heights v. Metropolitan Housing Development Corp., 429 US 252 (1977).
[70] Id. at 564.
[71] Audrey Daniel, "The Intent Doctrine and CERD: How the United States Fails to Meet Its International Obligations in Racial Discrimination Jurisprudence," *DePaul Journal for Social Justice* 4 (2011): 263.

operates in society and the doctrinal requirements that claimants must be able to show to prove that they have been subject to intentional discrimination. For instance, research on "institutional racism" has examined how organizations can operate through systemic practices and procedures that replicate exclusion of racial minorities or indifference to the cumulative impact of choices that disadvantage those who are already disadvantaged.[72] Communities of color bringing claims in the context of environmental harms have had a difficult time due to the intent doctrine. A doctrinal approach addressing the causes as well as the effects of racial disparities and the disparate impacts of facially neutral policy decisions could better promote racial justice and provide more protection for the principle of equality.

B. *Disparate Environmental Impacts: Establishing Intentional Inequality in US Courts*

Environmental justice cases in the United States frequently fail because plaintiffs have been unable to establish discriminatory intent.[73] For example, in *East-Bibb Twiggs Neighborhood Association v. Macon-Bibb Planning and Zoning Commission*,[74] plaintiffs brought a Fourteenth Amendment equal protection action to enjoin a commission permit allowing a landfill to be located in a census tract which was 60% African American. Plaintiffs presented evidence that other landfills in the area were also located in majority minority census tracts that were 70% black and that there was deviation from usual decision-making procedures when the permit was issued.[75] Noting that the "only other" commission-approved landfill permit was located in a majority white census tract undermined the plaintiffs' claim of a "clear pattern, unexplainable on grounds other than race."[76] Accordingly, "unable to discern a series of official actions taken ... for invidious purposes," the Court did not find the zoning commission decision to be racially motivated.[77]

In *R.I.S.E. Inc. v. Kay*,[78] plaintiffs brought a Fourteenth Amendment equal protection action seeking to reverse a county board's approval for development of a landfill in a predominately African American section of a community. The plaintiffs presented evidence of a long history of placing waste in sites where 95%–100% of the people living within a two-mile radius were African American. The Court held that plaintiffs failed to prove intent, explaining that "equal protection does not impose an affirmative duty to equalize the impact of official decisions on different racial groups. Rather, it merely prohibits government officials discriminating based on race."[79] The Court concluded that in this instance, the decision to locate the landfill was based on economic considerations, explaining that "the Board appears

---

[72] Id. at 288–89.   [73] Keenheel, "Need for New Legislation," 105.
[74] East-Bibb Twiggs Neighborhood Association v. Macon-Bibb Planning and Zoning Commission, 706 F. Supp. 880 (M.D. Ga. 1989).
[75] Id.   [76] Id.   [77] Id.
[78] R.I.S.E. Inc. v. Kay, 768 F. Supp. 1144 (Ed. Va. 1991).   [79] Id. at 1150.

to have balanced the economic, environmental, and cultural needs of the County in a responsible and conscientious manner."[80] Prior to the litigation, the composition of the county's board had been expanded pursuant to federally ordered redistricting and a special election that resulted in increased minority representation. Arguably, an equal protection analysis able to look beyond intent could have considered the cumulative effects of racial exclusion and disparate impact differently.

In *South Bronx Coalition for Clean Air Inc. v. Conroy*,[81] plaintiffs sought to enjoin a solid waste facility. Plaintiffs, residents of the area, and environmental public interest organizations alleged violations of the National Environmental Policy Act (NEPA), federal antidiscrimination laws, and state environmental quality laws. Plaintiffs claimed that the defendants, private companies and public agencies, made waste transfer agreements restricting the handling and transportation of solid waste in Queens and Long Island, creating a burden for the minority communities of the Bronx. As a result of the agreements, residents of the Bronx would be subjected to the adverse impacts of waste to a greater degree than the white residents of Long Island. Plaintiffs produced evidence that their community was 79% African American and Hispanic and that rates of asthma for residents were among the highest in the country. The Court dismissed the Coalition's complaint as too general and conclusory to support an actionable claim of intentional discrimination under Title VI of the Civil Rights Act of 1964. The Court declined to entertain a "disparate impact" claim of discrimination due to the plaintiffs' failure to submit analytical comparisons of the affected locations.

For a while, private environmental justice plaintiffs tried, largely unsuccessfully, to use Title VI of the Civil Rights Act of 1964 to combat discrimination in decision making. Title VI prohibits entities receiving federal funding from engaging in conduct that would have discriminatory consequences, regardless of intent. Prior to the 2001 Supreme Court's decision in *Alexander v. Sandoval*,[82] some federal courts had interpreted Title VI provisions to create an implied right of action allowing private plaintiffs to challenge discrimination. Impacts, regardless of intent, could constitute a violation of federal civil rights laws, while intent had to be proved to establish a violation of the equal protection clause of the Constitution. In *Lau v. Nichols*,[83] Chinese children refused English instruction in public schools successfully challenged the decision of education administrators. The Supreme Court found that the Health and Welfare Department Regulations prohibiting discrimination based solely on effects even where no purposeful intent to discriminate had been established by plaintiffs created an implied right of action.

Prior to *Sandoval*, a federal court in New Jersey ruled that the New Jersey Department of Environmental Protection had violated Title VI of the Civil Rights Act by failing to consider "the potential adverse, disparate impact" of its decisions

---

[80] Id. [81] South Bronx Coalition for Clean Air Inc. v. Conroy, 20 F. Supp. 2d 565 (S.D.N.Y. 1998).
[82] Alexander v. Sandoval, 532 US 275 (2001). [83] Lau v. Nichols, 414 US 563 (1974).

"on individuals based on their race, color or national origin."[84] In *South Camden Citizens in Action v. New Jersey Department of Environmental Protection*, the court found that when the state environmental department failed to consider evidence beyond technical compliance with emissions standards in siting the proposed facility, it did not act in compliance with regulations promulgated by the US Environmental Protection Agency to implement Title VI of the Civil Rights Act of 1964. The Court held that the state environmental department should have considered the circumstances more holistically, giving attention to adverse impacts likely to affect minority communities. After *Sandoval*, a federal appeals court reversed *South Camden Citizens*, concluding that the statute could not be construed to provide a disparate impact cause of action to a private plaintiff.[85]

In *Sandoval*, the Supreme Court decided private individuals do not have a right to file lawsuits to enforce federal antidiscrimination regulations issued pursuant to Title VI under which demonstrating disparate impact was sufficient to establish a civil rights violation. The *Sandoval* plaintiffs sought to enjoin the Alabama Department of Public Safety from administering exams required to obtain a license to drive only in English. Pursuant to amendments to the state's constitution adopting English as the official and only language of the state, the Department stopped providing exams in other languages. Plaintiffs argued that the English-only policy violated Federal Title VI regulations prohibiting the use of criteria or methods of administration that would have discriminatory effects. Plaintiffs maintained that the policy had a discriminatory effect on non-English speakers based on national origin. The Supreme Court found that the relevant statutory provisions did not contain the rights-creating language required to recognize a private right of action.

Before and after the *Sandoval* decision, several other similar cases raising claims of environmental inequality have followed a similar pattern to dismissal. These cases illustrate how the intent requirement erects high evidentiary hurdles in the environmental justice context as other justifications are offered to courts and accepted, despite significant suffering on the part of affected communities, predominately people of color. The only course of action remaining for environmental justice plaintiffs seeking redress in the United States is to file federal administrative complaints because courts are effectively closed to environmental justice concerns.

With other avenues effectively foreclosed, environmental justice plaintiffs have sought redress through filing administrative complaints with the Environmental Protection Agency. However, after more than 20 years of agency enforcement and more than 250 complaints filed as of 2013, the EPA has yet to issue a violation.[86]

---

[84] South Camden Citizens in Action v. New Jersey Department of Environmental Protection, 145 F. Supp. 2nd 446, 481 (D.N.J. 2001).
[85] South Camden Citizens in Action v. New Jersey Department of Environmental Protection, 274 F.3d 771, 780–81(3rd Cir. 2001).
[86] Tony LoPresti, "Realizing the Promise of Environmental Civil Rights: The Renewed Effort to Enforce Title VI of the Civil Rights Act of 1964," *Administrative Law Review* 65 (2013): 757.

IV. ENVIRONMENTAL JUSTICE IN THE UNITED STATES AND INTERNATIONAL HUMAN RIGHTS INSTITUTIONS

While US judgments on environmental justice do not cite or reference international law in making determinations, the US government does present court decisions as evidence of compliance with international human rights standards. This section surveys the role of international law in US law, the US presentation of environmental justice cases before international human rights institutions, and the alternative advocacy avenues some environmental justice activists are using to press claims that are impossible to have heard in US courts under current interpretations of equal protection.

A. International Law in US Courts

Under article VI of the US Constitution, duly ratified treaties become part of the "supreme law of the land" equal in legal effect to enacted federal statutes. Accordingly, international treaties to which the United States is a party will prevail over previously enacted federal law in the event of any conflict. International accords will also take precedence over any inconsistent state or local law. The United States ratified the International Convention on the Elimination of All Forms of Racial Discrimination (CERD) in 1994. The United States had already been a party to the International Covenant on Civil and Political Rights (ICCPR). Both of these international human rights instruments to which the United States has agreed to be bound contain antidiscrimination provisions with which the country must comply.

There is no single statute or institution in the United States through which internationally recognized human rights and fundamental freedoms are guaranteed or enforced. It is the position of the United States that domestic law provides sufficient protection through various constitutional provisions and statutes that usually allow access to administrative and judicial remedies at both the federal and state levels. As a result, the United States recognized that responsibility for identifying violations and enforcing compliance with international legal obligations is shared among the various branches at all levels of government. Individual remedial actions, and advocacy by nongovernmental organizations and a free press, are significant drivers toward compliance supplementing legislative and federal agency monitoring and oversight.[87]

Courts in the United States have uniformly refused to evaluate claims based on the ICCPR and the CERD because the instruments are not self-executing. The ICCPR and CERD would require implementing legislation to be given binding effect in the United States. However, several cases cite the Covenant. The author's

---

[87] CERD/C/351/Add.1.

2016 search yielded 444 cases making reference to the ICCPR and 49 cases making reference to the CERD.

The CERD was deemed not self-executing at its ratification, with the US Senate making a clear declaration to that effect, leading some commentators to argue that the United States has opted out of CERD in practice.[88] When signing on to CERD, the United States refused to recognize the competence of the Committee to receive and consider individual or organization complaints, thus preventing an individual or organization in the United States from bringing a CERD claim within the US court system based on the CERD, as well as preventing claims being brought to the Committee. The Senate placed conditions on the CERD ratification, most notably, a stipulation that no US domestic policy should be amended as a result of the ratification, further limiting any legal consequences for violations. The reservations take the teeth out of CERD, preventing any claims from being brought under it. As a result, the Covenant does not do any work in the 49 cases citing it, and it cannot as a matter of current law.

B. *The Convention on Racial Discrimination and US Equal Protection Obligations*

The United States is a party to the International Convention on the Elimination of All Forms of Racial Discrimination (CERD).[89] The US government has taken the position that because existing US law provides through constitutional and statutory measures protections against and allows remedies for racial discrimination, it already fully complies with obligations assumed under CERD, making it unnecessary to propose and enact implementing legislation.[90]

CERD defines racial discrimination as "any distinctions, exclusion, restriction or preference based on race, colour, descent, or national or ethnic origin which has the purpose *or* effect of nullifying or impairing the recognition, enjoyment or exercise, on equal footing of human rights and fundamental freedoms in the political, economic, social, cultural, or any other field of public life."[91] Significantly, the CERD's definition of racial discrimination is not limited to discrimination that is intentional, as US equal protection jurisprudence has become. It defines racial discrimination as extending to state actions that have the effect of preventing equal enjoyment of fundamental human rights and freedoms. Parties to the CERD have a duty to review and "amend, rescind or nullify all laws and regulations which have *the effect of creating* or *perpetuating* racial discrimination wherever it exists."[92] Taking seriously the CERD definition of discrimination would reach the disparate impact that the intent doctrine does not. For example, under the intent doctrine, policy decisions in the United States can have disparate effects but not be based on race

---

[88] Daniel, "The Intent Doctrine and CERD," 263.
[89] International Convention on the Elimination of All Forms of Racial Discrimination, December 21, 1965, 600 UNTS 195.
[90] CERD/C/351/Add.1   [91] Art. 2.   [92] Art. 2.

explicitly and escape scrutiny. For example, racial justice advocates have pointed to different penalties for possession of the less expensive illegal substance "crack cocaine" versus the more expensive powder cocaine as a facially neutral rule with disparate racial impact.[93] Crack possession was more common in poor and minority communities, and these communities bore a disproportionate penalty for possession without regard to race or poverty.

The Committee on the Elimination of All Forms of Racial Discrimination (CERD Committee), the international body that monitors state compliance with commitments assumed under the treaty, has entertained environmental justice issues recently.[94] The CERD Committee has requested information from state parties to the treaty on environmental issues. For example, the CERD Committee requested information from Nigeria on government efforts to respect the rights of minority groups that had been adversely affected by environmental deterioration associated with practices of the extractives industry sector operating in the country.[95]

The Committee reported to the Independent Expert on Human Rights and the Environment identifying the right to property and the right to health as particular concerns covered in the treaty relevant to the enjoyment of equality environmental protection.[96] Article 5 of CERD provides that "States Parties undertake to prohibit and to eliminate racial discrimination in all its forms and to guarantee the right of everyone, without distinction as to race, colour, or national or ethnic origin, to equality before the law, notably in the enjoyment of... the right to own property alone as well as in association with others."[97] The CERD Committee has described conduct such as the transfer of indigenous lands to extractive sector firms, the siting of waste facilities, weapons tasting, and the issuance of geothermal energy leases and open pit mining activities as adversely affecting property rights through ecological depletion of traditional lands contrary to CERD.[98]

Article 5(e)(iv) of CERD provides that "States Parties undertake to prohibit and to eliminate racial discrimination in all its forms and to guarantee the right of everyone, without distinction as to race, colour, or national or ethnic origin, to equality before the law, notably in the enjoyment of... the right to public health."[99]

---

[93] Nkechi Taifa, "Codification or Castration? The Applicability of the International Convention to Eliminate All Forms of Racial Discrimination to the US Criminal Justice System," *Howard Law Journal* 40 (1997): 641.

[94] Kristen Marttila Gast, "Environmental Justice and Indigenous Peoples in the United States: An International Human Rights Analysis," *Transnational Law and Contemporary Problems* 14 (2004): 253.

[95] Id.

[96] Individual Report on the International Convention on the Elimination of All Forms of Racial Discrimination Mapping Human Rights Obligations Relating to the Enjoyment of a Safe, Clean, Healthy and Sustainable Environment, December 2013.

[97] Id.

[98] Report of the Committee on the Convention on the Elimination of All Forms of Racial Discrimination for the Sixty-Eighth and Sixty-Ninth Sessions, Prevention of Racial Discrimination Including Early Warning and Urgent Procedures: Decision 1(68) on the United States, UN Doc. A/61/19 (October 1, 2006), paras. 7–10.

[99] Id.

The Committee has recommended measures to ensure the right to health in response to environmental pollution.[100]

The text of CERD does not explicitly articulate environmental rights, but the Committee has acknowledged that environmental damage can compromise the enjoyment of rights protected by CERD; however, the Committee has participated in international environmental policy-making processes submitting comments.

> At its sixty-first session in March 2002, the CERD Committee issued a statement to the participants at the World Summit on Sustainable Development that recognized the interwoven nature of human rights and the environment. The Committee stated that "policies, practices and the lack of enforcement of certain laws perpetuate racial discrimination, 'environmental racism' and other forms of oppression which violate the rights to freedom, equality and adequate access to basic needs such as clean water, food, shelter, energy, health and social care," and that "some negative aspects of globalization, including unbalanced economic growth, unfair terms of trade, unabated production and consumption, land and water pollution, displacements of people, the hoarding of natural resources and mismanagement of external debt, all undermine efforts to combat racial discrimination at national and international levels."
>
> The Committee also called Agenda 21 a document "of paramount importance, not only for the preservation of the Earth's environment and the promotion of sustainable development, but also, and above all, a fundamental instrument for the worldwide observance of human rights." The Committee called upon States to "respect and protect all human rights" and to recognize that diversity is an essential precondition for sustainable development, encouraged the World Summit on Sustainable Development to ensure the inclusion of human rights and the prohibition of racial discrimination in its final documents, and welcomed the opportunity to cooperate with State parties and other UN bodies in upholding those human rights norms and standards relevant to sustainable development and set forth in CERD.[101]

The CERD Committee has not yet heard individual complaints concerning environmental justice issues but has indicated a willingness to recognize environmental racism. Given the CERD Committee's long-standing adherence to a standard definition of racial discrimination that is concerned with effects, it can be expected that issues of environmental justice will become a subject given greater attention in the Committee's future comments and concluding observations.[102]

---

[100] Report of the Committee on the Convention on the Elimination of All Forms of Racial Discrimination for the Fifty-Sixth and Fifty-Seventh Sessions, Consideration of Reports, Comments and Information Submitted by State Parties: Slovakia, UN Doc.A/55/18 (October 17, 2000), at para. 265.

[101] Individual Report on the International Convention on the Elimination of All Forms of Racial Discrimination Mapping Human Rights Obligations Relating to the Enjoyment of a Safe, Clean, Healthy and Sustainable Environment, December 2013.

[102] The CERD Committee derives its authority from Article 8 of the International Convention on the Elimination of All Forms of Racial Discrimination. It has the power to review legislative, judicial,

The present inability of American jurisprudence to recognize the discriminatory effects of decisions that disadvantage people of color and leave communities of color with disproportionate disease burden associated with environmental pollution and to ensure access to remedy for the victims of environmental racism remains at sharp variance with the government's obligations under international human rights law.

While the US reservations to the CERD are legally effective, the reservations arguably could be challenged by other state parties to the CERD as inconsistent with the spirit and purpose of the very definition of discrimination contained in the treaty. This is not to say court citations to CERD could not have significant symbolic influence were more courts to make reference to it.

C. US Reporting to the CERD Committee and Environmental Justice

Submissions the Committee on the Elimination of Racial Discrimination made by the US government have acknowledged environmental justice issues and highlighted US judgments, even though US equal protection jurisprudence has not been favorable for bringing disparate impact claims of race discrimination.

1. US Representations Regarding Environmental Justice

The first submission to the CERD Committee, prepared by the US Department of State with assistance from the White House, the Civil Rights Division of the US Department of Justice, the Equal Employment Opportunity Commission, and other relevant departments and agencies of the federal government and states, was provided in 2000. Contributions from civil society organizations were also received by the US government and the CERD Committee. The 2000 CERD Report acknowledged environmental justice issues:

> The United States recognizes that low-income and minority communities frequently bear a disproportionate share of adverse environmental burdens and is working to implement existing laws that better protect all communities. "Environmental justice" is the fair treatment and meaningful involvement of all people regardless of race, colour, national origin, culture or income with respect to the development, implementation, enforcement and compliance of environmental laws, regulations

> policy, and other measures they have taken to give effect to the Convention, generally receiving reports from members every two years, or they can request information if a complaint is logged. CERD then produces a report analyzing the policies and providing recommendations to improve compliance. Furthermore, when a complaint is logged, under Article 14, CERD produces an opinion on the matter so long as the State has agreed to "recognize the competence of the Committee to receive and consider communications from individuals or groups of individuals within its jurisdiction claiming to be victims of a violation by that State Party of any of the rights set forth in this Convention." The opinions produced contain recommendations to remedy the matter at hand. CERD in essence relies on States to do what it says to avoid the public shaming that may come from continually falling short of the recommendations.

and policies. Fair treatment means that no group of people, including racial, ethnic, or socio-economic groups, should bear a disproportionate share of negative environmental consequences resulting from industrial, municipal and commercial operations or the execution of federal, state, local and tribal programmes and policies.[103]

This statement, made before the *Sandoval* decision, does not reflect the present challenges faced by environmental justice plaintiffs. While it acknowledges the disproportionate impact of harmful environmental burdens on poor communities and minority communities, it does not address the inability to seek redress based on claims of racial discrimination. The primary significance is that the matter of environmental justice even made it into the country report.

The 2000 report highlighted President Clinton's Executive Order 12898 requiring "all departments and agencies of the Federal Government directing them to take action to address environmental justice with respect to minority populations and low-income populations." Pursuant to Order 12898, US agencies were directed to address disproportionate human health or environmental effects of programs on such populations, to collect additional data on these subjects, and to coordinate their efforts through newly established interagency working groups, among other things.[104]

The 2000 Report to the Committee also acknowledged that while most environmental laws do not address potential impacts on low-income and minority communities, Executive Order 12898 would now direct the EPA "[t]o the greatest extent practicable and permitted by law... [to] make achieving environmental justice part of its mission by identifying and addressing, as appropriate, disproportionately high and adverse human health or environmental effects of its programmes, policies, and activities on minority populations and low-income populations."[105] The government directed the Committee to more detailed information about the EPA's environmental justice initiatives available to the general public.

As evidence of the country's commitment to environmental justice, the US CERD report points to what it deemed environmental justice successes:

> Recently, American Indian and Alaska Natives argued successfully to the EPA that Indian tribes had suffered environmental injustice because the Federal Government had not provided them equitable funding and other agency resources necessary to develop environmental programmes. Federally recognized Indian tribes generally have the authority to regulate activities on their reservations that affect their environment. Thus, such Indian tribes are in the process of developing comprehensive tribal environmental laws and regulations. However, unlike the states of the United States, Indian tribes had not, until recently, been provided the federal resources to assist them in the development of their environmental programmes. Today, the EPA has significantly increased its funding and technical assistance to

---

[103] Report 2000 at para. 389. [104] Id. at para. 390. [105] Id. at para. 391.

Indian tribes. As a result, many tribes are now developing and enacting their own tribal environmental codes and beginning to take charge of their own environments through the enforcement of these codes and through an improved partnership with EPA.[106]

The government conceded that several organizations remained concerned that existing civil rights legal remedies did not offer sufficient protection from environmental hazards for people of color. The report specifically cites several failed environmental justice cases, including *R.I.S.E. v. Kay*.

In 2007, the US submission to the CERD Committee addressed environmental justice directly. On the state of environmental justice in the United States, the report offered:

> Federal agencies continue to address issues concerning the environmental impacts of activities such as the locating of transportation projects and hazardous waste clean-up projects, on certain population groups, including minority and low income populations. As required by US Executive Order 12898, and informed by the National Environmental Justice Advisory Council, the Environmental Protection Agency (EPA) and other federal agencies integrate environmental justice considerations into their day-to-day decision making processes, principally through environmental impact analysis under the National Environmental Policy Act (NEPA). EPA also runs three programs designed to address environmental justice concerns. The first is the Environmental Justice Collaborative Problem-Solving Cooperative Agreements Program, which provides financial assistance to eligible community-based organizations working to address local environmental or public health concerns in their communities. The second is the Environmental Small Grant Program, which provides small grants to eligible community-based organizations for education and training programs concerning local environmental or public health issues. Finally, the Environmental Justice Community Intern Program places students in local community organizations to experience environmental protection at the grass-roots level. In addition, the Federal Interagency Working Group on Environmental Justice coordinates government-wide efforts through three task forces: (1) Health disparities; (2) Revitalization Demonstration Projects; and (3) Native American. The Native American group works to protect tribal cultural resources and sacred places.[107]

Like the 2000 Report, the 2007 Report lists cases. In the 2007 Report, the cases presented are offered to demonstrate that environmental justice analysis is being assessed by US courts. The Report highlights National Environmental Policy Act (NEPA) analyses of the impacts of potential federal projects on the human environment.[108] In *Coliseum Square Ass'n v. HUD*,[109] a court upheld a Department of Housing and Urban Development's consideration of environmental justice issues involving a

---

[106] Id. at para. 392.   [107] Id.   [108] See 40 CFR 1508.14.
[109] No. 03-30875, No. 04-30522, 206 US App. LEXIS 23726 (5th Cir. Sept. 18, 2006).

housing development revitalization project. In *Communities against Runway Expansion Inc. v. F.A.A.*,[110] a court upheld an environmental justice analysis of construction of a new airport runway. In *Senville v. Peters*,[111] a court upheld an environmental justice analysis prepared by the Federal Highway Administration with regard to the effects of a new highway project on low-income and minority persons. Finally, in *Washington County v. Department of Navy*,[112] a court issued an order temporarily halting construction of an aircraft landing field due to an inadequate environmental justice analysis.[113] These instances are identified and offered by the government as evidence of progress in the area of environmental justice potentially consistent with CERD obligations.

The Obama administration identified environmental justice as an EPA priority in 2010, mandating that the agency consider environmental justice issues in permitting decisions and policy making.[114] In its 2013 Report, the United States again includes express reference to environmental justice:

> Recognizing that low income and minority communities often are exposed to an unacceptable amount of pollution, the Obama Administration is committed to making environmental justice a central part of the everyday decision-making process. The Administration has re-energized the Federal Interagency Working Group on Environmental Justice (EJ IWG), founded in 1994 under Executive Order 12898. In addition, the White House Forum on Environmental Justice, held in December 2010, focused on addressing environment and health disparities and on how low income and minority communities can prepare for the environmental and health impacts of climate change. Administration initiatives include: issuing final environmental justice strategies, implementation plans and/or progress reports for 15 agencies, including Plan Environmental Justice ("EJ") 2014, which is EPA's strategy to develop stronger community relationships and increase agency efforts to improve environmental and health conditions in overburdened communities; and increasing collaboration between the EJ IWG and other federal partnerships, such as the Partnership for Sustainable Communities and the Action Plan to Reduce Racial Ethnic Asthma Disparities. The Asthma Action Plan recognizes that poor and minority children suffer a greater burden of the disease, and focuses on ensuring that the populations most severely affected receive evidence-based comprehensive care."[115]

---

[110] 355 F.3d 678 (DC Cir. 2004).   [111] 327 F. Supp. 2d 335 (D. Vt. 2004).
[112] 317 F. Supp. 2d 626 (E.D.N.C. 2004).
[113] Reports Submitted by States Parties under Article 9 of the Convention, Sixth Periodic Reports of the States Parties Due in 2005 CERD/C/USA/6 (October 24, 2007) (document submitted by United States contains the fourth, fifth, and sixth periodic reports of the United States of America due previously submitted in a single document).
[114] Rebecca Bratspies, "Human Rights and Environmental Regulation," *New York University Environmental Law Journal* 19 (2012): 225, 275.
[115] Reports Submitted by States Parties under Article 9 of the Convention, CERD/C/USA/7-9 (October 3, 2013) at para. 144.

In the 2013 Report, attention is also directed to the "specific information on the legislative, judicial or other measures taken" to give effect to ending racial discrimination. For example, the Report highlighted the EPA's leadership of the government's efforts to enhance the Federal Working Group on Environmental Justice (EJIWG) under Executive Order 12898, including the execution of a Memorandum of Understanding formally recommitting all agencies to environmental justice and establishing priorities, structures, and procedures for the EJIWG. The EJIWG conducted 20 community listening sessions across the country, and in 2012, 15 federal agencies issued final agency environmental justice strategies, implementation plans, and/or progress reports.[116]

2. CERD Committee Comments and Observations

Many of the challenges environmental justice plaintiffs confront in US courts would be overcome more easily were the recommendations made by the CERD Committee in response to the US government adopted. The Committee's concluding observations on US compliance with CERD contained concerns over the absence of specific legislation implementing the provisions of the CERD Convention in domestic law.[117] The Committee also expressed concerns about the "far-reaching" reservations, understandings, and declarations made by the United States upon ratification of the CERD Convention and recommended reform and review of legislation to prevent and combat racial discrimination and protect against acts of racial discrimination.[118]

Most important for removing impediments to disparate impact actions, the Committee was critical of the failure of the United States to meet its obligations under the Convention, pursuant to Article 1, paragraph 1 and general recommendation XIV, to endeavor to prohibit and eliminate racial discrimination in all forms, including laws, policies, and practices that, while not discriminatory on purpose, are in effect.[119] The Committee called upon the United States to take measures to review existing legislation and federal, state, and local policies and practices to ensure "effective protection" against any form of racial discrimination as well as any "unjustifiably disparate impact."[120]

Significant for addressing the pollution and adverse environmental impacts attributable to private actors, the Committee also expressed concern with respect to obligations under Article 2, paragraphs 1(c) and (d), which require state parties to endeavor to bring an end to all racial discrimination by any person, group, or organization, including the discriminatory conduct of private actors. The Committee

---

[116] Reports Submitted by States Parties under Article 9 of the Convention, CERD/C/USA/7-9 (October 3, 2013) at para. 28 (document includes the seventh, eighth, and ninth periodic reports of the United States due previously submitted in a single document).
[117] A/56/18 para. 390.   [118] Id. at para. 391.   [119] Id. at para. 393.   [120] Id.

recommended that the United States review and reform laws to reach "the largest possible sphere of private conduct that is discriminatory on racial or ethnic grounds."[121]

D. The Inter-American Commission on Human Rights Considers Claims from Louisiana's "Cancer Capital"

Before the International CERD Committee, the United States has asserted a position acknowledging that the government has environment justice obligations, at least under federal civil rights and environmental protection laws. The United States has asserted an arguably inconsistent position before a regional human rights body. In response to a 2010 petition filed by environmental justice activists from Advocates for Environmental Human Rights with the Inter-American Commission on Human Rights (IACHR), seeking a declaration that there is a human right to a clean and healthy environment representing residents Mossville, Louisiana, the United States has denied that there is a right to a healthy environment it is obligated to protect or respect. The Commission summarized the position of the United States contesting the admissibility of the Mossville petition as follows:

> The State rejects the allegations of violations of the American Declaration because it asserts that they are based on an erroneously expansive interpretation of state commitments, unsupported by the texts of those articles or by customary law, and rely on a flawed analysis of international law. The State contends that there is no such right as the right to a healthy environment, either directly, or as a component of the rights to life, health, privacy and inviolability of the home, or equal protection and freedom from discrimination.[122]

In 2004, Mossville residents, through Mossville Environmental Action Now and with the Sierra Club, first sought review of an EPA rule for failure to meet Clean Air Act requirements.[123] The result turned on technical considerations. The opinion does not speak of victim's rights or international law but rather regulatory agency authority. A condition of accessing regional and international human rights institutions is that a petitioner first exhaust all domestic remedies. The IACHR explained that where "domestic legislation does not afford due process of law for protection of the right allegedly violated, if the party alleging the violation has been denied access to domestic remedies or is prevented from exhausting them, or if there has been an unwarranted delay in reaching a final judgment under domestic remedies" that it would be appropriate for it to admit such a petition.[124] Because both the US

---

[121] Id. at para. 392.
[122] Report No. 43/10; Petition 242–05 Admissibility Mossville Environmental Action Now, United States (March 2010) at para. 18.
[123] Mossville Environmental Action Now v. EPA, 370 F.3d DC Cir. 1232 (2004).
[124] Petition 242–05 at para. 25.

government and the petitioners agreed it would not be possible to bring an action in US courts for disproportionate impact without a clear showing of discriminatory intent, the IACHR concluded that "the claims of the petitioners regarding the alleged disproportionate discriminatory pollution burden on Mossville residents and the related consequences on the community would have no reasonable prospect of success through domestic proceedings."[125] Over the objection of the United States, the Inter-American Commission did not dismiss the Mossville petition. It remains pending.

CONCLUSION

Given the difficulty of providing discriminatory intent required in US equal protection decisions interpreting the Fourteenth Amendment's equal protection clause and federal civil rights laws, plaintiffs have been forced to put forward new theories. Plaintiff's now seek recognition of claims and legitimation of environmental injustice in international forums. For example, representatives of the Native American nations contesting the construction of the Dakota Access Pipeline have also appealed to an international body to acknowledge rights abuses by the US government. Several Sioux tribes have asked the Inter-American Commission on Human Rights to call on the US government to adopt precautionary measures to prevent irreparable damage to the environment and to protect protesters against violence.[126] The plaintiffs allege that US law and international law require the government to consult with indigenous people likely to be adversely impacted by government action.[127] International human rights bodies have been critical of the US approach to equal protection. The impact–intent distinction is a judicial creation, and it stands in sharp contrast to international standards that advance a more substantive and robust understanding of equality. The story of US judgments in the area of environmental justice remains for plaintiffs one of certain defeat, but this story may not be over. International human rights law instructs that the impact–intent distinction in US antidiscrimination jurisprudence to the extent it cannot address demonstrated discriminatory effects be revisited and preferably reversed.

---

[125] Id. at para. 33.
[126] "Tribes Ask International Human Rights Commission to Stop Violence against Water Protectors at Standing Rock," December 2, 2016, available at http://standwithstandingrock.net/tribes-ask-international-human-rights-commission-stop-violence-water-protectors-standing-rock/.
[127] Id.; see also Sam Levin, "Dakota Access Pipeline Protests: UN Group Investigates Human Rights Abuses," October 31, 2016.

3

Incorporation, Federalism, and International Human Rights

David Sloss

A *New York Times* article recently declared that the United States is the only country in the world with "a self-assigned global role that is based on universal values rather than national interests."[1] The recent election of Donald Trump notwithstanding, the national commitment to a foreign policy based on universal values has been a core feature of American national identity since the eighteenth century. However, from the Founding until World War II, principles of constitutional federalism meant that state governments, not the national government, had the primary responsibility for defining the content of those universal values.

Consider three examples. The Fourth Amendment prohibits "unreasonable searches and seizures." The Sixth Amendment provides that all criminal defendants "shall enjoy the right to a speedy and public trial, by an impartial jury." The Eighth Amendment bars "cruel and unusual punishments." All three provisions express universal values. As of 1947, though, despite our national commitment to universal values, the Fourth, Sixth, and Eighth Amendments were not binding on state governments. Indeed, as of 1947, most provisions of the Bill of Rights did not bind state governments. (The "Bill of Rights" refers to the first eight Amendments to the US Constitution.) Each state decided for itself the specific content of the broad, general principles enshrined in those amendments.

The United Nations adopted the Universal Declaration of Human Rights (UDHR) in 1948. Like the US Bill of Rights, the UDHR also expresses universal values. It establishes "a common standard of achievement for all peoples and all nations."[2] Like the Fourth Amendment, Article 9 of the UDHR stipulates that "no one shall be subjected to arbitrary arrest." Like the Sixth Amendment, Article 10 provides that "everyone is entitled in full equality to a fair and public hearing by an independent

---

[1] "Syrian War Magnifies Tension in America's Global Mission," *New York Times*, October 9, 2016, 16.
[2] Universal Declaration of Human Rights, GA Res. 217A (III), UN Doc. A/810 (December 10, 1948) at 71.

and impartial tribunal." Like the Eighth Amendment, Article 5 states that "no one shall be subjected to torture or to cruel, inhuman or degrading treatment or punishment." This essay contends that the development of international human rights law after World War II exerted pressure on the United States to nationalize protection for the rights codified in the Bill of Rights.

The US Supreme Court developed "incorporation doctrine" between 1948 and 1971.[3] The doctrine holds that most, but not all, of the rights codified in the Bill of Rights are binding on the states by virtue of the Fourteenth Amendment due process clause. Before 1948, a firm consensus held that the Bill of Rights applied only to the federal government; it was not directly binding on state and local governments. Entrenched principles of constitutional federalism meant that each state decided for itself the proper application of the universal values expressed in the Bill of Rights. By 1971, though, the Supreme Court had decided that most Bill of Rights provisions were directly binding on state governments and that the Court itself would define the specific content of the universal values expressed in the Bill of Rights. Thus, the Court's incorporation doctrine had two significant consequences. First, the doctrine altered the constitutional balance between the states and the federal government by transferring power over individual rights from state governments to the Supreme Court. Second, the Court used that power to align the standards for protection of constitutional rights in the United States with the universal values expressed in the UDHR and other international human rights instruments.

The first consequence was purposeful, or at least conscious. As the justices developed incorporation doctrine through a series of judicial decisions, they knew they were shifting the balance of power between the states and the federal courts. Indeed, Justice Harlan emphasized this point in several dissenting opinions.[4] The second consequence was not purposeful. However, I contend, it was not entirely accidental either. The Supreme Court's incorporation doctrine, developed between 1948 and 1971, defined the specific content of universal values that bind all state governments. During roughly the same time period, the United Nations developed an International Bill of Rights to define the content of universal values that bind all national governments. The International Bill of Rights consists of three documents: the UDHR, adopted in 1948; the International Covenant on Civil and Political Rights (ICCPR),[5] adopted in 1966; and the International Covenant on Economic,

---

[3] See Part II.A. There is an extensive body of scholarship on incorporation doctrine. For a concise summary, see John E. Nowak and Ronald D. Rotunda, *Constitutional Law*, 7th ed. (St. Paul, MN: West, 2004), §§10.2 and 11.6.

[4] See especially Benton v. Maryland, 395 US 784, 807–9 (1969) (Harlan, J., dissenting); Duncan v. Louisiana, 391 US 145, 171–83 (1968) (Harlan, J., dissenting); Malloy v. Hogan, 378 US 1, 27–33 (1964) (Harlan, J., dissenting); Mapp v. Ohio, 367 US 643, 678–86 (1961) (Harlan, J., dissenting).

[5] International Covenant on Civil and Political Rights, 999 UNTS 171 (December 19, 1966) [hereinafter ICCPR].

Social, and Cultural Rights (ICESCR),[6] also adopted in 1966. Although the Court's major incorporation decisions did not explicitly reference the International Bill of Rights, incorporation doctrine had the practical effect of creating a fairly close alignment between US constitutional law and the human rights norms codified in the International Bill of Rights. By 1971, the Court had held that *every provision* in the US Bill of Rights that had an analogue in the International Bill of Rights bound the states under the Fourteenth Amendment.[7] However, as of 1971, subject to two significant exceptions, provisions in the US Bill of Rights that did not have analogues in the International Bill of Rights did not bind the states under the Fourteenth Amendment.[8] Part II contends that the close fit between the Court's incorporation doctrine and the content of the International Bill of Rights can be explained as a product of "acculturation."[9]

The relationship among incorporation doctrine, federalism, and human rights norms is not merely of historical interest. In its October 2015 term, the Court issued 62 decisions (not counting per curiam opinions). Seven of those decisions relied, at least implicitly, on incorporation doctrine.[10] Since at least the 1970s, the dominant policy discourse in the United States has assumed that federalism and human rights are mutually antagonistic values. Promotion of human rights is seen as a liberal cause, whereas promotion of federalism is seen as a conservative cause. Several scholars have amassed evidence tending to show that federalism can be a useful tool for promoting the cause of human rights.[11] Conversely, this chapter contends that human rights can be a useful tool for promoting the cause of federalism. Specifically, application of international human rights norms as a limitation on incorporation doctrine would partially reverse the centralizing effects of incorporation doctrine

---

[6] International Covenant on Economic, Social, and Cultural Rights, 999 UNTS 3 (December 16, 1966) [hereinafter ICESCR].

[7] See Part II.B.

[8] The two exceptions are Duncan v. Louisiana, 391 US 145 (1968), and Mapp v. Ohio, 367 US 643 (1961).

[9] See Ryan Goodman and Derek Jinks, *Socializing States: Promoting Human Rights through International Law* (New York: Oxford University Press, 2013) (introducing and explaining the concept of acculturation); see also David Sloss, "Book Review," *American Journal of International Law* 108 (2014): 576 (reviewing the book by Goodman and Jinks).

[10] See Birchfield v. North Dakota, 136 S. Ct. 2160 (2016) (applying the Fourth Amendment to North Dakota); Utah v. Strieff, 136 S. Ct. 2056 (2016) (applying the Fourth Amendment to Utah); Betterman v. Montana, 136 S. Ct. 1609 (2016) (applying the Sixth Amendment to Montana); Heffernan v. City of Paterson, 136 S. Ct. 1412 (2016) (applying the First Amendment to a city in New Jersey); Montgomery v. Louisiana, 136 S. Ct. 718 (2016) (applying the Eighth Amendment to Louisiana); Kansas v. Carr, 136 S. Ct. 633 (2016) (applying the Eighth Amendment to Kansas); Hurst v. Florida, 136 S. Ct. 616 (2016) (applying the Sixth Amendment to Florida).

[11] See, e.g., Cynthia Soohoo and Suzanne Stolz, "Bringing Theories of Human Rights Change Home," *Fordham Law Review* 77 (2008): 459; Judith Resnik, "Law's Migration: American Exceptionalism, Silent Dialogues, and Federalism's Multiple Ports of Entry," *Yale Law Journal* 115 (2006): 1564; Catherine Powell, "Dialogic Federalism: Constitutional Possibilities for Incorporation of Human Rights Law in the United States," *University of Pennsylvania Law Review* 150 (2001): 245.

and return control over the application of some Bill of Rights provisions from the federal courts to the states. Therefore, the widespread assumption that domestic application of international human rights norms would be antithetical to principles of constitutional federalism is mistaken.

The doctrine developed by the Warren Court in the 1960s is known as "selective incorporation." Selective incorporation doctrine is best understood as an uneasy compromise between two incompatible theories: the "total incorporation" theory and the "fundamental rights" theory. Total incorporation theory holds that the rights codified in the Bill of Rights bind the states because the Fourteenth Amendment "incorporates" the first eight amendments and makes them applicable to the states. In contrast, fundamental rights theory rejects the proposition that the Bill of Rights binds the states. It holds that the Fourteenth Amendment due process clause prohibits state governments from infringing "fundamental rights." Justice Black was the leading proponent of total incorporation theory. Black acknowledged that, as an original matter, the Bill of Rights was intended to constrain only the federal government, not the states. However, he argued, one purpose of the Fourteenth Amendment was to make the Bill of Rights binding on state governments.[12] Therefore, in his view, the Fourteenth Amendment should be construed to make the *entire* Bill of Rights binding on the states. In the 1960s, Justice Harlan was the chief proponent of fundamental rights theory. Under that theory, the Fourteenth Amendment due process clause merely prohibits state governments from violating "rights basic to a free society"[13] – those fundamental rights that are so important "that neither liberty nor justice would exist if they were sacrificed."[14] Although some of the rights codified in the Bill of Rights qualify as fundamental under this theory, others do not.

Justice Black never persuaded a majority of the justices to endorse his total incorporation theory. However, most of the justices were uncomfortable with the natural law premises that were integral to the traditional fundamental rights theory.[15] Unable to reconcile the tension between the two theories, the Court adopted a strategy of "selective incorporation." The Court's selective incorporation doctrine transferred power over a wide range of individual rights from state governments to the federal courts. But the Court never articulated a coherent theory to justify the exercise of federal judicial power over subjects that, under the original Constitution, were reserved to the states under the Tenth Amendment.

---

[12] See Adamson v. California, 332 US 46, 71–75 (1947) (Black, J., dissenting).
[13] Ker v. California, 374 US 23, 44 (1963) (Harlan, J., concurring).
[14] Malloy v. Hogan, 378 US 1, 23 (1964) (Harlan, J., dissenting) (quoting Palko v. Connecticut, 302 US 319, 326 (1937)).
[15] I refer to the "traditional fundamental rights theory" to distinguish between Justice Harlan's views and those of justices who served on the Court during the first half of the twentieth century. In contrast to many of the earlier justices, Justice Harlan was not entirely comfortable with natural law reasoning. Accordingly, his version of fundamental rights theory relied heavily on respect for judicial precedent, a strong commitment to federalism, and a narrow view of the proper scope of judicial power.

This essay introduces a new theory, the "human rights theory," that helps explain and justify selective incorporation doctrine. The human rights theory holds that rights codified in the Bill of Rights should bind state governments if, but only if, those rights are included in the International Bill of Rights. If the Supreme Court were to adopt the human rights theory today, it would partially reverse the centralizing effects of incorporation doctrine by returning control over the application of some Bill of Rights provisions from the federal courts to the states.

This essay consists of three parts. Part I describes the precursors to incorporation doctrine before 1948. Part II analyzes the application of selective incorporation doctrine from 1948 to 1971. The analysis demonstrates that Supreme Court decisions during this period conformed closely to the results that the Court would have reached by applying the human rights theory. Part II also contends that the close correlation between Supreme Court precedent and the human rights theory was not purely coincidental. International human rights norms exerted a subtle influence over the Court's development of selective incorporation doctrine through a process of acculturation. The concept of acculturation helps explain the close correlation between the human rights theory and the actual pattern of Supreme Court decisions.

Part III turns from explanation to justification. It compares the human rights theory to the Court's current selective incorporation doctrine. This essay does not specifically advocate adoption of the human rights theory. However, Part III demonstrates that the theory has two significant advantages over current doctrine. First, the Court has never articulated a coherent, principled rationale to justify selective incorporation doctrine. The human rights theory provides a principled rationale to support the doctrine. Second, there is a significant tension between selective incorporation doctrine and the Court's stated commitment to principles of constitutional federalism. Adoption of the human rights theory would not eliminate that tension, but it would alleviate the tension by returning control over the application of some Bill of Rights provisions from the federal courts to the states.

I. PRECURSORS TO INCORPORATION DOCTRINE BEFORE 1948

Scholars agree that the Bill of Rights was not originally intended to address violations of individual rights by state governments. Rather, the Bill of Rights was designed to prevent the federal government from infringing individual rights. Consistent with this understanding, as of 1947, the Second, Third, Fourth, Seventh, and Eighth Amendments did not constrain state governments. Moreover, most of the rights protected under the Fifth and Sixth Amendments applied only to the federal government, not the states. However, by 1947, the Court had held that the Constitution protects the following rights against state infringement: the First Amendment protections for freedom of speech,[16] freedom of the press,[17] the right of peaceful assembly,[18] free exercise of religion,[19] and the prohibition against establishment of religion;[20] the Fifth Amendment right to just compensation for takings of private property;[21] and the Sixth Amendment right to assistance of counsel.[22]

The Court applied natural law concepts of fundamental rights to determine which Bill of Rights provisions were binding on the states. For example, in *Palko v. Connecticut*, the Court said that the Fourteenth Amendment due process clause protects against state infringement rights that are "implicit in the concept of ordered liberty" because "neither liberty nor justice would exist if they were sacrificed."[23] Justice Black referred to the *Palko* standard as a "due process-natural law formula."[24] From the late 1890s until the late 1930s, the Court was quite comfortable with fundamental rights theory. Indeed, the natural law premises underlying fundamental rights theory provided a foundation for much of the Court's *Lochner*-era jurisprudence.[25] Moreover, during the *Lochner* era, the Court explicitly rejected the central tenet of total incorporation theory – that the Bill of Rights binds the states *because* the Fourteenth Amendment makes the first eight amendments binding on the states. Thus, in *Powell v. Alabama*, the Court said that although "some of the personal rights safeguarded by the first eight Amendments against national action may also be safeguarded against state action . . . it is not because those rights are enumerated in the first eight Amendments, but because they are of such a nature that they are included in the conception of due process of law."[26]

In sum, before 1940, judicial decisions holding that the due process clause protected specific Bill of Rights provisions against state infringement relied heavily on natural law reasoning. However, between 1937 and 1943, President Roosevelt appointed eight new justices to the Supreme Court, many of whom were deeply skeptical of natural law reasoning. Roosevelt's appointees accepted the earlier decisions protecting First, Fifth, and Sixth Amendment rights against state infringement, but most of them rejected the fundamental rights theory that justified those decisions.

Then, in 1947, Justice Black's dissent in *Adamson v. California*[27] presented a novel rationale for applying the Bill of Rights to the states. *Adamson* involved a criminal defendant who chose not to testify in his own defense. Under California law, the prosecutor and judge were permitted to comment on the defendant's failure to

---

[16] Stromberg v. California, 283 US 359 (1931); Fiske v. Kansas, 274 US 380 (1927); Gitlow v. New York, 268 US 652 (1925).
[17] Near v. Minnesota, 283 US 697 (1931); Gitlow, 268 US 652.
[18] De Jonge v. Oregon, 299 US 353 (1937). [19] Cantwell v. Connecticut, 310 US 296 (1940).
[20] Everson v. Board of Education, 330 US 1 (1947).
[21] Chicago B&Q R. Co. v. Chicago, 166 US 226 (1897). [22] Powell v. Alabama, 287 US 45 (1932).
[23] 302 US 319, 325–26 (1937) (citing Twining v. New Jersey, 211 US 78 (1908)).
[24] Adamson v. California, 332 US 46, 80 (1947) (Black, J., dissenting).
[25] On the link between natural law and the Court's *Lochner*-era jurisprudence, see Edward A. Purcell Jr., *Brandeis and the Progressive Constitution* (New Haven, CT: Yale, 2000), 46–56.
[26] 287 US 45, 67–68 (1932) (quoting Twining, 211 US 78, 99). [27] 332 US 46 (1947).

testify, and the jury was permitted to draw negative inferences from his silence.[28] The Court assumed, without deciding, that California law and practice "would infringe defendant's privilege against self-incrimination under the Fifth Amendment if this were a trial in a court of the United States under a similar law."[29] However, the Court said, "[s]uch an assumption does not determine appellant's rights under the Fourteenth Amendment. It is settled law that the clause of the Fifth Amendment, protecting a person against being compelled to be a witness against himself, is not made effective by the Fourteenth Amendment as a protection against state action."[30] The law was "settled" because the Court held in *Twining v. New Jersey*[31] that the Fifth Amendment privilege against self-incrimination was not "protected by the Fourteenth Amendment against state invasion."[32]

Writing on behalf of himself and Justice Douglas, Black argued that the *Twining* "decision and the 'natural law' theory of the Constitution upon which it relies, degrade the constitutional safeguards of the Bill of Rights and simultaneously appropriate for this Court a broad power which we are not authorized by the Constitution to exercise."[33] Black believed that *Twining* and its progeny degraded constitutional safeguards because the fundamental rights theory allowed state governments to infringe key rights codified in the Bill of Rights, such as the Fifth Amendment protection from double jeopardy,[34] the Sixth Amendment right to confront witnesses,[35] and the Sixth Amendment right to appointed counsel.[36] Additionally, Black argued that *Twining*'s fundamental rights theory violated separation of powers principles by conveying legislative power to courts. In his words: "I further contend that the 'natural law' formula which the Court uses . . . [is] itself a violation of our Constitution, in that it subtly conveys to courts, at the expense of legislatures, ultimate power over public policies in fields where no specific provision of the Constitution limits legislative power."[37]

Black contended that the Bill of Rights should apply to the states because that was the purpose of the Fourteenth Amendment. His argument began with the premise that *Barron v. Baltimore*[38] – which held that the Bill of Rights does not constrain the states – "was the controlling constitutional rule when the Fourteenth Amendment was proposed in 1866."[39] However, he contended, "one of the chief objects that the provisions of the [Fourteenth] Amendment's first section, separately, and as a

---

[28] See id. at 48–49. [29] Id. at 50. [30] Id. at 50–51. [31] 211 US 78 (1908).
[32] Adamson, 332 US at 52 (citing *Twining*). [33] Id. at 70 (Black, J., dissenting).
[34] See Palko v. Connecticut, 302 US 319 (1937) (rejecting application of the Double Jeopardy Clause to the states) (overruled by Benton v. Maryland, 395 US 784 (1969)).
[35] See West v. Louisiana, 194 US 258 (1904) (rejecting application of the Confrontation Clause to the states) (overruled by Pointer v. Texas, 380 US 400 (1965)).
[36] See Betts v. Brady, 316 US 455 (1942) (holding that Fourteenth Amendment does not require states to appoint counsel for indigent criminal defendants) (overruled by Gideon v. Wainwright, 372 US 335 (1963)).
[37] Adamson, 332 US at 75 (Black, J., dissenting). [38] 32 US 243 (1833).
[39] Adamson, 332 US at 71 (Black, J., dissenting).

whole, were intended to accomplish was to make the Bill of Rights, applicable to the states."[40] Black attached to his opinion a lengthy appendix reviewing the drafting history of the Fourteenth Amendment.[41] Thus, Black's opinion, with the appendix, provided a detailed historical argument in support of his view that the Framers of the Fourteenth Amendment intended to make *the entire* Bill of Rights binding on state governments. Justices Douglas, Murphy, and Rutledge endorsed Black's historical argument in support of "total incorporation." However, two years after the Court decided *Adamson*, Professor Charles Fairman published an influential law review article that cast doubt on Black's central historical claim.[42] Thanks in part to Fairman's article, Black never persuaded a majority of justices to endorse his total incorporation theory. Nevertheless, between 1948 and 1971, the Court issued a series of decisions that made most of the Bill of Rights binding on the states. Unfortunately, the Court never articulated a principled rationale for its selective incorporation doctrine. As Justice Harlan pointedly observed, the Court decided several key incorporation cases by judicial fiat, declaring "that the clause in question is 'in' rather than 'out,'"[43] without offering a principled rationale for deciding which clauses are "in" or "out."

II. THE HUMAN RIGHTS THEORY AND INCORPORATION FROM 1948 TO 1971

Part II analyzes the application of incorporation doctrine between 1948 and 1971. The year 1948 is a good starting point for three reasons. First, Justice Black's dissent in *Adamson* in 1947 set the terms for the modern incorporation debate. Second, the Court issued two key incorporation decisions in 1948–49.[44] Third, the UN adopted the Universal Declaration of Human Rights in 1948, giving birth to modern international human rights law. The year 1971 is a good ending point because Justices Black and Harlan, the two key protagonists in the incorporation debate, both retired from the Supreme Court in 1971. Additionally, the Court decided an important case in 1971 in which it assumed that the Eighth Amendment bail clause restricted the states, although that provision had not previously been incorporated.[45] After 1971, the Court did not decide another major incorporation case until 2010.[46]

The International Bill of Rights consists of three documents: the UDHR, the ICCPR, and the ICESCR. Human rights theory holds that a right codified in the Bill of Rights binds the states under the Fourteenth Amendment if, but only if, that

---

[40] Id. at 71–72.   [41] See id. at 92–123.
[42] Charles Fairman, "Does the Fourteenth Amendment Incorporate the Bill of Rights? The Original Understanding," *Stanford Law Review* 2 (1949): 5.
[43] Duncan v. Louisiana, 391 US 145, 180–81 (1968) (Harlan, J., dissenting).
[44] See Wolf v. Colorado, 338 US 25 (1949); In re Oliver, 333 US 257 (1948).
[45] Schilb v. Kuebel, 404 US 357 (1971).   [46] See McDonald v. City of Chicago, 561 US 742 (2010).

right is also protected under the International Bill of Rights. Part II demonstrates that the human rights theory is generally consistent with the Court's application of selective incorporation doctrine between 1948 and 1971. Indeed, the human rights theory yields a closer fit with the actual results of the Court's decisions than either the total incorporation theory or the fundamental rights theory.

The analysis is divided into three sections. The first section summarizes selective incorporation doctrine as applied by the Supreme Court from 1948 to 1971. The second evaluates the consistency of all three theories with Supreme Court precedents during the relevant time frame. The final section contends that the concept of acculturation helps explain why the Court's decisions during this period were generally consistent with the human rights theory.

A. *Selective Incorporation Doctrine from 1948 to 1971*

To understand selective incorporation doctrine, one must consider both cases and clauses. As of 1971, five specific provisions in the Bill of Rights were not binding on the states (the five unincorporated clauses). Between 1948 and 1971, the Court decided 13 cases in which it held explicitly that particular Bill of Rights provisions were binding on the states (the express incorporation cases). Also between 1948 and 1971, the Court decided two cases in which it assumed that other Bill of Rights provisions were binding on the states (the implied incorporation cases). This section summarizes the unincorporated clauses, the implied incorporation cases, and the express incorporation cases.

As of 1971, only five provisions in the Bill of Rights were *not* binding on the states: the Second Amendment right to bear arms;[47] the Third Amendment prohibition on quartering of soldiers;[48] the Fifth Amendment grand jury clause;[49] the Seventh Amendment right to a jury trial in civil cases;[50] and the Eighth Amendment excessive fines clause.[51] The Supreme Court decided in the nineteenth century that the Second Amendment, the Fifth Amendment grand jury clause, and the Seventh Amendment do not bind the states.[52] The Court has never ruled explicitly on the

---

[47] US Const. Amend. II ("A well regulated Militia, being necessary to the security of a free State, the right of the people to keep and bear Arms, shall not be infringed").
[48] US Const. Amend. III ("No Soldier shall, in time of peace be quartered in any house, without the consent of the Owner, nor in time of war, but in a manner to be prescribed by law").
[49] US Const. Amend. V ("No person shall be held to answer for a capital, or otherwise infamous crime, unless on a presentment or indictment of a Grand Jury").
[50] US Const. Amend. VII ("In suits at common law, where the value in controversy shall exceed twenty dollars, the right of trial by jury shall be preserved, and no fact tried by a jury, shall be otherwise reexamined in any Court of the United States, than according to the rules of the common law").
[51] US Const. Amend. VIII ("nor excessive fines imposed").
[52] See Presser v. Illinois, 116 US 252 (1886) (Second Amendment); United States v. Cruikshank, 92 US 542 (1876) (Second Amendment); Hurtado v. California, 110 US 516 (1884) (grand jury clause); Walker v. Sauvinet, 92 US 90 (1875) (Seventh Amendment).

Third Amendment or the excessive fines clause. However, in an important case decided in 2010, the Court included both provisions in a list of unincorporated clauses.[53]

The Court's express incorporation decisions between 1948 and 1971 addressed various aspects of the First, Fourth, Fifth, Sixth, and Eighth Amendments. *Edwards v. South Carolina*[54] incorporated the First Amendment right to petition the government for a redress of grievances. *Wolf v. Colorado*[55] incorporated the Fourth Amendment prohibition on unreasonable searches and seizures, *Aguilar v. Texas*[56] incorporated the Fourth Amendment warrant requirement, and *Mapp v. Ohio*[57] incorporated the Fourth Amendment exclusionary rule. *Malloy v. Hogan*[58] incorporated the Fifth Amendment self-incrimination clause, and *Benton v. Maryland*[59] incorporated the Fifth Amendment double jeopardy clause. The Court decided six cases addressing discrete portions of the Sixth Amendment: *In re Oliver* incorporated the right to a public trial;[60] *Klopfer v. North Carolina* incorporated the right to a speedy trial;[61] *Pointer v. Texas* incorporated the right to confront adverse witnesses;[62] *Washington v. Texas* incorporated the right to compulsory process;[63] *Gideon v. Wainwright* incorporated the right to appointed counsel;[64] and *Duncan v. Louisiana* incorporated the right to a jury trial in criminal cases.[65] Finally, *Robinson v. California* incorporated the Eighth Amendment cruel and unusual punishments clause.[66]

The Court decided two other cases between 1948 and 1971 that implicitly incorporated other Bill of Rights provisions not previously incorporated. In *Irvin v. Dowd*, the Court assumed without deciding that the Sixth Amendment right to an impartial jury binds the states under the Fourteenth Amendment due process clause.[67] In *Schilb v. Kuebel*, the Court said, "The Eighth Amendment's proscription of excessive bail has been assumed to have application to the States through the Fourteenth Amendment."[68]

Viewed together, the 5 unincorporated clauses, 13 express incorporation cases, and 2 implied incorporation cases provide 20 data points that can be used to evaluate competing theories. For ease of expression, I refer to the 20 data points as 20 "decisions," even though the Court did not issue decisions regarding the unincorporated clauses. The next section evaluates three competing theories – the total incorporation theory, the fundamental rights theory, and the human rights theory – by testing their consistency with these 20 decisions.

---

[53] See McDonald v. City of Chicago, 561 US 742, 765 n. 13 (2010). Justice Alito also included the Sixth Amendment right to a unanimous jury verdict in his list of unincorporated provisions. I do not include that right here because the text of the Sixth Amendment does not explicitly require unanimity.
[54] 372 US 229 (1963). [55] 338 US 25 (1949). [56] 378 US 108 (1964). [57] 367 US 643 (1961).
[58] 378 US 1 (1964). [59] 395 US 784 (1969). [60] 333 US 257 (1948). [61] 386 US 213 (1967).
[62] 380 US 400 (1965). [63] 388 US 14 (1967). [64] 372 US 335 (1963). [65] 391 US 145 (1968).
[66] 370 US 660 (1962). [67] 366 US 717 (1961). [68] 404 US 357, 365 (1971).

B. Comparing Theories to Precedents

The total incorporation theory holds that the entire Bill of Rights applies to the states. That theory is consistent with all of the express and implied incorporation cases. However, it is inconsistent with the five unincorporated clauses. Therefore, the theory is consistent with 15 of the 20 decisions that provide our baseline for comparison.

The human rights theory holds that rights codified in the Bill of Rights bind state governments if, but only if, those rights are included in the International Bill of Rights. In contrast to the total incorporation theory, the human rights theory is entirely consistent with the five unincorporated clauses. The International Bill of Rights does not protect the right to bear arms or the right to a jury trial in civil cases, nor does it include any provision similar to the Eighth Amendment ban on excessive fines or the Third Amendment rule on quartering of soldiers. ICCPR Article 14 includes provisions whose purpose is similar to the goals underlying the Fifth Amendment grand jury clause.[69] However, the grand jury clause requires a federal prosecutor to present his case to a grand jury (not a judge) and to proceed by way of indictment (not information). The International Bill of Rights does not include any similar restrictions.

The human rights theory is also consistent with almost all of the express and implied incorporation cases. Articles 20 and 21 of the UDHR, and Articles 19 and 21 of the ICCPR, protect rights similar to the First Amendment right of petition at issue in *Edwards v. South Carolina*. Articles 9 and 12 of the UDHR, and Articles 9(1) and 17(1) of the ICCPR, protect rights comparable to the Fourth Amendment rights at issue in *Wolf v. Colorado* and *Aguilar v. Texas*. Articles 14(3)(g) and 14(7) of the ICCPR are similar, respectively, to the Fifth Amendment self-incrimination and double jeopardy clauses (at issue in *Malloy v. Hogan* and *Benton v. Maryland*). Article 10 of the UDHR and Article 14(1) of the ICCPR protect the right to a public trial, as in *In re Oliver*. Articles 9(3) and 14(3)(c) of the ICCPR protect the right to a speedy trial, as in *Klopfer v. North Carolina*. Article 10 of the UDHR and Article 14(1) of the ICCPR guarantee an impartial tribunal, as in *Irvin v. Dowd*.[70] Article 14(3)(e) of the ICCPR protects both the right to confront adverse witnesses and the right to compulsory process, at issue in *Pointer v. Texas* and *Washington v. Texas*, respectively. Articles 14(3)(b) and 14(3)(d) of the ICCPR protect the right to counsel, as in *Gideon v. Wainwright*. Article 5 of the UDHR and Article 7 of the ICCPR are

---

[69] See ICCPR, Art. 14(3)(a) (protecting the right of a criminal defendant "[t]o be informed promptly and in detail in a language which he understands of the nature and cause of the charge against him").

[70] The Sixth Amendment protects the right to trial "by an impartial jury." This right can be divided analytically into two parts: the right to a jury trial and the right to an impartial tribunal. Article 10 of the UDHR and Article 14(1) of the ICCPR protect the right to an "independent and impartial tribunal," but neither document guarantees the right to a jury trial. *Irvin v. Dowd*, decided in 1961, implicitly incorporated the right to an impartial tribunal. The Court did not incorporate the right to a jury trial until its 1968 decision in *Duncan v. Louisiana*.

similar to the Eighth Amendment cruel and unusual punishments clause, at issue in *Robinson v. California*. Finally, Article 9(3) of the ICCPR protects the right to release from custody pending trial; it is similar to the Eighth Amendment bail clause noted in *Schilb v. Kuebel*.

Mapp v. Ohio and *Duncan v. Louisiana* are the only two incorporation decisions between 1948 and 1971 that are inconsistent with the human rights theory. The International Bill of Rights does not include any provision similar to the exclusionary rule at issue in *Mapp*. Article 14(1) of the ICCPR guarantees "a fair and public hearing by a competent, independent and impartial tribunal," but neither the UDHR nor the ICCPR specifically protects the right to a jury trial at issue in *Duncan*. Overall, the human rights theory is consistent with 18 of the 20 decisions that provide our baseline for comparison. In other words, the Court would have reached the same results in 18 out of 20 cases if it had applied the human rights theory. Thus, the human rights theory is broadly consistent with the actual pattern of Supreme Court decisions in incorporation cases between 1948 and 1971.

The fundamental rights theory holds that many Bill of Rights provisions do not bind the states because the Fourteenth Amendment due process clause protects against state infringement only those rights that qualify as "fundamental." Different justices expressed conflicting views about which rights qualify as "fundamental." For present purposes, I consider Justice Harlan's views to be the best indicator of the scope of protection under the fundamental rights theory because he was the leading proponent of that theory on the Warren Court.[71] Inasmuch as Justice Harlan was generally opposed to incorporation, he would surely agree that the five unincorporated clauses should not be incorporated. Therefore, the fundamental rights theory is consistent with the five unincorporated clauses.

Justice Harlan participated in 11 of the 13 express incorporation cases[72] and in 1 of the 2 implied incorporation cases.[73] He dissented in 4 of the 12 cases in which he participated: *Mapp v. Ohio*, *Malloy v. Hogan*, *Duncan v. Louisiana*, and *Benton v. Maryland*. Therefore, the fundamental rights theory is inconsistent with those four cases. Let us assume that the fundamental rights theory is consistent with the three cases in which Harlan did not participate, because that assumption yields the highest plausible estimate of consistency between the fundamental rights theory and the Court's decisions.[74] Given that assumption, the fundamental

---

[71] If one were to rely on cases decided before 1940 to determine the scope of protection under the fundamental rights theory, then the scope of protection would be narrower and the inconsistency between the theory and the Court's selective incorporation doctrine would be greater.

[72] The Court decided *In re Oliver*, 333 US 257 (1948), and *Wolf v. Colorado*, 338 US 25 (1949), before Justice Harlan joined the Court.

[73] Justice Harlan was in the majority in *Irvin v. Dowd*, 366 US 717 (1961), but he retired before the Court decided *Schilb v. Kuebel*, 404 US 357 (1971).

[74] In fact, Harlan would probably have dissented in *Oliver* because Justices Jackson and Frankfurter dissented in *Oliver*, and Harlan's judicial philosophy was close to theirs. Moreover, Harlan concurred separately in several cases where he agreed with the majority's result but not its rationale.

rights theory would be consistent with 16 of the 20 decisions that provide our baseline for comparison (all except the four cases in which Harlan dissented). Thus, the final tally is that the human rights theory is consistent with 18 of 20 decisions, the fundamental rights theory is consistent with no more than 16 of 20 decisions, and the total incorporation theory is consistent with 15 of 20 decisions. Therefore, insofar as consistency with Supreme Court precedents is a valid metric for testing competing theories, the human rights theory compares favorably to the other two. Part III addresses other relevant criteria for evaluating the merits of the human rights theory. First, though, the next section provides an explanation for the observed correlation between selective incorporation doctrine and the human rights theory.

C. Selective Incorporation and International Human Rights

What explains the close fit between the Court's actual decisions in incorporation cases and the results it would have reached by applying the human rights theory? One possible answer is that the Supreme Court and the United Nations were pursuing similar goals: both sought to articulate a catalog of "fundamental rights." Indeed, the Court repeatedly said that only "fundamental rights" bind the states under the Fourteenth Amendment.[75] Similarly, the Universal Declaration of Human Rights affirms people's "faith in *fundamental* human rights" as a cornerstone of modern international human rights law.[76] Thus, one could argue that the concept of fundamental rights functioned as a "supernorm" that linked incorporation doctrine to international human rights law.[77]

This explanation is not without merit. However, the concept of "fundamental rights" manifested in Supreme Court decisions changed over time. In 1942, the Court held in *Betts v. Brady* that the right of an indigent criminal defendant to have counsel appointed for him or her was not a fundamental right.[78] Twenty years later, the Court held that indigent criminal defendants do have a fundamental right to appointed counsel.[79] In 1937, the Court held in *Palko v. Connecticut* that subjecting a criminal defendant to double jeopardy did not violate "fundamental principles of liberty and justice."[80] Thirty years later, though, the Court decided "that the double jeopardy prohibition of the Fifth Amendment represents a fundamental ideal in our constitutional heritage, and that it should apply to the States through the Fourteenth

---

[75] See, e.g., Benton v. Maryland, 395 US 784, 794 (1969); Duncan v. Louisiana, 391 US 145, 149 (1968); Klopfer v. North Carolina, 386 US 213, 223 (1967); Pointer v. Texas, 380 US 400, 403 (1965).
[76] Universal Declaration of Human Rights, Preamble.
[77] The term "supernorm" has been part of the lexicon of international law scholars since at least 1983. See Prosper Weil, "Towards Relative Normativity in International Law," *American Journal of International Law* 77 (1983): 413, 427.
[78] 316 US 455 (1942).   [79] Gideon v. Wainwright, 372 US 335 (1963).   [80] 302 US 319, 328 (1937).

Amendment."[81] One could cite other, similar examples.[82] The point is that the abstract idea of "fundamental rights" is not self-defining. Before World War II, applying the *Palko* standard, the Supreme Court classified a very narrow set of rights as "fundamental." Between 1948, when the UN adopted the Universal Declaration, and 1966, when it adopted the two Covenants, the United Nations articulated a more expansive concept of fundamental rights that encompassed a broader range of rights. During roughly the same time period, the Court's selective incorporation doctrine also embraced a more expansive concept of fundamental rights that encompassed many of the rights codified in the International Bill of Rights that the Court had previously held were not "fundamental." So, the question remains: why did the Court expand its concept of fundamental rights to incorporate rights similar to those codified in the International Bill of Rights, but not to incorporate other clauses in the US Bill of Rights?

Some scholars have argued that codification of the International Bill of Rights between 1948 and 1966 was the result of a successful US effort to export American values to the rest of the world.[83] They note that Eleanor Roosevelt, a leading spokeswoman for American values, was one of the key architects of the Universal Declaration, the document that laid the foundation for the subsequent drafting of the two Covenants.[84] Under this view, the alignment of federal constitutional law with international human rights norms by means of incorporation doctrine is best explained as a "re-importation" of American values that were exported to other countries and codified in the International Bill of Rights. This explanation also has merit. However, standing alone, it does not explain the key feature of incorporation doctrine: the decision to override traditional principles of constitutional federalism by making the Bill of Rights binding on the states. For more than 150 years, the Supreme Court had assumed that state law provided adequate protection against infringement by state governments for most of the rights codified in the Bill of Rights. Why, between 1948 and 1971, did the Court decide that reliance on state law would no longer suffice?

I suggest that Supreme Court decisions aligning US constitutional law with the International Bill of Rights can be explained as a product of both foreign policy and psychological factors. Begin with foreign policy. During the period under review, the United States was engaged in the Cold War struggle with the Soviet Union. In that context, a key goal of US foreign policy was to persuade the developing world that the United States was the true champion of human rights and that the

---

[81] Benton v. Maryland, 395 US 784, 794 (1969).
[82] See, e.g., Pointer v. Texas, 380 US 400 (1965) (overruling West v. Louisiana, 194 US 258 (1904)); Malloy v. Hogan, 378 US 1 (1964) (overruling Adamson v. California, 332 US 46 (1947)).
[83] See generally Louis Henkin, *The Age of Rights* (New York: Columbia University Press, 1990); Mary Ann Glendon, *A World Made New: Eleanor Roosevelt and the Universal Declaration of Human Rights* (New York: Random House, 2001).
[84] See id.

US democratic system was superior to the Soviet communist system.[85] However, many countries in the developing world were highly critical of the US failure to adhere to international human rights norms.[86] For example, the Universal Declaration guarantees "men and women of full age" the right to marry "without any limitation due to race."[87] Until 1967, though, when the Supreme Court decided *Loving v. Virginia*, many states in the United States prohibited interracial marriage.[88] Similarly, the Universal Declaration prohibits "cruel, inhuman or degrading treatment or punishment."[89] Until 1962, though, when the Supreme Court's decision in *Robinson v. California*[90] made the Eighth Amendment binding on the states, state governments were free to impose cruel punishments on criminals, subject only to the very permissive "shocks the conscience" test that the Court applied to states under the Fourteenth Amendment.[91] After the Court's decision in *Robinson*, though, "federal courts ended up promulgating a comprehensive code for prison management [for the states], covering such diverse matters as residence facilities, sanitation, food, clothing, medical care, discipline, staff hiring, libraries, work, and education."[92]

The Court's decisions in *Loving* and *Robinson* advanced US foreign policy goals by adding substance to the claim that the US democratic system was superior to the Soviet communist system. Similarly, many of the Court's incorporation decisions during this period advanced US foreign policy goals by aligning US constitutional norms with international human rights norms, thereby adding substance to the claim that the United States was the true champion of human rights. The Court did not explicitly articulate a foreign policy rationale to support its incorporation decisions, but the justices were undoubtedly aware that decisions aligning constitutional doctrine with international human rights norms would advance the nation's Cold War foreign policy goals. For example, in *Brown v. Bd. of Education*, the federal government submitted an amicus brief to the Supreme Court that explicitly advanced a foreign policy rationale to support the argument that racial segregation in public schools was unconstitutional.[93] The government submitted similar briefs in other cases as well.[94]

---

[85] See Mary L. Dudziak, *Cold War Civil Rights: Race and the Image of American Democracy* (Princeton: Princeton University Press, 2000).

[86] See id. at 18–46 (documenting third world criticisms of the US human rights record).

[87] Universal Declaration, Art. 16.   [88] Loving v. Virginia, 388 US 1 (1967).

[89] Universal Declaration, Art. 5.   [90] Robinson, 370 US 660 (1962).

[91] Justice Harlan described the test as follows: "In the absence of anything in the conduct of the state authorities which shocks the conscience or does more than offend some fastidious squeamishness or private sentimentalism about combatting crime too energetically," state practices did not violate the Fourteenth Amendment. Fikes v. Alabama, 352 US 191, 201 (1957) (Harlan, J., dissenting).

[92] Malcolm M. Feeley and Edward L. Rubin, *Judicial Policy Making and the Modern State: How the Courts Reformed America's Prisons* (Cambridge: Cambridge University Press, 1998), 41.

[93] See Brown, 347 US 483 (1954) (Nos. 1, 2, 3, 4, 5), Brief for United States as Amicus Curiae, available at 1952 WL 82045.

[94] See David L. Sloss, *The Death of Treaty Supremacy: An Invisible Constitutional Change* (New York: Oxford University Press, 2016), 191–94.

Foreign policy considerations aside, psychological factors also help explain the development of incorporation doctrine between 1948 and 1971. Professors Goodman and Jinks define acculturation as "the general process by which actors adopt the beliefs and behavioral patterns of the surrounding culture."[95] They argue that "acculturation narrows the gap between public acts and private preferences through internal cognitive processes: Under certain conditions people change their beliefs to avoid the unpleasant state of cognitive dissonance between what they profess in public and what they believe in private."[96]

During the period under review, many Supreme Court justices held two inconsistent beliefs. First, as of 1948, most believed that principles of American federalism meant that states had the primary responsibility to protect rights codified in the Bill of Rights from infringement by state governments. Second, they believed in American exceptionalism: the view that the United States has the best constitutional system in the world because the United States offers more robust protection for human rights than any other country in the world. The advent of modern international human rights law – and the juxtaposition of the International Bill of Rights with the (very narrow) *Palko* standard for determining which rights qualify as fundamental – created cognitive dissonance for the justices.[97] Continued reliance on the *Palko* standard would have meant that constitutional rules protecting individual rights against infringement by state governments fell below international standards. As Professor Charles Fairman wrote in 1952, "it would seem, indeed, a reproach to our constitutional system to confess that the values it establishes fall below any requirement of [international human rights law]. One should think very seriously before admitting such a deficiency."[98] (Fairman referred to the human rights provisions of the UN Charter, but the argument applies equally to the International Bill of Rights.) The justices did not wish to concede that the Constitution permitted state governments to infringe rights codified in the International Bill of Rights. That would have been, in Fairman's words, a "reproach to our constitutional system." To avoid reproaching our constitutional system and to preserve their faith in American exceptionalism, the justices reinterpreted the Fourteenth Amendment to override traditional principles of state autonomy and to make most Bill of Rights provisions binding on the states.

Consider *Gideon v. Wainwright* as an example.[99] *Gideon* presented the question whether, in a criminal case in state court, the Fourteenth Amendment requires the state to provide a lawyer for an indigent criminal defendant at no expense to the defendant. Article 11 of the Universal Declaration provides that "everyone

---

[95] Goodman and Jinks, *Socializing States*, 4.   [96] Id. at 153.
[97] See Sloss, *Death of Treaty Supremacy*, 247–48, 283–84 (explaining that the advent of modern international human rights law created cognitive dissonance for American lawyers and judges and that cognitive dissonance was a key factor contributing to constitutional change).
[98] Charles Fairman, "Editorial Comment, Finis to Fujii," *American Journal of International Law* 46 (1952): 682, 689.
[99] 372 US 335 (1963).

charged with a penal offence has the right to... all the guarantees necessary for his defence."[100] Article 14(3) of the ICCPR, which existed in draft form when *Gideon* was decided, makes clear that those guarantees include the right to appointed counsel.[101] Just 20 years before *Gideon*, the Supreme Court decided in *Betts v. Brady* that the Fourteenth Amendment does not obligate states to provide appointed counsel for indigent criminal defendants, absent special circumstances.[102] Given the facts in *Betts*, the Court held that denial of the request for appointed counsel was not "shocking to the universal sense of justice," and therefore, consistent with traditional federalism principles, the state could decide for itself whether to provide appointed counsel.[103]

In *Gideon*, though, presented with facts very similar to *Betts*, the Court concluded that the Sixth Amendment, which guarantees a right to appointed counsel for federal criminal defendants, is "fundamental and essential to a fair trial" and is therefore "made obligatory upon the states by the Fourteenth Amendment."[104] Given the codification of the right to counsel in the International Bill of Rights – which occurred between the Court's decisions in *Betts* (1942) and *Gideon* (1963) – it would have been a reproach to our constitutional system to hold otherwise. Since the justices believed in American exceptionalism, it would have created cognitive dissonance for them to hold that human rights protections available under the Fourteenth Amendment fell below international standards. As Goodman and Jinks note, "under certain conditions people change their beliefs to avoid the unpleasant state of cognitive dissonance between what they profess in public and what they believe in private."[105] Between *Betts* and *Gideon*, the justices changed their beliefs about the relationship between the Fourteenth Amendment and principles of constitutional federalism to avoid the unpleasant state of cognitive dissonance between their private belief in American exceptionalism and their public statements about the meaning of the Fourteenth Amendment.

Granted, the Court did not cite the International Bill of Rights in any of its major incorporation decisions. In my view, though, the absence of explicit citations does not prove that the Court was immune to the influence of international human rights law. As I have explained elsewhere, between 1948 and 1954, litigants repeatedly invoked international human rights norms in US courts to challenge the validity of state laws.[106] However, two developments in the early 1950s persuaded human rights advocates that continued reliance on international norms was neither wise nor necessary. First, the debate over the proposed Bricker Amendment between 1950 and 1954 – which was largely a response to judicial decisions applying international

---

[100] Universal Declaration, Art. 11.
[101] See ICCPR, Art. 14(3)(d) (guaranteeing the right of a criminal defendant "to have legal assistance assigned to him, in any case where the interests of justice so require, and without payment by him in any such case if he does not have sufficient means to pay for it").
[102] Betts, 316 US 455 (1942). [103] Id. at 462. [104] Gideon, 372 US at 342.
[105] Goodman and Jinks, *Socializing States*, 153. [106] See Sloss, *Death of Treaty Supremacy*, 187–91.

human rights norms – persuaded human rights advocates that they would provoke less political resistance by framing their arguments in terms of US constitutional rights rather than using the rhetoric of international human rights.[107] Second, the Supreme Court's 1954 decision in *Brown v. Bd. of Education* signaled the Court's willingness to enforce the Fourteenth Amendment more vigorously.[108]

Thus, the combination of *Brown* and Bricker closed the human rights door at the same time that it opened the Fourteenth Amendment door. In response, the human rights advocates who had previously invoked international norms to advance their political agenda chose instead to rely on the Fourteenth Amendment. Hence, many of the individuals and organizations who litigated human rights claims in US courts in the early 1950s were litigating Fourteenth Amendment incorporation claims in the 1960s.[109] Indeed, Thurgood Marshall, who was a prominent advocate for the domestic application of the UN Charter's human rights provisions in his role as lead counsel for the NAACP,[110] later became an important proponent of incorporation doctrine in his role as an Associate Justice of the Supreme Court.[111] Between 1954 and 1971, leading human rights advocates did not forsake their goals, but they made a tactical decision to employ the rhetoric of constitutional rights, rather than the rhetoric of international human rights, to advance those goals. The development of selective incorporation doctrine during this period demonstrates that they were remarkably successful in persuading the Court to reinterpret the

---

[107] See id. at 248–53 (discussing the Bricker Amendment) and at 178–79 (noting the disappearance of international human rights litigation in US courts after 1954).

[108] Brown v. Bd. of Education, 347 US 483 (1954).

[109] Detailed support of this claim is beyond the scope of this essay. I note here one important example. In the late 1940s and early 1950s, the ACLU played a lead role in efforts to persuade US courts to apply the human rights provisions of the UN Charter. See Sloss, *Death of Treaty Supremacy*, 187–90. Later, in the 1960s, the ACLU filed amicus briefs supporting incorporation in several key incorporation cases. See Klopfer v. North Carolina, 386 US 213 (1967) (No. 100), Motion of the American Civil Liberties Union and the American Civil Liberties Union of North Carolina for Leave to File a Brief as Amici Curiae and Brief Amici Curiae, available at 1966 WL 100766; Malloy v. Hogan, 378 US 1 (1964) (No. 110), Brief for American Civil Liberties Union, Amicus Curiae, available at 1963 WL 105806; Gideon v. Wainwright, 372 US 335 (1963) (No. 155), Brief of the American Civil Liberties Union and the Florida Civil Liberties Union, Amici Curiae, available at 1962 WL 115121; Mapp v. Ohio, 367 US 643 (1961) (No. 236), Brief Amici Curiae on Behalf of American Civil Liberties Union and Ohio Civil Liberties Union, available at 1961 WL 101785.

[110] See McGhee v. Sipes, 331 US 804 (1947) (No. 87), Brief for Petitioners, available at 1947 WL 44154 (Marshall was lead counsel for petitioners); Bob-Lo Excursion Co. v. Michigan, 333 US 28 (1948) (No. 374), Motion and Brief for the National Association for the Advancement of Colored People, American Civil Liberties Union, and National Lawyers Guild as Amici Curiae, available at 1947 WL 44321 (Marshall was lead counsel for NAACP); Takahashi v. Fish & Game Comm'n, 334 US 410 (1948) (No. 533) Motion and Brief for the National Association for the Advancement of Colored People as Amicus Curiae, available at 1948 WL 47434 (Marshall was lead counsel for NAACP).

[111] Marshall joined the Court in fall 1967, after most of the major incorporation cases had been decided. However, he wrote the majority opinion in *Benton v. Maryland*, 395 US 784 (1969), and he joined the majority in *Duncan v. Louisiana*, 391 US 145 (1968). Both *Benton* and *Duncan* were important incorporation cases.

Fourteenth Amendment to align with international human rights norms, albeit without mentioning those norms explicitly.

III. HUMAN RIGHTS AND FEDERALISM

As noted previously, the dominant political discourse in the United States since at least the 1970s has assumed that federalism and human rights are mutually antagonistic values. Part III challenges that assumption by comparing the human rights theory to the Court's current selective incorporation doctrine. Part III evaluates the "federalism friendliness" of both approaches by comparing the extent to which they grant power to the states, or the federal courts, to control the application of rights codified in the Bill of Rights. A theory or doctrine is "federalism friendly," compared to other approaches, if it grants more power to the states and less power to the federal courts. The analysis demonstrates that the human rights theory is more federalism friendly than the Court's current selective incorporation doctrine.

This essay does not specifically advocate adoption of the human rights theory. However, Part III demonstrates that the theory has two significant advantages over current doctrine. First, the Court has never articulated a coherent, principled rationale to justify selective incorporation doctrine. The human rights theory provides a principled rationale to support the doctrine. Second, there is a significant tension between selective incorporation doctrine and the Court's stated commitment to principles of constitutional federalism. Adoption of the human rights theory would not eliminate that tension, but it would alleviate the tension by returning control over the application of some Bill of Rights provisions from the federal courts to the states.

A. Articulating a Principled Rationale for Incorporation Doctrine

Justice Black launched modern incorporation doctrine with his dissenting opinion in *Adamson v. California*.[112] He relied exclusively on history to justify his total incorporation theory, contending that the original understanding of the Fourteenth Amendment required application of the entire Bill of Rights to the states. However, Black's originalist defense of total incorporation never garnered support from a majority of justices. Lacking a consensus in favor of an originalist rationale, the Court has struggled to articulate a principled rationale to justify its selective incorporation doctrine.

Before *Adamson*, the Court typically applied some version of the *Palko* standard, which invoked natural law concepts of fundamental rights to justify constitutional limitations on state governments under the Fourteenth Amendment. For example, the Court said, "This court has never attempted to define with precision the words

---

[112] *Adamson*, 332 US 46, 68–123 (1947) (Black, J., dissenting).

'due process of law,' nor is it necessary to do so in this case. It is sufficient to say that there are certain immutable principles of justice, which inhere in the very idea of free government, which no member of the Union may disregard."[113] After 1948, though, most of the justices were reluctant to base their decisions on the premise that there are "immutable principles of justice, which inhere in the very idea of free government." Nevertheless, they continued to use the rhetoric of "fundamental rights," unhinged from its natural law foundations, as a test for selective incorporation.

For example, in *Duncan v. Louisiana*, petitioner claimed that the Sixth Amendment right to a jury trial binds the states under the Fourteenth Amendment. In evaluating that claim, Justice White repudiated the traditional test: whether "a civilized system could be imagined that would not accord the particular protection."[114] Instead, he argued, a "particular procedure is fundamental" if it "is necessary to an *Anglo-American* regime of ordered liberty."[115] He concluded that "trial by jury in criminal cases is fundamental to the *American* scheme of justice."[116] More recently, in *McDonald v. City of Chicago*, the City argued that the Second Amendment right to bear arms is not fundamental because "it is possible to imagine a civilized country that does not recognize the right."[117] Justice Alito cited *Duncan* approvingly for the proposition "that the governing standard is not whether *any* civilized system [can] be imagined that would not accord the particular protection." Instead, he maintained, the proper test is "whether a particular Bill of Rights guarantee is *fundamental* to our [American] scheme of ordered liberty and system of justice."[118] In short, both Justice White in *Duncan* and Justice Alito in *McDonald* invoked American traditions as the touchstone for determining which rights qualify as "fundamental" and therefore bind the states.

Unfortunately, the *Duncan–McDonald* methodology does not withstand close scrutiny because both cases ignore the long-standing American tradition of granting states broad discretion to decide for themselves the scope of the jury trial right (at issue in *Duncan*) and the scope of gun rights (at issue in *McDonald*). In both cases, the Court invoked American traditions to justify its decision to create a new, uniform federal rule in areas that had previously been governed exclusively by state law. Before *Duncan*, there was no federal jury trial right that bound the states. Before *McDonald*, there were no federal gun rights that bound the states. The key move in both cases involved a judicial decision to replace an entrenched tradition of state autonomy with a new rule of federal uniformity. Justice Black's originalist argument provides a plausible rationale for applying a federal rule to override state autonomy. Similarly, the traditional "immutable principles of justice" test provides a plausible rationale for applying a federal rule to override state autonomy. However, the Court's modern selective incorporation doctrine rejects both of those tests.

---

[113] Holden v. Hardy, 169 US 366, 389 (1898). [114] Duncan, 391 US 145, 149 n.14 (1968).
[115] Id. (emphasis added). [116] Id. at 149 (emphasis added).
[117] McDonald, 561 US 742, 753 (2010). [118] Id. at 764.

Instead, *Duncan* and *McDonald* both invoke a purely fictitious "American tradition" as a rationale for replacing a deeply entrenched tradition of state autonomy with a newly minted federal constitutional rule. Regardless of whether one agrees with the outcomes in those cases, it defies logic to invoke "American traditions" as a rationale for creating a novel federal constitutional rule to override an established tradition of state autonomy.

Duncan and *McDonald* illustrate the broader point that the Court never articulated a principled rationale for its selective incorporation decisions. In case after case, the Court cited federal rules that had previously bound only the federal government, and state rules that had previously bound only the relevant state government, to justify its decision to classify a right as "fundamental" and make the federal rule binding on state governments. The Court never explained why the existence of similar rules at the state and federal levels justified a decision to override state law by applying a federal Bill of Rights provision to the states that was not previously binding on the states.

In contrast, human rights theory does offer a principled rationale for selective incorporation. Human rights theory begins with the premise "that there are certain immutable principles of justice, which inhere in the very idea of free government, which no ... [state] may disregard."[119] This idea has deep roots in American jurisprudence, beginning with the Declaration of Independence, which affirmed the "self-evident" proposition that all people "are endowed by their Creator with certain unalienable rights." The very same idea is the foundation of modern international human rights law. The preamble to the Universal Declaration affirms "the equal and inalienable rights of all members of the human family." If one accepts the premise that there are immutable principles of justice that protect the inalienable rights of all people, then it makes perfect sense to conclude that the Supreme Court has a duty to apply those immutable principles of justice to protect the inalienable rights of individuals against infringement by state governments.

The primary objection to this line of argument is that the "immutable principles of justice" test, in practice, leaves each individual Supreme Court justice free to apply his or her own subjective preferences in deciding which rights are inalienable. The human rights theory addresses this objection by providing an objective test for determining which rights are inalienable: a right qualifies as inalienable (or fundamental) if it is included in both the US Bill of Rights and the International Bill of Rights. Both the US Bill of Rights and the International Bill of Rights represent efforts to develop a catalog of fundamental rights – that is, rights that "inhere in the very idea of free government, which no ... [state] may disregard."[120] The International Bill of Rights was written more than 150 years after the US Bills of Rights, in a very different historical era. Given the separation in time and historical circumstances between the two bills of rights, the fact that a particular right is

---

[119] Holden v. Hardy, 169 US 366, 389 (1898).   [120] Id.

included in both provides compelling, objective evidence that it really does embody an immutable principle of justice that inheres in the very idea of free government.

Skeptics who reject the proposition that there are any immutable principles of justice will undoubtedly remain unpersuaded by this argument. Regardless, the human rights theory provides a principled rationale to support the Court's selective incorporation doctrine. Moreover, as demonstrated in Part II, the theory yields results that are broadly consistent with the relevant Supreme Court precedents. In contrast, the Court's actual decisions in selective incorporation cases provide no principled rationale whatsoever. They merely offer a fig leaf for arbitrary decision making by judicial fiat.

B. Federalism and the Human Rights Theory

If the Supreme Court were to adopt the human rights theory, it would require reversal of three key precedents that are part of current selective incorporation doctrine. *Mapp v. Ohio* held that the Fourth Amendment exclusionary rule binds the states.[121] *Duncan v. Louisiana* held that the Sixth Amendment right to a jury trial binds the States.[122] And *McDonald v. City of Chicago* held that the Second Amendment right to bear arms binds the states.[123] Under the human rights theory, none of these rules would bind the states because none of them are included in the International Bill of Rights. (The International Bill of Rights includes provisions similar to the Fourth Amendment ban on unreasonable searches and seizures,[124] but it does not include any provision analogous to the exclusionary rule.) However, in all other respects, the human rights theory would yield results consistent with current doctrine because the other Bill of Rights provisions that bind the states under current selective incorporation doctrine have analogues in the International Bill of Rights.[125]

The human rights theory is more federalism friendly than the Court's current selective incorporation doctrine because, under the human rights theory, states would be free to decide for themselves the appropriate gun control regulations to adopt, the particular circumstances in which a jury trial is required, and the proper application of the exclusionary rule. It bears emphasis that reversal of *Mapp* and *McDonald* would be ideologically neutral in terms of contemporary political ideology. Most liberals would celebrate the reversal of *McDonald* and criticize the reversal of *Mapp*. Most conservatives would celebrate the reversal of *Mapp* and mourn the reversal of *McDonald*. However, those who place a high value on the constitutional principle of state autonomy would presumably welcome reversal of both *Mapp* and *McDonald*, because both decisions mandated federal uniformity in areas that were originally reserved to the states under the Tenth Amendment.

---

[121] 367 US 643 (1961).   [122] 391 US 145 (1968).   [123] 561 US 742 (2010).
[124] See Universal Declaration, Arts. 9 and 12; ICCPR, Arts. 9(1) and 17(1).   [125] See Part II.B.

Reversal of *Duncan v. Louisiana* would necessarily entail reversal of two more recent Supreme Court decisions – *Apprendi v. New Jersey*[126] and *Ring v. Arizona*[127] – both of which built on the foundation established by *Duncan*. *Duncan* held that the Sixth Amendment right to a jury trial binds the states. *Apprendi* held that the Sixth Amendment, as applied to the states through the Fourteenth Amendment, "requires that a factual determination authorizing an increase in the maximum prison sentence for an offense" must be made by a jury, not a judge.[128] *Ring* applied *Apprendi* to capital sentencing, holding that the Sixth Amendment requires the key factual determinations in the sentencing phase of a capital trial to be made by a jury, not a judge. Judicial adoption of the human rights theory would require reversal of all three decisions because the International Bill of Rights does not recognize a human right to a jury trial. The human rights theory is federalism friendly because, compared to current doctrine, it would leave states greater discretion to decide for themselves how to allocate functions between judges and juries.

The trifecta of *Duncan*, *Apprendi*, and *Ring* shows how the Court has used selective incorporation doctrine to expand the reach of federal constitutional lawmaking into areas previously reserved to the states. Before *Duncan*, states decided for themselves how to allocate the functions of judges and juries in state criminal trials. *Duncan* restricted their discretion in this regard. *Apprendi* and *Ring* tightened the noose further, leaving states very little leeway to formulate their own rules regarding the appropriation division of responsibility between judges and juries. The federal constitutional rules created by the Supreme Court in *Duncan*, *Apprendi*, and *Ring* are not required by the Sixth Amendment, as originally understood, because the original Sixth Amendment applied only to the federal government, not the states. The human rights theory provides no support for *Duncan*, *Apprendi*, and *Ring* because the right to trial by jury is not a recognized human right. Justice Black's total incorporation theory offers a plausible rationale to support the Court's Sixth Amendment decisions, but the Court has abjured reliance on Justice Black's theory. Lacking any coherent rationale, the Court's current Sixth Amendment incorporation doctrine imposes significant constraints on state autonomy by the force of arbitrary judicial fiat.

Both *Ring* and *Apprendi* created unusual coalitions of liberal and conservative justices. In *Apprendi*, Justices Scalia and Thomas joined three liberals – Justices Stevens, Souter, and Ginsburg – to create a 5–4 majority. In *Ring*, Justice Kennedy bowed to the precedential force of *Apprendi* and joined the *Apprendi* majority,[129] but Justices O'Connor and Rehnquist continued to dissent.[130] (Justice Breyer concurred separately in *Ring*, but he relied on the Eighth Amendment, not the Sixth Amendment.[131]) The nose counting is significant because it shows that the

---

[126] 530 US 466 (2000).   [127] 536 US 584 (2002).   [128] Apprendi, 530 US at 469.
[129] See Ring, 536 US at 613 (Kennedy, J., concurring).
[130] See id. at 619–21 (O'Connor, J., dissenting).   [131] See id. at 613–19 (Breyer, J., concurring).

human rights theory is neither liberal nor conservative. Contemporary political mythology holds that judicial application of international human rights norms would promote a liberal political agenda at the expense of constitutional federalism principles. In fact, though, a more refined analysis demonstrates that judicial application of international human rights norms in accordance with the human rights theory would promote constitutional federalism principles without advancing either a liberal or conservative political agenda.

CONCLUSION

This essay has introduced a new theory, the human rights theory, to help explain and justify the Supreme Court's selective incorporation doctrine. The theory holds that a particular right binds the states under the Fourteenth Amendment if the right is included in both the US Bill of Rights and the International Bill of Rights. The preceding analysis supports four main conclusions. First, the human rights theory is generally consistent with the actual pattern of Supreme Court decisions in selective incorporation cases. Second, the concept of acculturation helps explain why there is a close fit between the human rights theory and selective incorporation doctrine. Third, in contrast to the Court's decisions – which have failed to articulate a coherent rationale for the doctrine – the human rights theory provides a principled rationale for selective incorporation doctrine. Finally, adoption of the human rights theory would return control over certain individual rights from the federal courts to the states, thereby alleviating the tension between selective incorporation doctrine and the Court's professed commitment to principles of constitutional federalism.

4

Why Do International Human Rights Matter in American Decision Making?

*Stephen A. Simon**

INTRODUCTION

The phrase "international human rights," for many people, has a strong and positive moral valence. It resonates with things we hold dear: justice, liberty, equality, and protection from oppression and exploitation. When used in a manner that simply conveys a cluster of cherished values at a high level of generality, the term "international human rights" sounds like the kind of thing that no right-thinking person could be against. After all, the idea of treating people with the respect and dignity they deserve seems difficult, if not impossible, to oppose. The term "international human rights," however, can be used in different ways. While it may seem irresistible as a broad ideal, it is used by some today as a means of buttressing quite specific and contested propositions that bear on live and heated political controversies. Across many policy areas, for instance, activists draw on principles of international human rights with the aim of affecting ongoing debates in concrete ways. Indeed, two of the contributions in this volume manifest ways in which scholars and activists draw on international human rights within the arena of domestic policy debates, as Cynthia Soohoo examines the criminal justice system's treatment of juveniles and Erika George explores the disproportionate harm done to racial minorities by policies that adversely affect the environment. The work by scholars like Soohoo and George is part of a larger school that is centrally concerned with the impact of international human rights norms on domestic policy, which includes attempts to better understand the factors shaping when such norms are likely to be most efficacious. The fact that the term "international human rights" can be used in such radically distinct ways makes it especially important to probe more carefully the roles that it is meant to play within different forums of discourse. The focus of this chapter is on the role

---

* Many thanks to William Brewbaker, Erika George, Austin Sarat, David Sloss, and Cynthia Soohoo for thoughts and comments that have been very helpful in making revisions to this chapter.

that references to international human rights law are meant to play in discourse over the domestic effect of international human rights law within the United States, particularly in the context of Supreme Court decision making.

As noted, much work on the connection between international human rights and domestic law approaches the subject with a primary interest in the practical impact of the former on the latter. Thus, a good deal of scholarship is focused on which empirical factors are most likely to promote the domestic adoption of international norms, or is directly interested in seeking to bring about changes in domestic policy. By contrast, the focus of this chapter is on how references to international human rights norms are meant to work as arguments in public discourse over domestic policies. That is, my interest here is not in assessing or promoting the pragmatic effectiveness of international human rights talk but rather in examining the substantive ways that references to international human rights norms in domestic discourse are presented as reasons for adopting particular positions.

An underlying premise of this discussion is that it is not only the outcomes of controversies that matter but also the kinds of factors or sources that the disputants recognize as relevant and the substantive reasons why they are willing to do so. While one may profitably ask these sorts of questions about any of the various kinds of arguments that enjoy at least some purchase within American political and legal discourse, there are at least two considerations that make the role of international human rights law in domestic discourse of special interest. One consideration is temporal. Certain other influential bases of argument within American discourse have long been taken for granted as at least being potentially relevant to public controversies, such as whether a policy violates the US Constitution or other American laws, is likely to achieve its objects, or enjoys popular support. By contrast, because the emergence of international human rights as a body of law is a recent phenomenon, ideas regarding its domestic role have had relatively little time to crystallize. Nations have had to confront questions about the domestic effect of international human rights norms only in the last several decades. For centuries, each state's sovereignty had traditionally insulated it from outside interference with internal affairs (at least in principle). In the wake of the Second World War, however, the Nuremberg Trials prominently and unmistakably rejected the notion that acts authorized by public officials were immune from international legal responsibility. Other mid-century events laid the groundwork for the gradual development of international human rights law, including the UN General Assembly's adoption of the Universal Declaration of Human Rights. Although the preamble stated that it presented aspirational ends, the Universal Declaration has come to be seen by many as an authority on protected international human rights.[1] Fewer than two decades later, the General Assembly adopted the International Covenant on Civil and Political Rights and the International Covenant on Economic, Social, and Cultural Rights, which together

---

[1] Jack Donnelly, *International Human Rights* (Boulder, CO: Westview Press, 2013), 3–6.

largely reiterated the Declaration's protections in the form of treaty law. Though in an incipient stage, the international human rights regime has continued to grow, as manifested by the establishment of UN bodies with monitoring and investigative responsibilities and the adoption of major treaties, including, for instance, the Convention on the Rights of the Child and the Convention on the Elimination of All Forms of Discrimination against Women.[2] Even after a norm is recognized as law, of course, the means of enforcement is a separate question.[3] Since international mechanisms are weak, enforcement depends on state institutions. With the continued development of the international human rights regime, questions about the domestic impact of international human rights law are continuing to grow in salience. Indeed, the issue of implementation is more urgent than ever due to the increasing significance of transnational norms,[4] particularly as foreign citizens seek avenues for pursuing human rights violators,[5] and many look to international law as a resource for ensuring that American policies properly respect crucial freedoms.[6]

A second reason for special interest in the way that international human rights arguments are supposed to work in the domestic context concerns the different senses of the term "international human rights." As alluded to above, the term is sometimes employed to evoke a moral ideal that human beings ought to be treated with dignity and respect. This use of the term appeals to the idea that, notwithstanding the diversity of cultures and practices around the world, certain standards of morality that are universal in origin and application restrict the ways that persons ought to be treated. This sense of international human rights may be characterized as aspirational or normative in character. It is often in play when people launch normative criticisms against official policies; indeed, one of the most compelling elements of international human rights talk is the premise that public or governmental practices are not necessarily acceptable simply because they enjoy the imprimatur of popular support or of those who hold the reins of political power.[7] The term, however, is also often used in a different manner: to invoke legal rules. This use of the term has been made plausible by the emergence since the mid-twentieth

---

[2] Id. at 14.
[3] David Sloss, *The Role of Domestic Courts in Treaty Enforcement* (Cambridge: Cambridge University Press, 2009), 5–6.
[4] Daniel Abebe and Eric A. Posner, "The Flaws of Foreign Affairs Legalism," *Virginia Journal of International Law* 51 (2011): 507, 508.
[5] Roger P. Alford, "Arbitrating Human Rights," *Notre Dame Law Review* 83 (2008): 505, 508–9.
[6] Cynthia Soohoo and Suzanne Stoltz, "Bringing Theories of Human Rights Change Home," *Fordham Law Review* 77 (2008): 459, 460.
[7] International human rights, to be sure, is not the only platform from which one may critique existing official policies. The long tradition of natural law, for instance, as well as any number of frameworks within moral and political theory may furnish grounds for normatively assessing positive laws. The idea of international human rights, however, has been instrumental in providing a contemporary vantage point from which to emphasize that the mere fact of legal enactment does not render public policies immune from normative attack.

century of an international human rights regime articulating norms meant to be recognized as binding law.

That the term is commonly used in such distinctive ways places a premium on understanding its intended meaning in public discourse on domestic policy, especially since some uses of the term are much more controversial than others. While the broad idea that human beings ought to be treated with dignity is not in itself particularly contentious, attempts to bring particular domestic policies in line with standards articulated in the arena of international human rights provoke considerable controversy. To see why references to international human rights as law are so disputed, we must note a feature of the manner in which international human rights have evolved. To set the stage, let us observe two potential approaches to how we might conceive of and construct systems of human rights. One approach would emphasize the system's role in preventing the very worst kinds of human rights abuses. It would prioritize the safeguarding of a hard core of well-established rights for which the achievement of broad consensus was not only feasible in a near future but actual in today's world. Moved by worries that an overly expansive use of the term would dilute its force, this sort of approach would jealously patrol the boundaries of international human rights protections. In contrast, an alternative approach would emphasize the system's role in facilitating the identification and articulation of emerging rights. It would prioritize the expansion of rights consciousness to embrace previously underappreciated threats to the well-being of persons. From this vantage point, one of the system's key functions would be to provide a frame for discourse over new categories of rights and creative ways of applying existing ones. As one of the crucial early events in the development of international human rights as law, Nuremberg reflected the first approach to a significant extent, as it targeted individuals who had committed the worst acts imaginable against other human beings. At least some of the charges brought against the defendants were based on principles that enjoyed an overwhelming consensus, norms with which it would be extraordinarily difficult for a reasonable person to disagree, such as the prohibition of genocide. While there was a good deal of controversy over the legal status of some of the charges and especially over the nature of the procedures that were employed in the Trials, the enormity of the allegations themselves was beyond any conceivable doubt. Whatever one might have thought about the procedural fairness of the Nuremberg Trials, no one could doubt the heinous nature of the acts that the defendants were accused of committing. Thus, moral diversity was no barrier to wide-scale agreement on the evil of the Nazi atrocities.

Now, it is true that since the Second World War, the international human rights regime has focused a good deal of attention on what we might call "core rights," as reflected, for instance, in the United Nations's creation of committees to review countries' performance under the Convention on the Elimination of All Forms of Racial Discrimination and the Convention against Torture. As the substantive scope of international human rights norms expanded significantly since World War II, however, major disagreements over the content of rights became inevitable.[8] Even constitutional democracies that have long viewed themselves as protective of liberty were charged with violations,[9] spotlighting the potential conflict between international human rights and democratic self-government. The point here is certainly not that constitutional democracies, or countries that self-identify as enlightened, are incapable of violating human rights. Rather, the point is that as the content of international human rights expands in its scope and specificity, it increasingly takes positions on matters of public controversy on which well-meaning people may disagree. The maturation of the international human rights regime means that provisions increasingly address matters that present extremely difficult and close normative questions. Different long-cherished rights may come into conflict in complicated ways. At the regional level, for instance, the European Court of Human Rights engages many issues that are similar in complexity and nuance to those faced by courts in the United States, particularly in interpreting the US Constitution. Relatedly, as the idea of international human rights as law has developed in recent decades, some have attempted to expand its scope to include new categories of rights, such as the right to peace, the right to development, and the right to a clean environment.[10] Indeed, the nature of international human rights as a potential source of law facilitates attempts to harness its power to advocate the recognition of emerging rights. Since there is no centralized legislature or governmental structure for establishing what counts as international human rights law at any moment, discerning existing norms is as much art as science. The relatively indefinite character of the rules for identifying the rules creates opportunities for those wishing to push the

---

[8] Donnelly, *International Human Rights*, 4–16. See John O. McGinnis and Ilya Somin, "Democracy and International Human Rights Law," *Notre Dame Law Review* 84 (2009): 1739, 1746 ("Accordingly, the trend in international human rights laws has moved from rights about which there is more consensus to rights about which there is less, and from rights which have a fairly definable core, like free speech, to those that are quite difficult to define, such as sustainable development. Moreover, by their very nature, positive rights to government-provided resources can conflict with negative individual rights to liberty and property").

[9] See generally Donnelly, *International Human Rights*, 95–96 (discussing the European Court of Human Rights).

[10] Fueled in part by the rising influence of international law more generally and enhanced awareness of the welfare of people in other parts of the world owing to innovations in media technology, for instance, the scope of topics covered by the international human rights regime expanded to place a greater emphasis on economic and social rights, as opposed to the civil and political rights associated with the "first generation" of protections. McGinnis and Somin, "Should International Law Be Part of Our Law?," *Stanford Law Review* 59 (2007): 1175, 1182–85. A greater proportion of this "second generation" of rights may be characterized as "positive rights" in the sense that they require proactive policies by governments, rather than requiring merely that public officials refrain from certain kinds of activities. Some observers have used the term "third generation" to refer to an emerging class of rights that are a further expansion in the scope of the international human rights regime in that they potentially impose positive obligations on nongovernmental actors, as in the case of protections relating to the state of the environment. McGinnis and Somin, "Democracy and International Human Rights Law," 1745.

boundaries. Acts by regional human rights regimes, for instance, along with ostensibly nonbinding statements issued by UN bodies and the practices of particular states, open space for the pressing of novel rights claims. As a consequence, the language of international human rights is increasingly brought to bear on policy questions that are highly contested, and with respect to which reasonable people can and do disagree.

Because the term, as used in some ways, carries the highly positive connotations associated with broad, aspirational ideals, it may be easier to overlook the challenging questions that are raised when it is used in more controversial ways. When employed simply to evoke a broad aspirational ideal or essentially undisputed core norms, references to international human rights draw on a rhetorical force that is rooted in long-established and overwhelming consensus. Appeals to respect dignity or to prevent genocide may not provoke fine questions about the basis of the norms under discussion. When relied on within the context of furthering concrete objectives on deeply contested domestic policy issues, however, it will be appropriate – and imperative – to inquire, why do norms articulated within the arena of international human rights law matter to American decision making? Referencing international human rights norms is an intentional move presumably evincing a claim that they provide reasons for adopting one view over another. Such a move prompts an interest in understanding how such norms are meant to work as reasons within a larger argument in favor of a particular position.

Questions about the domestic role of international human rights law are made more pressing and controversial by a fundamental tension in American politics. On one hand, the idea of universal human rights has roots in American thought dating to the nation's Founding, and the United States took a leading role in the early movement to give them a tangible reality, playing an active part, for instance, in the creation of the Universal Declaration of Human Rights. At the same time, recognizing the legal force of norms developed outside the country is potentially problematic in light of the weight that American politics has long placed on the consent of the governed – understood increasingly in majoritarian terms – as the grounds of legitimate authority.[11] We can see, then, why advancement in the specificity of the matters addressed by international human rights law raises difficult questions about the relation between international and domestic law, as members of a democratic polity may well wonder why an externally formed norm should take precedence over the prevailing views of the national citizenry. The centrality of this tension makes it especially worthwhile to focus attention not only on the outcomes of disputes touching on human rights but also on the nature of the discourse employed by those engaged in the debate. Of course, even if an international human rights norm attains the status of law, the means of ensuring its protection is a separate

---

[11] See Stephen A. Simon, *The US Supreme Court and the Domestic Force of International Human Rights Law* (Lanham, MD: Lexington Books), 2–3.

question.¹² Since the mechanisms of international enforcement are weak – where they exist at all – implementation depends on state institutions. Issues regarding implementation continue to grow more urgent due to the increasing significance of transnational norms,¹³ particularly as foreign citizens seek avenues for pursuing human rights violators¹⁴ and many look to international law as a resource for ensuring that American policies properly respect crucial freedoms.¹⁵

While examining the function of international human rights law in any number of discursive contexts is worthwhile, this chapter focuses in particular on the context of Supreme Court decision making. Not surprisingly in light of the American tendency to judicialize disagreements, debate over the domestic force of international human rights has been channeled into a number of litigated disputes that have reached the US Supreme Court. The justices' opinions serve as an especially useful target of examination not only because the Court's decisions are influential but also because issues impinging on international human rights law are crystallized through extensive litigation. While other institutions grapple with questions relating to international human rights, only the judiciary carries the responsibility of explaining the legal reasoning underlying their determinations. Even in the judicial context, however, larger questions about the relevance of international human rights law may be overshadowed by concerns about the effect that its application would have on particular cases. To capture themes transcending the immediate impact for individual disputes, this study will concentrate not on doctrine, but on discourse. In broad terms, the focus will be on the role that international human rights norms have played in the justices' analysis of prominent cases. More specifically, the discussion revolves around the following queries: (1) in cases raising questions about the domestic force of international human rights norms, to what extent have the justices treated such norms as exerting the force of binding law in the domestic context? and (2) to the extent that the justices have referenced international human rights norms without treating it as binding law, what kinds of justifications have they offered for taking it into account at all?¹⁶

---

¹² Sloss, *The Role of Domestic Courts in Treaty Enforcement*, 5–6.
¹³ Abebe and Posner, "The Flaws of Foreign Affairs Legalism," 508.
¹⁴ Alford, "Arbitrating Human Rights," 508–9.
¹⁵ Cynthia Soohoo and Suzanne Stoltz, "Bringing Theories of Human Rights Change Home," *Fordham Law Review* 77 (2008): 459, 460.
¹⁶ The analysis, then, presumes a distinction between two different kinds of appeals to international human rights norms: appeals that present these norms as imposing mandatory legal rules in the domestic context, and those that do not, but which might, nevertheless, be relevant for other reasons. Of course, the relation between legal and other kinds of norms (such as moral ones) is one of the central questions in legal theory and has been debated for thousands of years. The manner in which the present discussion leans on the distinction, however, does not require us to settle such a vexed set of questions. It is plain that formation of the law is shaped by underlying moral norms and that the application and interpretation of the law reflect normative judgments. We may acknowledge the inevitable interrelationship while still noting that it means something distinctive to invoke a norm as law. Indeed, if this were not the case, the entire discussion of the relationship between legal and other

We are interested here, then, in how international human rights work as arguments (to the extent they do at all) in the hands of the justices.[17] Since the judiciary does not issue free-standing commentaries, investigating the Court's approach demands analysis of individual cases with an eye to what they reveal about the justices' discourse on the domestic force of international human rights.[18] Parts I, II, III, and IV analyze cases bearing on the topic, organized around the respective doctrinal area in which they fall: the force of treaties, the Alien Tort Statute, limitations on policies designed to combat terrorism, and reliance on foreign law in constitutional interpretation.[19] The concluding section discusses general points that emerge from consideration of the Court's jurisprudence.

I. THE DOMESTIC FORCE OF TREATIES

Two of the Court's most significant recent cases addressing the force of treaties – *Sanchez-Llamas v. Oregon* (2006) and *Medellín v. Texas* (2008) – highlight the uphill battle that international human rights law faces in gaining recognition as binding law, while also reflecting disagreement over the relative weight that treaty commitments should be accorded. As a documented agreement between countries, a treaty has the character both of a domestic law and of a contract regulating the relations between distinct sovereigns.[20] A treaty becomes law when the Senate

---

norms would be unnecessary. The inquiry, then, will focus on whether references to international human rights are meant to invoke those norms as binding law. How to interpret those legal norms, if they are accepted as such, is a subsequent and important question. I am grateful to Austin Sarat and William Brewbraker for noting the potential for confusion on this point in their comments on an earlier draft of this chapter.

[17] Given the focus on international human rights as a form of domestic discourse, my interest will be in the arguments that the justices have actually articulated in their opinions. The justices, like others engaged in public debate, are sometimes accused of offering arguments insincerely. That is, they are often charged with writing opinions that mask the real reasons underlying their decisions. While this kind of critique and analysis has its place, the present discussion is interested instead in the nature of the discourse itself rather than in seeking to uncover unarticulated considerations that might be the "real reason" for particular outcomes.

[18] In exercising their judicial function, the justices pronounce their understandings of law exclusively in deciding actual disputes because the Court held early on that its jurisdiction extended only to "cases and controversies" between parties with a stake in the outcome. See Muskrat v. US, 219 US 346, 361 (1911); Hayburn's Case, 2 US 408 (1792).

[19] This discussion employs the term "international human rights" in a broader sense than would be conventional in some contexts. Discussion of the Geneva Conventions (which appears below in the section on military commissions), for instance, is typically referred to as "humanitarian law," understood as a body of norms applicable to the conduct of warfare. The more liberal, wider employment of the idea of international human rights here is advantageous not merely due to the very limited engagement by the justices with norms traditionally recognized as international human rights law but especially due to the present focus on a kind of discourse, namely, one that seeks to affect debate on domestic policies by reference to international norms that centrally concern the treatment and protection of persons.

[20] Curtis A. Bradley, "Self-Execution and Treaty Duality," *Supreme Court Review* 2008 (2008): 131, 133.

votes by a two-thirds margin to ratify an international agreement presented to it by the president.[21] In the ordinary course, a ratified treaty places the United States under obligations to the other parties from the perspective of international law, but the domestic effect of that obligation is another question.[22] When ratification is not followed up by implementing legislation, issues often arise about the extent to which treaty provisions are self-executing – whether they have binding force on their own account. Moreover, even when treaties are recognized as self-executing, disputes often arise over the manner in which they should be interpreted.

Regarding the interaction of treaties with domestic law, no treaty provision has drawn more attention in recent years than Article 36 of the Vienna Convention on Consular Relations (VCCR), which affords individuals detained in a foreign country the right to communicate with consular officials. Although the United States was a key player in the creation of the VCCR and ratified it in 1969, state and local law enforcement authorities frequently overlooked its requirements. By the mid-1990s, in response to widespread disregard of the treaty, many foreign defendants had sought relief from their prosecutions or convictions by appealing to the rights enshrined in the VCCR.[23] In *Sanchez-Llamas* and *Medellín*, there was no dispute that law enforcement officials failed to inform foreign nationals of their right to communicate with the consulate, yet in both cases, the Court determined that the defendants in question could find no solace in the Convention's protections.

On trial for attempted murder, Moises Sanchez-Llamas unsuccessfully moved to suppress self-incriminating statements on the grounds that they were obtained in violation of the Convention. Before the Court, he contended that the Convention mandated access to a judicially enforceable remedy. While Article 36 provided that parties "must enable full effect to be given to the purposes for which the rights . . . are intended," however, Chief Justice John Roberts's opinion for the majority stressed that it also said the rights protected in Article 36 were to "be exercised in conformity with the laws and regulations of the receiving State."[24] This language left the means of implementation up to each country, and American law did not offer grounds for the justices to impose a remedy on state courts.

Justice Stephen Breyer's dissenting opinion for a four-member minority challenged the majority's view that the treaty never required suppression.[25] The dissenters

---

[21] US Const., Art. II, § 2.
[22] Anthony Aust, *Modern Treaty Law and Practice* (Cambridge: Cambridge University Press, 2013), 87. In special cases, it is possible for internal features of the American legal system, however, to deprive a duly ratified treaty of any domestic force, as, for example, where its provisions violate the Constitution or subsequent congressional legislation. Sloss, *Role of Domestic Courts in Treaty Enforcement*, 510.
[23] Oona A. Hathaway, Sabria McElroy, and Sara Aronchick Solow, "International Law at Home: Enforcing Treaties in US Courts," *Yale Journal of International Law* 37 (2012): 51, 52.
[24] VCCR, Art. 36(2).
[25] The opinion was joined by Justices John Paul Stevens and David Souter, and in part by Ruth Bader Ginsburg.

would have advised lower courts to employ a pragmatic analysis, balancing the interests at stake on a case-by-case basis and ordering "suppression if and when there are circumstances in which suppression provides the only effective remedy."[26] Chief Justice Roberts had minimized the Convention's practical import, arguing that it did not implicate the exclusionary rule since the treaty did not concern the gathering of evidence.[27] While Justice Breyer conceded that there could be instances in which a defendant's establishment of contact with the consulate would have no connection to law enforcement's pursuit of incriminating evidence, he rejected the majority's blanket determination that fulfillment of a defendant's VCCR rights would never have implications for the prosecution's preparation of a convincing case. Chief Justice Roberts might have been right that VCCR protections would be superfluous in some cases as a practical matter. "Much depends upon the circumstances," he wrote, contending that it was impossible to rule out the possibility that the defendant's ability to consult with the consulate could impact law enforcement's access to incriminating evidence. It was especially important to recall in this regard that some foreign arrestees were from countries with dramatically different legal and political systems. In addition to experiencing a heightened fear of police brutality, many defendants were not familiar with the use of confessions at trial or the role of public defenders.[28]

The Court's consideration of another defendant's conviction in *Sanchez-Llamas* centered on procedural default and the relevance of international rulings. Mario Bustillo, a Honduran national, was convicted in Virginia on a murder charge and sentenced to 30 years in prison. He invoked the Convention for the first time in state habeas proceedings, claiming that communication with the consulate would have significantly impacted his defense. The state court held that Bustillo defaulted the claim by failing to raise it earlier. A recent precedent seemed to potentially cut against Bustillo's position: *Breard v. Greene* (1998) held that the court hearing Breard's habeas petition had not erred in finding that the defendant defaulted his treaty claims since international law left procedural questions up to domestic law.[29] Hoping to defuse *Breard*, Bustillo cited the *LaGrand* and *Avena* cases, in which the International Court of Justice ruled that by applying default rules to block defendants from raising their claims, the United States failed to give "full effect" to the treaty's protections.[30]

---

[26] 548 US 331, 393–94 (Breyer, J., dissenting).   [27] Id. at 349.   [28] Id. at 393 (Breyer, J., dissenting).
[29] 523 US 371. A difference between the two cases was that the defendant in *Breard* had alleged in federal habeas proceedings a conflict between the treaty and a federal procedural rule, while Bustillo in state habeas proceedings alleged a conflict between the treaty and a state procedural rule. This was a distinction without a difference, however, for the majority in *Sanchez-Llamas*, as Chief Justice Roberts's opinion treated as Breard as a binding precedent that was directly on point. (I am grateful to David Sloss, who, in private correspondence on an earlier draft, noted this distinction between the two cases.)
[30] Sanchez-Llamas, 548 US at 369–70 (Breyer, J., dissenting).

The Court's handling of the ICJ rulings was revealing, as none of the justices believed that the Court was required to treat the ICJ rulings as conclusive, yet the majority and dissenting opinions nevertheless treated the rulings in very different ways. For the majority, the fact that the international rulings did not function as binding law had pivotal significance. In expounding on why the majority would not defer to the ICJ's determinations, Chief Justice Roberts emphasized ways in which American legal institutions differed from those of other countries and expressed concern that deferring to outside judgments would threaten cherished principles of domestic law.[31] By contrast, Justice Breyer highlighted reasons for honoring the ICJ's determinations, even though they were not binding on the Court. For instance, he highlighted that interpretive harmony across nations was a key aim in the implementation of treaties, and that the ICJ was uniquely well positioned to further this objective, as it represented "a natural point of reference for national courts seeking [international] uniformity."[32] Justice Breyer also appealed to the substantive aims of international law and the importance of the nation's living up to its commitments. By failing to give effect to the treaty's protections, Justice Breyer charged, the majority left the states "free to deny effective relief for Convention violations, despite America's promise to provide just such relief." Such an approach risked "weakening respect abroad for the rights of foreign nationals" and undermined "the role that law can play in assuring all citizens, including American citizens, fair treatment throughout the world."[33] Comparative advantages in decision making also figured in the dissenters' reasoning, as Justice Breyer noted that the ICJ's expertise also counseled deference.[34]

While, as noted, *Sanchez-Llamas* had raised the import of ICJ determinations on similar issues to those before the Court, *Medellín v. Texas* (2008) brought the impact of international rulings into even sharper relief, as it concerned ICJ rulings on the same case that was before the Court. After lower courts held that José Ernesto Medellín defaulted his VCCR claims, the Court considered whether the ICJ's judgment in *Avena* was directly enforceable as domestic law in state court.[35] With the Court dividing on nearly identical lines as in *Sanchez-Llamas*, Chief Justice Roberts again wrote the majority opinion, holding that not even an ICJ ruling that directed reconsideration of a specific case was enforceable in American courts. Applying a general presumption that treaties were to be implemented according to the forum state's procedural rules, he found as applied to the VCCR that there was no "clear and express statement to the contrary." It is notable that the majority made this finding despite two provisions of international law that arguably supported the opposite conclusion: first, the VCCR's Optional Protocol stated that "[d]isputes arising out of the interpretation or application of the Convention shall lie within the compulsory jurisdiction of the International Court of Justice," and second, Article 94(1) of the

---

[31] Id. at 357. [32] Id. at 383 (Breyer, J., dissenting). [33] Id. at 398 (Breyer, J., dissenting).
[34] Id. at 383–84 (Breyer, J., dissenting). [35] 552 US 491, 498.

United Nations Charter provided, in part, "Each Member of the United Nations undertakes to comply with the decision of the International Court of Justice in any case to which it is a party." In supporting the Court's holding, the chief justice drew a distinction between, on one hand, agreeing to submit disputes to a court and, on the other hand, agreeing to abide by that court's decision; the United States, he contended, had promised only to allow the ICJ to hear disputes.[36] In critiquing the approach to the issue employed by the dissenters, Chief Justice Roberts complained that Justice Breyer's case-by-case methodology allowed too much judicial discretion in an area where the Constitution delegated authority to the political branches.[37] He also worried about the possibility of foreign rulings having the effect of overriding domestic authorities, since accepting ICJ judgments as binding would allow an international court to "annul criminal convictions and sentences, for any reason [it] deemed sufficient."[38]

Justice Breyer's dissenting opinion (joined by Justices Souter and Ginsburg) applied a multifactored approach to find that the ICJ judgments were self-executing. In Justice Breyer's view, the majority's application of a clear-statement rule revealed a failure to appreciate inherent challenges involved in creating international agreements. In light of these challenges, he argued, the absence of text calling for self-execution should not be understood as a dictate of non-self-execution but rather as a reflection of the need to reach consensus among states with differing legal systems.[39] He further charged that the majority's view that the nation had agreed merely to let the tribunal hear cases would render the ratification of a treaty a "near useless act,"[40] and would "undermine longstanding efforts... to create an effective international system for interpreting and applying many... self-executing treaty provisions."[41] Disregarding the domestic relevance of international bodies "threatens to deprive individuals... of the workable dispute resolution procedures that many treaties... provide."[42] Whereas the majority had worried about a potential undermining of national autonomy, the dissenters worried about national credibility; as a result of the Court's ruling, Justice Breyer wrote, "the Nation may well break its word"[43] and find it "more difficult to negotiate new [treaties]."[44] Even more broadly, by making "it more difficult to enforce the judgments of international tribunals," the Court's determinations "weaken that rule of law for which our Constitution stands."[45]

II. THE ALIEN TORT STATUTE

The Alien Tort Statute (ATS) provides federal courts with jurisdiction over "any civil action by an alien for a tort only, committed in violation of the law of nations."[46]

---

[36] Id. at 507–8, 517. [37] Id. at 514–16, 522. [38] Id. at 517–18.
[39] Id. at 547–48 (Breyer, J., dissenting). [40] Id. at 553 (Breyer, J., dissenting).
[41] Id. at 560 (Breyer, J., dissenting). [42] Id. at 562 (Breyer, J., dissenting).
[43] Id. at 567 (Breyer, J., dissenting). [44] Id. at 548 (Breyer, J., dissenting).
[45] Id. at 566 (Breyer, J., dissenting). [46] 28 USC § 1350.

Enacted as part of the Judiciary Act of 1789, it lay dormant until the Second Circuit Court of Appeals decision in *Filártiga v. Peña-Irala* (1980). Two Paraguayan nationals, Dr. Joel Filártiga and his daughter Dolly, brought an ATS action against a former Paraguayan police official for allegedly kidnapping, torturing, and killing Dr. Filártiga's 17-year-old son. The Court of Appeals found that "an act of torture committed by a state official against one held in detention violates established norms of the international law of human rights, and hence the law of nations." Underscoring its significance, the opinion closed by proclaiming that the decision was "a small but important step in the fulfillment of the ageless dream to free all people from brutal violence."[47]

Filártiga gave life to the ATS by treating violations of customary international law as violations of the "law of nations" under the statute. Unlike treaty provisions, norms of customary international law do not depend on explicit agreements; they gain their status from being widely followed by states out of a sense of legal obligation.[48] Ever evolving, customary international law did not encompass human rights until the twentieth century; it now prohibits, for instance, genocide, slavery, and "systematic racial discrimination."[49] *Filártiga* made the ATS the chief American vehicle for international human rights litigation, but it was controversial from the start. One objection was that the statute did not create a cause of action and that federal courts consequently lacked constitutional authority to hear ATS cases. Proponents of this position maintained that the statute merely bestowed jurisdiction on the courts to decide a class of lawsuits; since Congress never adopted legislation creating a cause of action, ATS cases did not present a federal question to underpin the federal judiciary's constitutional authority.[50] One counterresponse to that position maintained that customary international law constituted federal law for purposes of federal question jurisdiction. Assessing the relation between customary international law and federal law requires consideration of significant shifts in legal understandings since the ATS's enactment. Upon gaining independence, the states broadly carried on common law traditions inherited from England, including the notion that the law of nations was part of the common law.[51] The development of common law doctrines was not strictly hierarchical; judges at all levels were engaged in the

---

[47] Filártiga, 630 F. 2d 876, 880.
[48] John M. Rogers, *International Law and United States Law* (Brookfield, VT: Ashgate, 1999), 2–4.
[49] Richard B Lillich, "The Growing Importance of Customary International Human Rights Law," *Georgia Journal of International and Comparative Law* 25 (1996): 1–2; Restatement (Third) of the Foreign Relations Law of the United States, § 702.
[50] See, e.g., William R. Casto, "The Federal Courts' Protective Jurisdiction over Torts Committed in Violation of the Law of Nations," *Connecticut Law Review* 18 (1986): 467, 479–80. Article III provides that the "judicial power shall extend to all cases ... arising under this Constitution, the laws of the United States, and treaties made, or which shall be made, under their authority." US Const., Art. III, § 2.
[51] Anthony J. Bellia Jr. and Bradford R. Clark, "The Federal Common Law of Nations," *Columbia Law Review* 109 (2009): 1, 29.

common enterprise of discerning common law rules that were "out there" to be discovered.[52] By the 1930s, however, many saw judges as creating law under the sway of their individual ideologies, preferences, and predispositions.[53] In *Erie Railroad Co. v. Tompkins* (1938), the Court gave concrete legal effect to long-developing transformations in American jurisprudence. In cases where federal jurisdiction was based on diverse state citizenship of the parties, federal courts previously had applied their own interpretations of common law. *Erie*, however, announced that federal courts would no longer apply principles of general common law in diversity cases; they would apply the law of the state in which they were sitting. In the post-*Erie* world, federal courts would have authority only to enforce laws with an identifiable source of positive law, as in the form of a statute or a particular state's application of common law.[54] Since customary international law had been part of the general common law before *Erie*, federal courts could enforce it even in the absence of implementing legislation by Congress. But what did *Erie*'s undermining of a general common law mean for the status of customary international law?

The first of the two major cases that the Court decided on the ATS, *Sosa v. Alvarez-Machain* (2004), kept it alive within constraints, and the second, *Kiobel v. Royal Dutch Petroleum Co.* (2013), imposed a hurdle to its use that seemed nearly insurmountable. *Sosa* concerned an ATS action brought by one Mexican national against another for participating in his kidnapping. After a Drug Enforcement Agent was killed in Mexico, the Agency enlisted a number of Mexican nationals to abduct a suspect in the killing (Humberto Álvarez Machaín) and bring him to the United States for trial. Following acquittal, Álvarez sued the abductors (including Jose Francisco Sosa). According to Álvarez, the abduction violated customary international law prohibitions on arbitrary arrest and detention.[55] Although the Court's decision to reject Álvarez's ATS claims was unanimous, Justice Antonin Scalia's concurring opinion (joined by Chief Justice William Rehnquist and Justice Clarence Thomas) indicated a divide among the justices on their understanding of the legal effect of the ATS more broadly. While conceding that the ATS by itself was jurisdictional and did not create a cause of action, Justice Souter's opinion for the Court found "that federal courts could entertain claims once the jurisdictional grant was on the books," because a limited number of "torts in violation of the law of nations would have been recognized within the common law of the time."[56] Specifically, Justice Souter's opinion found that the Congress that enacted the ATS intended it to

---

[52] Carlos M. Vázquez, "Customary International Law as US Law: A Critique of the Revisionist and Intermediate Positions and a Defense of the Modern Position," *Notre Dame Law Review* 86 (2004): 1495, 1534.

[53] See generally Michael Heise, "The Past, Present, and Future of Empirical Legal Scholarship: Judicial Decision Making and the New Empiricism," *University of Illinois Law Review* 2002 (2002): 819.

[54] See Lawrence Lessig, "Understanding Changed Readings: Fidelity and Theory," *Stanford Law Review* 47 (1995): 395, 426–33.

[55] 542 US 692, 697–99.   [56] Id. at 714.

support lawsuits regarding offenses against ambassadors, violations of safe conduct, and piracy.[57]

Though acknowledging that *Erie* provided reasons for containing the scope of ATS actions, he stressed that the *Erie* Court did not say federal courts could never develop new substantive legal principles.[58] Translating the ATS into the post-*Erie* context, Justice Souter concluded that "federal courts should not recognize private claims under federal common law for violations of any international law norm with less definite content and acceptance among civilized nations than the historical paradigms familiar when [the ATS] was enacted."[59] The opinion held against Alvarez's claim because the principle of customary international law that Sosa allegedly violated was not yet sufficiently well-established under customary international law.[60] Notwithstanding agreement on the outcome, Justice Scalia objected to Justice Souter's all-things-considered approach, arguing that *Erie*'s abrogation of general common law definitively cut off the federal courts' ability to draw directly on customary international law as a source of authority.[61]

Kiobel threatened to shut the door that *Sosa* had left ajar. Owing to a variety of procedural difficulties in pursuing actions against public officials, many plaintiffs had shifted to seeking recovery from corporations on the theory that they had aided and abetted government actors. While the dispute initially appeared to be a vehicle for the Court to consider the permissibility of corporate liability under the ATS, the decision ultimately turned on the issue of extraterritoriality. The case concerned a suit by residents of Ogoniland in Nigeria against an oil corporation for allegedly aiding and abetting the Nigerian government's violations of customary international law prohibitions on extrajudicial killings and other abuses. Like *Sosa*, the opinions in *Kiobel* revealed significant disagreements among the justices despite the unanimous vote on the outcome. Chief Justice John Roberts's opinion for the Court rested on a presumption that statutes did not have extraterritorial application in the absence of a clearly expressed intention by Congress, a presumption that "helps ensure that the Judiciary does not erroneously adopt an interpretation of US law that carries foreign policy consequences not clearly intended by the political branches."[62] The opinion found no reason to believe that the founding generation's leaders intended "to make the United States a uniquely hospitable forum for the enforcement of international norms."[63] Although it concluded with the cryptic remark that "even where the claims touch and concern the territory of the United States, they must do so with sufficient force to displace the presumption against extraterritorial application," the decision represented an impediment to ATS

---

[57] Id. at 712–14, 720.   [58] Id. at 726–29.   [59] Id. at 732–33.
[60] Id. at 734–38.   [61] Id. at 749–51 (Scalia, J., concurring).
[62] 133 S.Ct. 1659, 1664. The opinion was joined by Justices Scalia, Thomas, Anthony Kennedy, and Samuel Alito.
[63] Id. at 1668.

suits, blocking litigation involving alleged abuses occurring entirely outside the country.[64]

In opposition to Chief Justice Roberts's opinion for the Court, Justice Breyer's concurring opinion (joined by Justices Ginsburg, Sotomayor, and Kagan) rejected the presumption against extraterritoriality with respect to legislation concerning foreign matters.[65] Even in suits alleging overseas conduct by a foreign defendant, Justice Breyer contended, the courts could hear ATS actions where "the defendant's conduct substantially and adversely affects an important American national interest, and that includes a distinct interest in preventing the United States from becoming a safe harbor (free of civil as well as criminal liability) for a torturer or other common enemy of mankind." Those who enacted the ATS intended it to eliminate safe harbors and to serve as a "weapon in the 'war' against those modern pirates who, by their conduct, have 'declar[ed] war against all mankind.'" International law, too, had "long included a duty not to permit a nation to become a safe harbor for pirates (or their equivalent)."[66] At the same time, Justice Breyer acknowledged the need for reasonable limitations on the ATS's reach and found that the plaintiff's claim in *Kiobel* could not stand given the minimal contacts with the United States.[67]

III. MILITARY COMMISSIONS

Many of the policies pursued by the administration of President George W. Bush in response to the September 11, 2001, attacks were criticized for infringing individual rights. The conflict with those responsible for the attacks added new wrinkles to the tension between liberty and security, for al-Qaeda was not an entity with which one could negotiate a truce. The administration framed the response in military terms, and Congress agreed, enacting the Authorization for the Use of Military Force Joint Resolution (AUMF), empowering the president "to use all necessary and appropriate force against those nations, organizations, or persons he determines planned, authorized, committed, or aided the terrorist attacks." During operations that the president initiated, American troops captured and sent hundreds of suspected terrorists to the US naval base at Guantánamo Bay in Cuba for detention and interrogation. The administration asserted the authority to hold them indefinitely without access to counsel.[68] Through an executive order stating that the war on terror presented the nation with a "new paradigm" necessitating "new thinking in

---

[64] Id. at 1669.
[65] The opinion was joined by Justices Ruth Bader Ginsburg, Elana Kagan, and Sonia Sotomayor.
[66] Id. at 1674 (Breyer, J., concurring).   [67] Id. at 1677–78 (Breyer, J., concurring).
[68] Melvin I. Urofsky and Paul Finkelman, *A March of Liberty: A Constitutional History of the United States*, vol. II, 3rd ed. (Oxford: Oxford University Press, 2011), 1119.

the law of war," the president also announced that the Geneva Conventions did not apply to the captured members of al-Qaeda and the Taliban.[69]

Of the several cases the Court heard on the treatment of suspected terrorists, the one that engaged most with questions about the domestic force of international human rights law – *Hamdan v. Rumsfeld* (2006) – concerned military commissions and the Geneva Conventions.[70] A form of tribunal used in wartime to try captured combatants for violations of the laws of war, military commissions date to the Revolutionary War. Their creation and development was a product of military necessity and evolving practice, and the acceptable procedures for military commissions have long been a subject of the customary international law of war.[71] The portion of customary international law dealing with the conduct of military conflict – the "law of war" or "international humanitarian law" – aims to mitigate avoidable horrors of war.[72] The distinction between combatants and civilians is central. The former must differentiate themselves by wearing uniforms and openly carrying weapons. Captured soldiers may be held throughout the duration of the hostilities (to prevent them from returning to the battlefield), but they may not be mistreated or prosecuted.[73] However, combatants who violate the law of war forfeit the protections enjoyed by "prisoners of war." Unlawful combatants must not be tortured or abused, but they may be prosecuted – either through the ordinary criminal justice system or by military commission.[74] Long governed by widely accepted understandings, humanitarian law more recently has been the subject of international agreements, including the Geneva Conventions.[75] Almost every country, including the United States, has signed on to the Conventions. The Third Convention codifies requirements for combatants retaining their status as lawful combatants and governs the prosecution of unlawful combatants. Shortly after September 11, President Bush authorized the use of military commissions and asserted that their use fell outside the scope of the Conventions.

---

[69] George W. Bush, "Human Treatment of al Qaeda and Taliban Detainees," memorandum, February 7, 2002, www.pegc.us/archive/White_House/bush_memo_20020207_ed.pdf.

[70] Other decisions involving the rights of suspected terrorists included Hamdi v. Rumsfeld, 542 US 507 (2004), and Rasul v. Bush, 542 US 466 (2004).

[71] Julian Ku and John Yoo, "Beyond Formalism in Foreign Affairs: A Functional Approach to the Alien Tort Statute," *Supreme Court Review* 2004 (2004): 153, 210.

[72] As "humanitarian law" has the specific meaning noted in the text, the term is frequently viewed as designating something distinct from what is often referred to as international human rights law. This chapter includes discussion of the Geneva Conventions, conventionally understood as humanitarian law, because this project is employing the term "international human rights" in a broader and less technical manner to encompass transnational norms meant to limit acts that might otherwise fall within the scope of public policy on the grounds of protecting the dignity and personhood of individuals.

[73] Joseph Marguiles, *Guantánamo and the Abuse of Presidential Power* (New York: Simon and Schuster, 2006), 54.

[74] Howard Ball, *Bush, the Detainees and the Constitution: The Battle over Presidential Power in the War on Terror* (Lawrence: University Press of Kansas, 2007), 41–42.

[75] Adopted initially in 1864, the currently governing Geneva Conventions were formed in 1949. Marguiles, *Guantánamo and the Abuse of Presidential Power*, 53.

After Salem Ahmed Hamdan, a Yemeni national, was captured and taken to Guantánamo Bay, the administration indicated its intention to try him by military commission for murder and conspiracy to engage in acts of terrorism. Conceding that he worked as Osama bin Laden's driver but denying involvement in terrorism, Hamdan argued that the use of a commission would violate procedural requirements established by the Geneva Conventions.[76] In a 5–3 decision, the Court held that the commission violated the Uniform Code of Military Justice and the Conventions. The reasoning in Justice Stevens's opinion for the Court rested on three key claims: the executive must act within constraints set by Congress, those constraints included compliance with the law of war, and the Court's role was to ensure that the executive operated within applicable constraints.[77] The interconnection between these components was critical, because it enabled the justices to frame their application of the Geneva Conventions as part of the judiciary's responsibility to ensure that the executive not flout the will of Congress.

In *Hamdan*, the majority rejected the administration's assertion of unilateral executive authority, insisting that even regarding national security matters, the president was subject to congressionally established requirements and to the judiciary's determinations on the legality of its policies. Against the administration's view that a World War II–era precedent established the executive's authority to employ military commissions whenever it deemed them necessary,[78] Justice Stevens's opinion for the majority emphasized that President Roosevelt had acted with the blessing of Congress, as expressed through adoption of the Articles of War (a precursor to the Uniform Code of Military Justice (UCMJ)).[79] Rather than endowing the president with unlimited authority to use military commissions, the Articles simply preserved the executive's power to use commissions within the limitations contained in the international law of war.[80] The executive had exceeded its authority by bringing conspiracy charges against Hamdan and by failing to provide required procedural protections.[81] The conspiracy charges ran afoul of the international law requirement that the "offense alleged must have been committed both in a theater of war and *during*, not before, the relevant conflict," because Hamdan's alleged acts occurred before September 11.[82] The commission's

---

[76] Hamdan, 548 US at 570, 635.
[77] Justice Stevens's opinion was joined by Justices Souter, Ginsburg, and Breyer, and in part by Justice Kennedy. Chief Justice Roberts did not participate in the Court's decision, as he had ruled on the case while sitting on the DC Circuit Court of Appeals.
[78] The earlier case was Ex Parte Quirin, 317 US 1 (1942).
[79] The opinion was joined, though only in part, by Justices Kennedy, Souter, Ginsburg, and Breyer.
[80] Hamdan, 548 US at 594–95.
[81] The finding regarding authority for the commission to bring conspiracy charges enjoyed the support of a plurality only, as Justice Kennedy declined to join this portion of Justice Stevens's opinion. Id. at 654 (Kennedy, J., concurring in part).
[82] Id. at 599, 611.

procedures violated Article 36 of the UCMJ, which required military commissions to follow the procedures required for courts-martial, unless that would be infeasible.

The Court found that the commission violated the Geneva Conventions as well. At an earlier stage of the litigation, the DC Court of Appeals had found that the Geneva Conventions were not judicially enforceable and would not apply in any event since al-Qaeda was not a party. Justice Stevens, however, found it unnecessary to address the independent force of the Conventions, because the UCMJ conditioned authority to use military commissions on compliance with the law of war. It was also unnecessary to address al-Qaeda's status under the Conventions because Common Article 3's applicability did not hinge on it. Common Article 3 – so called because it appears in each of the four Conventions – applies to conflicts "not of an international character occurring in the territory of one of the High Contracting Parties" and requires party states to observe certain minimum protections for individuals "taking no active part in the hostilities, including members of armed forces who have laid down their arms and those placed hors de combat by... detention." These protections included a prohibition on "the passing of sentences and the carrying out of executions without previous judgment pronounced by a regularly constituted court affording all the judicial guarantees which are recognized as indispensable by civilized peoples." Justice Stevens interpreted this language as requiring a trial according to the procedures of a court-martial unless deviations could be justified by "practical need" and as incorporating at least the barest of those trial protections that had been recognized by "customary international law," which included the right to be present at one's trial. The administration, however, had failed to proffer justifications for its departures from such procedures, which included depriving the defendant of access to the proceedings and the evidence used against him.[83] Thus, the commissions were unlawful both because they violated specific requirements of the UCMJ directly and because they violated the law of war, which the UCMJ imposed on the executive by reference.

Justice Thomas's dissenting opinion (joined by Justice Scalia and in part by Justice Samuel Alito) criticized the majority for not deferring to the executive's role in national security and foreign affairs; the holding represented "an unprecedented departure from the traditionally limited role of the courts with respect to war and an unwarranted intrusion on executive authority." He denied that the UCMJ was a constraint on the executive, pointing to Article 36's statement that military commissions "shall, *so far as* [the president] *considers practicable*, apply the principles of law and the rules of evidence generally recognized in the trial of criminal cases in the United States district courts."[84] In Justice Thomas's view, the UCMJ did not incorporate the Geneva Conventions since the UCMJ wasn't a limitation on the president's use of commissions in the first place. In any event, he argued, the Conventions were not

---

[83] Id. at 633.   [84] Id. at 684 (Thomas, J., dissenting).

judicially enforceable since it was part of the law of war that the Conventions gave rise to no judicially imposed remedies.[85]

The majority and dissenting opinions, then, advanced strikingly opposed approaches to the requirements of international law. Engaging in an independent analysis of Common Article 3, the majority rejected the administration's position. Interestingly, the dissenters allowed that Court's interpretation was "admittedly plausible."[86] The deeper problem for them was that the Court misunderstood the relation between the executive and judicial branches, failing to recognize that "the meaning attributed to treaty provisions by the Government agencies charged with their negotiation and enforcement is entitled to great weight."[87]

IV. FOREIGN LAW IN CONSTITUTIONAL INTERPRETATION

A trio of decisions between 2002 and 2005 sparked debate on whether constitutional interpretation should find guidance in foreign sources that do not impose obligations on the United States under international law.[88] Most of the Court's reliance on foreign law has occurred in opinions interpreting the Eighth Amendment's prohibition on "cruel and unusual punishments," especially as applied to capital punishment.[89] Uses of foreign law in this area have generally appeared in portions of opinions considering whether challenged punishments were consistent with prevalent legal practices and societal attitudes. Crystallizing principles expressed earlier, Chief Justice Earl Warren's plurality opinion in *Trop v. Dulles* articulated the now well-established doctrine that the Eighth Amendment "draw[s] its meaning from the evolving standards of decency that mark the progress of a maturing society."[90] "The basic concept underlying the ... Amendment is nothing less than the dignity of man," he wrote; by imposing a "prohibition against inhuman treatment," it mandated that the state's power to punish "be exercised within the limits of civilized standards."[91] Discerning the meaning of this prohibition, Chief Justice Warren indicated, would entail examination of prevalent practices, including consideration of foreign jurisdictions. Citing a UN study showing that only 2 of 84 countries prescribed denationalization as a punishment for desertion, he concluded that statelessness was "a condition deplored in the international community of democracies" and that there was "virtual unanimity" among the "civilized nations of the world" that it should not be imposed.[92]

As developed in the Court's jurisprudence since *Trop*, the examination of evolving societal standards has predominantly focused on domestic considerations, such as

---

[85] Id. at 717 (Thomas, J., dissenting). [86] Id. (Thomas, J., dissenting).
[87] Id. at 718 (Thomas, J., dissenting).
[88] The three decisions were Atkins v. Virginia, 536 US 304 (2002); Lawrence v. Texas, 539 US 558 (2003); and Roper v. Simmons, 543 US 551 (2005).
[89] Stephen A. Simon, "The Supreme Court's Use of Foreign Law in Constitutional Rights Cases: An Empirical Study," *Journal of Law and Courts* 1, no. 2 (2013): 279, 293–94.
[90] 356 US 86, 101.   [91] Id. at 100, 101 n. 32.   [92] Id. at 102–3, n. 35.

the percentage of American states following a particular practice. Nevertheless, the justices have supplemented their analysis of domestic sources with references to foreign law in a number of opinions concerning the constitutionality of death as punishment for certain classes of crimes or defendants. For instance, supporting its conclusion that "the imposition of the death penalty on a 15-year-old offender is now generally abhorrent to the conscience of the community," Justice Stevens's opinion announcing the Court's decision in *Thompson v. Oklahoma* (1988) not only cited American practices but also observed that opposition to execution of juveniles was consistent with the views of "other nations that share our Anglo-American heritage, and ... the leading members of the Western European community."[93] In disallowing execution of persons who were mentally retarded, *Atkins v. Virginia* (2002) cited evidence that the challenged punishment was "overwhelmingly disapproved" by the "world community."[94] Justice Kennedy's majority opinion in *Roper v. Simmons* (2005) – disallowing execution of persons under 18 – observed that only seven countries other than the United States had executed minors since 1990, and all of them later abolished or disavowed the practice. Noting that the United States was one of only two countries that had not ratified the UN Convention on the Rights of the Child, which banned the execution of minors, Justice Kennedy asserted that "the United States now stands alone in a world that has turned its face against the juvenile death penalty."[95] Although the "opinion of the world community" was "not controlling," it did provide instruction and "respected and significant confirmation for our own conclusions."[96] Similarly, *Graham v. Florida* (2010), which barred the sentencing of a juvenile to life imprisonment without the possibility of parole where the defendant had not committed homicide, found support for the holding in the evidence indicating that the challenged punishment had been "rejected the world over."[97] In response to arguments that no binding international law barred the practice at issue, Justice Kennedy wrote,

> The Court has treated the laws and practices of other nations and international agreements as relevant to the Eighth Amendment not because those norms are binding or controlling but because the judgment of the world's nations that a particular sentencing practice is inconsistent with basic principles of decency demonstrates that the Court's rationale has respected reasoning to support it.[98]

Justices have also cited foreign law in a number of cases involving the liberty protected by the Fourteenth Amendment's due process clause,[99] most famously in *Lawrence v. Texas* (2003). In invalidating a state law that made it illegal for two persons of the same sex to engage in certain sexual acts, Justice Kennedy's majority

---

[93] 487 US 815, 830–32. The opinion was joined by Justices Thurgood Marshall, William Brennan, and Harry Blackmun.
[94] 536 US 304, 316 n. 21.   [95] Id. at 577.   [96] Id. at 578.   [97] 560 US 48, 80.   [98] Id. at 82.
[99] The amendment provides, in relevant part: "No state shall ... deprive any person of life, liberty, or property, without due process of law." US Const. Amend. XIV.

opinion referenced foreign law to support its identification of an "emerging awareness" of the rights at issue in the case. Specifically, it observed that the British Parliament in the late 1960s had repealed laws criminalizing homosexual conduct and that the European Court of Human Rights in 1981 had invalidated Northern Ireland's laws criminalizing homosexual acts. Moreover, other countries had "taken action consistent with an affirmation of the protected right of homosexual adults to engage in intimate, consensual conduct."[100]

While, as noted, a number of the justices have shown a willingness to reference foreign law in certain constitutional rights cases, the practice has repeatedly met with opposition on the grounds that it exceeds the judiciary's authority and is undemocratic. In an opinion for three dissenters in *Thompson*, for instance, Justice Scalia asserted that only American attitudes were relevant to analysis of contemporary values; the punishment at issue was constitutional "even if that position contradicts the uniform view of the rest of the world. We must never forget that it is a Constitution for the United States of America that we are expounding."[101] Justice Scalia's dissent in *Roper* (joined by Chief Justice Rehnquist and Justice Thomas) similarly argued that the "basic premise ... that American law should conform to the laws of the rest of the world ought to be rejected out of hand."[102] He further accused the Court of inconsistency in the weight it accorded international practices. The rest of the world rejected strict application of the exclusionary rule, for example, and the United States was one of only six countries in the world that allowed abortion on demand up to the point of viability. In a similar vein, Justice Scalia's dissent in *Lawrence* (again joined by Rehnquist and Thomas) attacked Justice Kennedy's reliance on foreign law, since the Court had no authority to "impose foreign moods, fads, or fashions on Americans."[103]

V. THEMES IN THE COURT'S JURISPRUDENCE

To examine the nature of the Court's discourse on the domestic force of international human rights norms, the introductory section posed the following queries about the role that such norms play in the justices' reasoning: (1) in cases raising questions about the domestic force of international human rights norms, to what extent have the justices treated such norms as exerting the force of binding law in the domestic context? and (2) to the extent that the justices have referenced international human rights norms without treating it as binding law, what kinds of justifications have they offered for taking it into account at all? This section reflects on larger themes that emerge from consideration of prominent opinions falling within particular doctrinal areas in the previous four sections.

---

[100] 539 US 558, 571, 577.   [101] 487 US at 868 n. 4 (Scalia, J., dissenting).
[102] 543 US at 624 (Scalia, J., dissenting).   [103] 539 US at 598 (Scalia, J., dissenting).

The first point that emerges will frame our analysis: there is not one principal way that the justices have talked about international human rights law, but two. Thus, while the fluidity of the Court's membership and the range of factors that shape opinion writing preclude the identification of fixed blocs, it will nevertheless be helpful to speak of opinions as manifesting one of two broadly opposing approaches. We will examine each of these two opposing methodologies in turn.

One approach has resisted any role for international human rights norms in the Court's decision making beyond the application of principles that have received a stamp of authority from the political branches. This approach – referred to here for convenience as "sovereigntist" – has emphasized the importance of the link between judicial decision making and legal norms that express the will of the American people as manifested through executive and legislative acts.[104] The underlying philosophy holds that political authority is derived from popular sovereignty: what makes it acceptable for public officials to exercise power over people is that the governed are also the ones who shape the direction of government. In the American context, then, it is specifically the will of the American people that grounds legitimate authority. It should be stressed that "sovereigntist" is simply a shorthand term of convenience for what might more accurately be summarized as a majoritarian interpretation of popular consent. The kernel meant to be captured by the term "sovereigntist" is that of an approach that prioritizes the link between the context of domestic judicial decision making and sources that bear the binding nature of legal norms enacted through the domestic procedures of democratic policy making. As discussed below, this understanding of "sovereigntism" reflects components that are characteristically combined in an approach that has been prominent on the Court. There is, to be sure, no a priori reason, however, why they must travel together; one might well conceive of popular consent in a manner that did not necessarily translate into the mechanisms of majoritarian decision making, for instance.[105]

For justices operating from what we shall call here a sovereigntist perspective, resistance to recognizing the domestic force of international human rights is intertwined with longstanding concerns over the scope of judicial power. As unelected officials, the argument goes, federal judges must exercise power carefully within the bounds prescribed by the nation's democratic institutions. They must only give force, therefore, to norms of international law that have been endorsed by the political branches. Sovereigntist opinions have placed pivotal significance on whether norms of international human rights enjoyed the imprimatur of the nation's democratic institutions. The absence of such an imprimatur provides a decisive reason

---

[104] I borrow the terminology contrasting "sovereigntist" and "internationalist" approaches from Donald Earl Childress III, "The Alien Tort Statute, Federalism, and the Next Wave of Transnational Litigation," *Georgetown Law Journal* 100 (2012): 709, 711.

[105] I am grateful to William Brewbaker for private correspondence on an earlier draft, bringing to my attention the potential for confusion in the use of the term "sovereigntist."

not to treat international norms as binding law. It also provides reason for magistrates to resist employing international norms in their arguments for other purposes, because the judicial power is limited to the interpretation and application of legal authorities. A sovereigntist methodology, then, has framed its analysis around the question of whether international human rights norms amounted to binding law. In principle, such an approach has been willing to consider the possibility that international norms were binding in the domestic context; indeed, that possibility is the prism through which this approach has viewed the problem. In practice, however, the sovereigntist opinions considered have always declined to find that international norms had the force of binding law in the domestic context. Because sovereigntist opinions have set up the analysis around the question of whether the norms constituted binding law, a negative conclusion on that question effectively closed out their consideration. The approach has been essentially binary in the sense that the international norms were binding, or they were not, and if they weren't then they did not figure in the analysis at all.

The primacy of the sovereigntist concern with filtering out reliance on international norms that lack the authority of binding law is reflected in the use of a variety of clear-statement rules and other interpretive canons; examples have included the majority's use of a presumption against the judicial enforceability of international agreements in *Sanchez-Llamas* and of a presumption against extraterritoriality in *Kiobel*. Justice Scalia's concurring opinion in *Sosa* captured core sovereigntist preoccupations:

> We Americans have a method for making the laws that are over us. We elect representatives to two Houses of Congress, each of which must enact the new law and present it for the approval of a President, whom we also elect. For over two decades now, unelected federal judges have been usurping this lawmaking power by converting what they regard as norms of international law into American law.[106]

The majority opinion in *Medellín* was a paradigmatic example of sovereigntist reasoning, as Chief Justice Roberts focused on reasons why the Court was not strictly bound to comply with the ICJ's ruling. In doing so, Chief Justice Roberts excoriated Justice Breyer's approach for arrogating discretion to the judiciary that properly pertained to the political branches, and he worried about the implications of yielding national sovereignty to external decision makers.[107] Other examples discussed above of arguments that manifested the commitments underpinning the sovereigntist school included the majority opinions in *Sanchez-Llamas* and *Kiobel*, Justice Thomas's dissenting opinion in *Hamdan*, and Justice Scalia's dissenting opinion in *Lawrence*.

The justices' disagreements over the domestic force of international human rights law intersect with long-standing larger debates about methods of interpretation and

---

[106] 542 US at 750 (Scalia, J., concurring).   [107] 552 US at 514–22.

the scope of judicial power. Indeed, while questions about the domestic force of international human rights law arise for any country, they are especially pointed for the United States due to a fundamental tension in American constitutionalism that traces to the nation's birth.[108] As reflected in the Declaration of Independence, the political thought that was prevalent among the Founding generation encompassed commitments both to the universal norms of natural law and to popular consent as the grounds of legitimate authority.[109] On one hand, the Declaration proclaimed the existence of universal human rights; it was the purpose of government to protect these rights, and the people could rightfully overthrow a regime that invaded them. While explaining that people established government to secure these rights, however, the Declaration also asserted that governments "deriv[e] their just powers from the consent of the governed." The standards for evaluating the legitimacy of political authority, then, were both substantive and procedural in nature. The substantive character of the laws was crucial – they had to sufficiently protect fundamental rights – but so was their procedural pedigree; the laws had to be enacted in a manner that reflected the will of the governed. Evincing a similar tension, the Constitution could be understood as an attempt to make good on the Declaration's aim of protecting natural rights, while also announcing in the opening words – "We the People of the United States . . . do ordain and establish this Constitution" – that its authority was rooted in the will of the people. An important strand in American jurisprudence has emphasized that the judiciary's role is to give legal effect to popular will as it has been expressed through the enactments of democratic institutions.[110] The opinions described as "sovereigntist" here with respect to the domestic force of international human rights law suggest philosophical commitments consistent with that understanding. On this view, in deciding the outcomes of legal controversies, judges should seek to maximize the guidance provided by democratic institutions while minimizing the influence of their own personal predilections.

In sum, then, sovereigntist opinions have framed analysis around the question of whether international human rights norms constitute binding law in the domestic context. The point of embarkation is a premise that the exercise of judicial authority must be traceable to a binding source of authority. The opinions have the overarching structure of a flow chart. A break in the circuit between binding authority and the Court deprives it of the power to act. In simplified terms, a sovereigntist methodology concludes that the Court should act if it is instructed to by applicable directives. In the absence of appropriate authorization, the Court must refrain from acting. This mind-set is manifested in a tendency to employ presumptions militating against exercises of judicial authority, particularly where foreign or unelected decision

---

[108] See Michael Ignatieff, ed., *American Exceptionalism and Human Rights* (Princeton, NJ: Princeton University Press, 2005), 1.
[109] See Stephen A. Simon, *Universal Rights and the Constitution* (Albany: SUNY Press, 2014), 20–21.
[110] Simon, *Universal Rights and the Constitution*, 23.

makers could interfere with the nation's democratic institutions. The reasoning inclines toward inquiries about authority that are binary and definitive. Since the analysis of international human rights norms is framed around whether they have the authority of binding law, a conclusion that they do not has been seen by sovereigntists as exhausting the need for their consideration.

The term "internationalist" serves as useful shorthand for a competing approach that has not viewed the potential relevance of international human rights norms as exhausted by the possibility that they operated in the domestic context strictly as binding law. Internationalist opinions have eschewed (and explicitly critiqued) the sovereigntists' imposition of an all-or-nothing methodology, preferring instead an all-things-considered approach to the relevance of international human rights norms. Whereas for sovereigntists, a finding that an international norm did not operate domestically as binding law effectively brought consideration of the norm's potential relevance to an end, internationalist opinions, in contrast, have harnessed the flexibility of multifactored frames of analysis to consider other reasons why international norms might merit the justices' consideration. More specifically, an internationalist mode of reasoning has been characterized by an emphasis on the importance of the system of international law and of the nation's living up to its responsibilities within that system. Internationalist opinions have presented international human rights as a joint venture offering concrete solutions and ideas and approaches from which American institutions can benefit. In the words of Justice Breyer's quintessentially internationalist dissent in *Sanchez-Llamas*, the continuing development of international norms helps to "strengthen the role that law can play in assuring all citizens, including American citizens, fair treatment throughout the world."[111] In an ever increasingly interconnected and interdependent world, international law is critical to objectives shared by all countries, including the provision of dispute resolution procedures for international transactions,[112] and bringing to justice those who make themselves "enemies of mankind," such as pirates and torturers.[113] Thus internationalist opinions have highlighted the positive ends that international law serves on a broad scale and in particular instantiations, as when noting the vital function that the Vienna Convention on Consular Relations serves as a "cultural bridge" between an individual arrested in a foreign country and the host government.[114] Since the effectiveness of international law depends on individual countries' cooperation and participation, it is crucial for the United States (like other countries) to live up to its international obligations and to operate as a responsible citizen within the international community.[115] American disregard for its international responsibilities may undermine respect for the global system of law

---

[111] 548 US at 398 (Breyer, J., dissenting). [112] Medellín, 552 US at 562 (Breyer, J., dissenting).
[113] Sosa, 542 US at 731–32; Kiobel, 133 S.Ct. at 1671 (Breyer, J., dissenting).
[114] Sanchez-Llamas, 548 US at 367–68 (Breyer, J., dissenting).
[115] Medellín, 552 US at 559, 567 (Breyer, J., dissenting); Sanchez-Llamas, 548 US at 398 (Breyer, J., dissenting). Hamdan, 548 US at 635.

generally while making it "more difficult to negotiate new [treaties]."[116] This kind of approach was particularly evident in the internationalists' portrayal of the ICJ as a body of magistrates whose expertise and institutional posture enabled them to serve purposes that the United States shares with other countries. From this vantage point, the ICJ appeared in a relation of assistance rather than one of command. By emphasizing what the United States stood to gain from international institutions while framing observance of international human rights norms as mediated through acts of Congress, internationalists have effectively foregrounded the benefits of participation in international human rights law while downplaying the costs.

From this kind of internationalist perspective, the judiciary fulfills its mission by acting in accordance with applicable international requirements, for the failure to do so would threaten to "weaken that rule of law for which our Constitution stands."[117] Since the judiciary is often the only institution that can give concrete life to the dictates of international law, judges must be mindful of interpreting its requirements in a manner that does not render them nugatory.[118] It follows that the Court must not blindly accept whatever position the executive advances on questions relating to the domestic force of international law,[119] nor should it be blithely assumed that legislative actions will be forthcoming if the judiciary bows out, given the practical limitations on Congress's ability to engage in an ongoing manner with the details of international law's enforcement.[120] Moreover, the mutually interdependent character of international law means that it must often be part of the Court's analysis to consider how its determinations affect the application of law within other countries as well as how other countries apply the same provisions that the justices are interpreting.[121] An internationalist orientation is open to acknowledging the comparative advantage that international tribunals enjoy with respect to certain disputes arising under international agreements. Not only will judges on international tribunals typically have greater expertise in the relevant areas of jurisprudence but their determinations also have a greater chance to promote an important objective: fostering uniformity in the way that different countries interpret and apply international obligations.[122] In sum, the Court must be mindful of the "harmony" that international law is "intended to promote."[123]

Justice Breyer's dissent in *Medellín* exemplified the contrast between the internationalist and sovereigntist interpretive methodologies, as the opinion rejected the

---

[116] Medellín, 552 US at 549 (Breyer, J., dissenting).
[117] Id. at 566 (Breyer, J., dissenting); Sosa, 542 US at 761 (Breyer, J., concurring).
[118] Medellín, 552 US at 552–53, 556–57 (Breyer, J., dissenting).
[119] Hamdan, 548 US at 594–95; Sanchez-Llamas, 548 US at 378 (Breyer, J., dissenting).
[120] Medellín, 552 US at 560 (Breyer, J., dissenting).
[121] Sosa, 542 US at 761–63 (Breyer, J., concurring); Kiobel, 133 S.Ct. at 1676–77 (Breyer, J., concurring); Sanchez-Llamas, 548 US at 377–78 (Breyer, J., dissenting).
[122] Sanchez-Llamas, 548 US at 382–84 (Breyer, J., dissenting).
[123] Sosa, 542 US at 761 (Breyer, J., concurring).

majority's binary framing of key issues in favor of a balancing approach that consulted a lengthy list of considerations in concluding that the VCCR was judicially enforceable.[124] The use of more flexible decisional criteria has enabled internationalists to incorporate arguments appealing to substantive desiderata – such as the value of American participation in a viable system of international law – without repudiating the relevance of questions about legal authority. The justifications that internationalist opinions have suggested for considering international norms beyond status as binding law may be seen as falling broadly within three categories: (1) substantive arguments about the merit of specific norms, (2) substantive arguments about the merit of an international system of norms more generally, and (3) references to the prevalence of international practices or attitudes. Justice Breyer's dissent in *Kiobel* was an example from the first category. In protesting the majority's far-reaching denial of the ATS's extraterritorial effect, the opinion extolled the VCCR's aim of ensuring that defendants receive fair trials when outside of their home country. Supporting the functioning of the Convention would also enhance the protection of the rights of American citizens traveling abroad.[125] Justice Breyer's dissenting opinion in *Medellín* was an example from the second category, as it cautioned that the nation's disregard of international judgments would threaten to undermine the system of international law as a whole. The third category is predominantly populated by opinions relying on foreign law in the interpretation of foreign law. In *Lawrence*, for instance, Justice Kennedy's reference to the European Court of Human Rights was part of an argument seeking to demonstrate the existence of an "emerging awareness" of the right at stake in the case – not only domestically but also internationally.

Although this chapter has focused on the particular context of Supreme Court decision making, the discussion brings into view the wider significance of questions about how references to international human rights are supposed to work as reasons for adopting one position over another. Owing to the stakes, it is easy to concentrate on the outcomes of specific disputes that potentially touch on international human rights. Discourse on specific disputes, however, may be importantly shaped by deeply underlying disagreements regarding the international human rights might play within the domestic context. It is critical, then, to inquire about the role that references to international human rights are supposed to play in arguments. Vital questions include the ones that have been the subject of this study. First, when one cites international human rights norms, is the claim that these norms exert a binding legal force within the context of American decision making? And, if not, then what is the basis for treating these norms as relevant at all? As noted earlier, these questions take on added import due to the tendency of contemporary human rights discourse not simply to enforce long-established norms that enjoy an overwhelming global

---

[124] Medellín, 552 US at 546–61 (Breyer, J., dissenting). See also Kiobel, 133 S.Ct. at 1673–76 (Breyer, J., dissenting); Sanchez-Llamas, 548 US at 378–79 (Breyer, J., dissenting).

[125] Sanchez-Llamas v. Oregon, 548 US at 393 (Breyer, J., dissenting).

consensus but to push the boundaries of rights talk into novel and highly contested policy areas. Engaging questions not only about *whether* international human rights norms are relevant but *why* they should be so considered can enhance the chances for parties to engage with one another's arguments. If one participant in the debate is focused exclusively on international norms as binding law, while another participant is focused on other kinds of reasons for relying on international norms, for instance, there is a significant risk that the parties will end up talking past one another.

It is worth stressing that my motivation in pressing on questions regarding the role of international human rights in domestic discourse is not to suggest that its role is excessive or ought to be curtailed. Indeed, though a full-throated defense of the proposition is beyond the present scope, I believe that international human rights can serve a crucial function in offering a language for expressing the idea that even officially enacted or democratically endorsed policies may violate fundamental freedoms. If this is true, however, it provides even stronger reason to call for articulating the ways that international human rights can support particular arguments. Failure to address why anyone ought to consider international human rights norms as having a rightful place in the discussion can hinder attempts to imbue them with a meaningful role in public discourse. Reliance on foreign law in Supreme Court opinions interpreting constitutional rights provides an illustration. In a series of international opinions, a number of justices appealed to international norms without offering a cogent line of justification to ground their pertinence within the arguments they were advancing. As discussed earlier, the bulk of the opinions in which justices have referenced international sources in constitutional interpretation have assumed that an accounting of prevalent practices was relevant to determining whether a challenged punishment violated the Eighth Amendment's prohibition on cruel and unusual punishments. Regardless of one's view on the merits of this initial move in Eighth Amendment jurisprudence, however, it is a fair question why the analysis of evolving societal values should include sources meant to capture trends in such attitudes outside the United States. The justices who wrote these opinions, however, did little by way of even attempting to justify consideration of foreign law in constitutional rights cases. Many simply note that earlier opinions did so – with Chief Justice Warren's opinion in *Trop v. Dulles* treated as the launching point for this proposition. The small number of cases that might be seen as beginning to offer a justification, upon closer examination, have not offered anything of substance. Justice Kennedy's comment in *Roper*, for instance, that the "opinion of the world community" provided "respected and significant confirmation for our own conclusions" seemed if anything to suggest that the international references were superfluous. The references to foreign law simply did not explain how they were supposed to work as support for a position. Was the mere fact that a particular practice is common around the world (or in certain countries) in itself mean to count as a reason? It is not clear why this would be the case, nor could such an approach readily be applied on a consistent basis since there are long-cherished principles of American law – such as the exclusionary rule – which are quite unusual on a global scale. Perhaps the justification for citing foreign practices lies in the substantive reasoning that underlies them. From such a perspective, it would not be the fact that foreign jurisdictions adopted particular practices that would be important in itself; rather, the justices would find useful and persuasive arguments in foreign sources. *Graham* seemed to suggest something like this in stating that the Court "has treated the laws and practices of other nations and international agreements as relevant to the Eighth Amendment... because [they] demonstrate[] that the Court's rationale has respected reasoning to support it." Moreover, some members of the Court – including Justices O'Connor, Ginsburg, and Breyer – in their work off the bench have appealed to reasons relating to the value of cross-national dialogue and openness to new ideas. Such rationales may be appealing in principle, but in neither *Graham* nor any other Eighth Amendment decision has the Court actually discussed the reasoning underlying foreign decisions or practices. There may well be powerful justifications for judicial reliance on foreign law in constitutional rights cases; the discussion above is not meant to advance a view on that question. Rather, the point here is that the justices' failure to provide a rationale may undermine their role by reinforcing an impression held by some that references to international sources generally are ultimately rooted in nothing more than particular judges' own personal predilections. More broadly, the point here is that appeals to international human rights norm in the context of American decision making may be bolstered by attention to the questions that such appeals plainly bring to the fore.

This chapter has focused on the specific context of Supreme Court decision making, which is of vital importance in itself. However, the discussion's broader purpose has been to shine a spotlight on a set of questions that may too easily be shunted off stage. It is natural and understandable for parties contesting particular issues to be centrally concerned with the policy outcomes within those issue areas. As a result, though, it is too easy to overlook the significance of questions about the basis for the arguments advanced in support of specific positions. The term "international human rights" is so connotatively powerful that its appeal may seem irresistible as a basis for social and political change. Given the nature of contemporary international human rights norms – especially their tendency to address and engage with highly disputed policy questions – participants in ongoing debates over national and local polices are justified in asking why these norms are relevant to American decision making. Seeking more fully developed responses to such questions may not only clarify the nature of our reasons but also enhance the force of arguments for taking seriously the implications of principles developed within the arena of international human rights law.

Afterword: Instrumental Human Rights

William S. Brewbaker III

In his contribution to the present volume, Stephen Simon offers a helpful twofold definition of human rights: human rights, he says, are sometimes "moral claims" – "aspirational ideals" that operate under a model of persuasion. Such claims have force because they persuade us to consider a practice as violative of obligations we owe to other human beings merely by virtue of their being human. In the alternative, human rights can may refer to a body of legal norms that operate under what Simon calls a model of compliance. Such norms are universal in that we are obligated to follow them whether we agree with them or not, because of larger claims about political authority.

In either case, to say that a person's human rights are being violated is to draw attention to the *seriousness* of the actions being complained about and the *absoluteness* of the entitlements at issue. In most understandings of rights, if I truly have a *right*, either in law or morality, my right is not to be balanced against the greater good that might be achieved by failing to honor it. (Indeed, relative disregard of the common good is one reason for complaints about "rights talk."[1]) When rights are recognized, they are powerful, either rhetorically or legally, and sometimes both.

This is familiar ground to lawyers and law students. Lawyers and other advocates are only too happy to frame moral and legal claims in terms of rights. Indeed, lawyers are trained to frame their arguments in terms of legal rights – to *use* rights as instruments to get results for their clients.

And yet, as accustomed as a law professor should be to the enterprise of using rights to secure desired outcomes, I couldn't help but be struck by one of the central assumptions underlying the discussion of international human rights in the preceding chapters. Beginning with the proposition that there is plenty of injustice in American society (a proposition from which few would dissent), activists

---

[1] See Mary Ann Glendon, *Rights Talk: The Impoverishment of Political Discourse* (New York: Free Press, 1991), 109–44.

rightly wonder whether our general situation might be better if we could deploy the persuasive rhetoric of international human rights and the compulsory force of international law to alter some of the decisions being made by local, state, and federal government officials. What stands out about this completely understandable reaction to injustice is that human rights are treated mainly as *instruments* we might be able to use to solve important problems.

I thus organize this brief commentary around the theme of *instrumental human rights*. I want to be clear that I am not criticizing human rights scholars and practitioners who are trying to make the world better and whom I generally (and genuinely) admire. Nevertheless, it seems to me that an instrumental approach to questions of international human rights, as inevitable as it may be, raises questions that may not be present with more ordinary moral or legal claims.

Erika George's fine contribution provides an opportune point of departure. She asks whether international human rights norms might fill in to assist communities of color seeking environmental justice, given that domestic law precludes liability in the absence of intentional discrimination. The problem is pressing; domestic legal remedies are largely absent. Might international norms provide some relief?

One of the things George teaches us is that international human rights law must be *made* before it can be *used*. Opponents of environmental racism initially could not even rely on a preexisting body of moral human rights norms requiring environmental justice. The moral spadework had to be done first – drawing attention to the concrete problems faced by people of color disproportionately affected by private siting decisions and government environmental policies, and then drawing a connection between these harms and other, more clearly recognized moral and policy norms: concern over environmental degradation, recognition of the value of every human life, and the grievous wrong of pervasive racial discrimination. The latter two moral concerns are frequently expressed in terms of individual and group *rights*. Proponents of environmental human rights were thus able to characterize environmental justice as a human rights issue.

It still remained to take the next step and to develop an enforceable legal obligation on the part of states to pursue environmental justice. Professor George suggests that this step may by now have been taken. I defer to her superior knowledge, but I confess I am not so sure. If she is correct – if, for example, the Mossville petition[2] is ultimately the basis for a grant of relief – it will be a monument to decades of tireless work.

Cynthia Soohoo's chapter likewise fits squarely into the *instrumental human rights* mold. She begins by conceding that, "for the most part, the United States's human rights obligations cannot be directly enforced in US courts." The silver lining, however, is that the lack of enforceable legal norms leaves the contours of purported human rights up for grabs in a way that "creates opportunities for

---

[2] See Chapter 2.

social justice activists." The public is "for" human rights; the term can be used to "provoke the listener to consider an issue in a different way." The payoff is that if the listener can be persuaded, the argued-for right will be seen as "ha[ving] some fundamental character rooted in human dignity that requires universal respect." It can then be "leveraged" in debates to change *domestic* laws and policies, or even to provoke change short of legislation. An especially promising use for human rights rhetoric, she argues, is to encourage the generation of new constitutional norms or "to encourage more progressive interpretations of recognized constitutional rights." Recall my earlier suggestion that proposals framed as implicating universal human rights are generally seen as more *absolute* and more *serious* than proposals that cannot claim that status. Soohoo urges her readers to capitalize on that fact.

From there, Soohoo provides a fascinating and astute analysis of when human rights–based claims are likely to be effective. I confess that I got a little queasy seeing how the human-rights sausage gets made: "Activists and government officials serve as intermediaries both by importing international human rights standards into local contexts and helping to build and reshape global dialogue and understandings of rights based on their contexts." They help build the case for a human rights norm, help get the norm recognized by an official acting under color of international law, then deploy the norm to force action on the part of a state, local, or national government. (I also confess I felt better about all this before I learned that the two United Nations Special Rapporteurs whose reports play important roles in George and Sokol's contributions to this book are law professors at Wake Forest and American University, respectively.[3] Far be it from me to cast aspersions on fellow law professors, especially those as distinguished as the two I have just mentioned.[4] Still, I confess I had hoped for a bit more psychic distance between me and the diviners of universal legal obligations!) Again, however, one cannot help but be inspired by the good work that helps get youth out of extended solitary confinement and that may yet help our system show bit more mercy toward juvenile offenders.

David Sloss's creative and elegant proposal to use human rights law to bring coherence to incorporation doctrine is likewise arguably instrumental but in a more modest way. To be sure, allowing the provisions of the International Covenant on Civil and Political Rights, and perhaps the Universal Declaration of Human Rights, to help specify the constitutional rights incorporated as against the states under the Fourteenth Amendment would have follow-on consequences – consequences that Sloss finds attractive. These consequences go beyond generating the merely aesthetic pleasure that legal theorists might derive from the coherence his proposal

---

[3] Juan Mendez, the United Nations Special Rapporteur on Torture, is Professor of Human Rights Law in Residence as Washington College of Law, American University. John H. Knox, the United Nations Special Rapporteur on Human Rights and the Environment, is Henry C. Lauerman Professor of International Law at Wake Forest University School of Law.

[4] Indeed, Mendez was detained and tortured in Argentina as a direct result of his courageous human rights legal advocacy.

would arguably bring to Fourteenth Amendment jurisprudence. Judicial discretion would be limited; states would be freed from the exclusionary rule, the jury trial right, and Second Amendment obligations; the balance between federal and state authority would be struck, by Sloss's lights, in a more attractive way.

Significantly, however, Sloss's proposal does not appear to trade on the independent moral force of international human rights norms. Rather than invoking the absoluteness and seriousness of human rights norms, Sloss's proposal trades on them as a fixed convention that could limit federal judges' discretion to impose greater burdens on the states. Strikingly, his proposal invokes "human rights" in a way that would result in more limited "human rights" enforcement against the states than currently exists. Not only that, his "silent incorporation" thesis further distances him from a fully instrumental approach to international human rights law.

Stephen Simon's paper invites reflection on a question that is notably absent from instrumental accounts of international human rights law – the vexing question of their authority. Why, he wonders, do international human rights matter in American decision making? On what grounds do they rest?

Years ago, in an article titled "Unspeakable Ethics, Unnatural Law," Arthur Allen Leff argued that "the so-called death of God turns out not to have been just *His* funeral; it also seems to have effected the total elimination of any coherent, or even more-than-momentarily convincing, ethical or legal system depending upon finally authoritative extrasystemic premises."[5] "Who cares," Leff might ask, "what the UN says about 'human rights'?" Whose vision of human rights do the UN documents articulate? On what basis are they picking and choosing? How will the grand terms be operationalized? Leff puts the question slightly differently elsewhere in the article: "[W]hen would it be impermissible to make the formal intellectual equivalent of what is known in barrooms and schoolyards as 'the grand sez who'?"[6]

My point is not to join the debate over whether human rights require the existence of God. Leff seems to think so, although he wasn't sure God existed.[7] Hugo Grotius, the father of international law, was sure God existed but not sure his existence was necessary to the existence of natural law.[8]

Regardless, small wonder – as Simon notes – that the American emphasis on popular sovereignty engendered resistance to the legal implementation of norms developed outside politically accountable channels – e.g., by international bodies.

It seems to me that Simon's description of sovereigntism and its reliance on "popular sovereignty" may be overstated. The concrete structure of the Constitution, I would argue, suggests as much. That structure – put into place by "the consent of the governed" – is less than fully committed to popular sovereignty: the most representative body in our republican federal government cannot enact law without

---

[5] Arthur Allen Leff, "Unspeakable Ethics, Unnatural Law," *Duke Law Journal* 1979 (1979): 1232.
[6] Id. at 1230.   [7] See id. at 1249 ("All I can say is this: it looks as if we are all we have").
[8] See Hugo Grotius, *On the Law of War and Peace* (1625), Prolegomena §11.

the concurrence of the other body, in which the states, not the population at large, are mainly represented; the president can veto legislation approved by both houses; Congress and the president cannot unite to enact laws in violation of the limitations set by the Constitution. Provided it relate to appropriate subject matter, federal law trumps the will of local majorities expressed through state and local popularly elected governments. And, of great significance for present purposes, a duly executed and ratified treaty has the status of a federal statute (provided it be self-executing), even though the approval of the House of Representatives is not required. Moreover, as a practical matter, congressional enactments are usually underdetermined and thus require elaboration by courts and regulatory agencies. Such decisions reflect moral and policy judgments not far removed from those invoked by the internationalists. Sovereigntism, it appears, has its limits.

Nevertheless, Simon is entirely right to draw attention to the questions of authority raised by international human rights norms, which purport to bind and exist independently of whether any government recognizes them, and collide with the concrete laws that a legal system, especially a democratic one, generates. Allow me to quote Arthur Allen Leff for a final time:

> As things now stand,
> everything is up for grabs.
> Nevertheless:
> Napalming babies is bad.
> Starving the poor is wicked.
> Buying and selling each other is depraved.
> Those who stood up to and died resisting Hitler, Stalin, Amin, and Pol Pot – and General Custer too – have earned salvation.
> Those who acquiesced deserve to be damned.
> There is in the world such a thing as evil.[9]

Leff follows this momentarily hopeful note with a call for a "Sez Who?" on the part of his audience. "God help us," he concludes.[10]

What has all this to do with a view of human rights as *instrumental*? As stated previously, one can't help but applaud the efforts of human rights activists to make the world better, and I don't blame them for using whatever tools they find available – including international human rights norms, moral and legal – to attempt to do that.

My fear, however, is that the more widely such norms are invoked, the more the *authority* and *seriousness* associated with human rights claims – and that make human rights law and rhetoric effective as a source of positive change – will be whittled away. I'm tempted to say that there is a limited pool of human rights capital, which we usually deplete when we trade on human rights claims. The more specific and concrete, and the less generally accepted, the norms we ascribe to

---

[9] Leff, "Unspeakable Ethics," 1249.   [10] Id.

international, universal human rights, it seems to me, the larger the depletion of this pool. In other words, our gains may often come at a long-term cost.

Although it has been said that "friends do not call friends natural law lawyers,"[11] I think we can learn something from the classical natural law tradition on this point. One of the things that is particularly surprising about the tradition is how modest it is about the norms natural law provides. Thomas Aquinas, writing in the thirteenth century, and certainly not timid in his assertion of the presence of a God-given natural order in the world and the human ability to discern it, was surprisingly careful to limit the norms he was willing to attribute to direct derivation from natural law.

In Thomas's system, the primary principles of the natural law were relatively few, and their relationship to positive law is usually rather indirect:

> something may be derived from the natural law in two ways: first, as a conclusion from premises, secondly, by way of determination of certain generalities. The first way is like to that by which, in sciences, demonstrated conclusions are drawn from the principles: while the second mode is likened to that whereby, in the arts, general forms are particularized as to details: thus the craftsman needs to determine the general form of a house to some particular shape. Some things are therefore derived from the general principles of the natural law, by way of conclusions; e.g. that "one must not kill" may be derived as a conclusion from the principle that "one should do harm to no man": while some are derived therefrom by way of determination; e.g. the law of nature has it that the evil-doer should be punished; but that he be punished in this or that way, is a determination of the law of nature.
>
> Accordingly both modes of derivation are found in the human law. But those things which are derived in the first way, are contained in human law not as emanating therefrom exclusively, but have some force from the natural law also. But those things which are derived in the second way, have no other force than that of human law.[12]

Thomas is warning against claiming too much "natural law" authority for most human law. Human law is contextual; it is the result of the application of reason (understood by Thomas as having moral as well as intellectual content), but human officials can and regularly do get it wrong. Elsewhere he says that while natural law cannot be abolished from the hearts of human beings, whole societies can run off the rails and cast deep darkness over moral principles that should otherwise have been obvious.[13]

So we are left with a dilemma. On one hand, international human rights law inevitably seems to trade on something very much like natural law. It gets our attention precisely because of its claims to universality, but, it appears, the number

---

[11] Patrick H. Martin, "Natural Law: Voegelin and the End of [Legal] Philosophy," *Louisiana Law Review* 62 (2002): 879.
[12] Thomas Aquinas, *Summa Theologiae*, IaIIae Q. 95.2.   [13] Id. at Q. 94.6.

of legal principles we are entitled to attribute to the direct force of natural rights is smaller than most of us would like.

I'm further tempted to suggest, then, that we might keep our human rights powder dry for just the sorts of situations that Leff finds universally acknowledged to be evil – lest we find ourselves on the receiving end of the grand "sez who" when the worst crises arise, and we most need the rhetorical and legal force of human rights claims. On the other hand, international human rights discourse as we know it is already under pressure from nationalist movements in some Western countries and from increasing awareness of its particularity and even its simultaneous indebtedness to conflicting strains of thought.[14] Perhaps, then, my suggestion is ill advised and we should take advantage of international human rights talk while we can. It may even be true that visible successes achieved under the banner of international human rights discourse will enhance its prestige and thus extend its life-span.

The last thing we might learn from the natural law tradition may give us some hope, however. The tradition holds that natural law is not just a legal theory but rather a *fact* about human nature. Whatever contingent obstacles and blindnesses human beings face, there are some things that people "can't not know."[15] Alongside the world's (and our own) intractable evil, there is within the human heart an inherent, perpetual ground for appeals to justice, regardless of the ultimate fate of a discourse of international human rights.

---

[14] See, e.g., Mark L. Movsesian, "Of Human Dignities," *Notre Dame Law Review* 91 (2016): 1517.

[15] J. Budziszewski, *The Revenge of Conscience: Politics and the Fall of Man* (Dallas, TX: Spence, 1999), 25.

Index

Action Plan to Reduce Racial Ethnic Asthma Disparities, 72
activism
 criteria for, 8
 targets for, 8
activists, 17–19
Adamson v. California, 81–82, 83, 94
Administration of Juvenile Justice (1985), 36
African Charter on Human and Peoples' Rights, 56–57
Agenda 21, 68
Aguilar v. Texas, 85, 86
Alexander v. Sandoval, 63, 64
Alien Tort Statute, 111–15
Alito, Samuel, 118
American Civil Liberties Union (ACLU), 18, 25, 37
Apprendi v. New Jersey, 98
Articles of War, 117
Atkins v. Virginia, 120
Authorization for Use of Military Force (AUMF), 115

Barron v. Baltimore, 82–83
Basu, Amrita, 4–5
Baton Rouge, Louisiana, 51
Benton v. Maryland, 85, 86, 87
Betts v. Brady, 88, 91–92
Bill of Rights, 76, 77, 80, 84, 96
Board of Corrections, 32
Boxed In, 25
Branded for Life, 37
Breard v. Greene, 109
Breyer, Stephen, 11, 108–09, 110, 111, 115
Bricker, John W., 4
Bricker Amendment, 92–93

Brooklyn Defender Services, 40
Brown v. Board of Education, 90, 92–93
Bush, George W., administration of, 4, 115, 116

Campaign for Alternatives to Isolated Confinement, 18
Campaign for Youth Justice (CFYJ), 39
Cancer Alley, 46, 48
Center for Constitutional Rights (CCR), 18
Center for Reproductive Rights, 18
Chavis, Benjamin, Jr., 48
children, right to special protection, 35–36
children's rights
 age as human rights issue, 37–38
 federal involvement in, 38–39
 human rights bodies/experts, 37–38
 in New York, 39–42
 reports, 37
 conflict with law and, 32–42
 criminal justice system and, 33–35
 international human rights standards and, 35–37
 prevention of torture/CIDT and, 36
 prosecution in adult court and, 37
Civil Rights Act of 1964, 63
Clean Air Act, 74
Clinton, Bill, 2, 70
Coliseum Square Association v. HUD, 71
Committee on the Elimination of Racial Discrimination (CERD Committee), 9, 38, 67–68, 69–74
 Agenda 21, 68
 comments and observations, 73–74
 US representations, 69–70
 World Summit on Sustainable Development statement, 68

139

Communities against Runway Expansion Inc. v. FAA, 72
Convention against Torture, 23, 26, 28, 103
Convention on the Elimination of All Forms of Discrimination against Women (CEDAW), 102
Convention on the Elimination of All Forms of Racial Discrimination (CERD), 26, 65, 103
　Article 5, 67–68
　US equal protection obligations, 66–69
Convention on the Rights of the Child (CRC), 7, 35–36, 102, 120
　Article 40(3), 36
　New York laws and, 40
Correctional Association of New York, 38
Covenant on Erasing Racial Discrimination (CERD), 9
cruel, inhuman, and degrading treatment (CIDT), 22, 36

Declaration of Independence, 124
democracy, 4–5
Department of Corrections, 32
discriminatory intent, 60–62
disparate impact, 60–62
Douglass, Frederick, 6
Draft Principles on Human Rights and the Environment, 57–58
due process clause, 77, 81, 87
Duncan v. Louisiana, 85, 87, 95–96, 97, 98

East-Bibb Twiggs Neighborhood Association v. Macon-Bibb Planning and Zoning Commission, 62
Edwards v. South Carolina, 85, 86
Eighth Amendment, 34, 76, 80, 83, 119
environmental injustice, 46
environmental justice, 46–75
　definition of, 53
　international human rights and, 54–60
　international human rights institutions and, 65–75
　　CERD and equal protection obligations, 66–69
　　CERD Committee, 69–74
　　Inter-American Commission on Human Rights, 74–75
　　international law, 65–66
　movements, 53
　racism and, 48–53
　US judgments and, 60–64
　　discriminatory intent, 60–62

　　disparate impact, 60–62
　　equal protection, 60–62
　　intentional inequality, 62–64
Environmental Justice Collaborative Problem-Solving Cooperative Agreements Program Agreements, 71
Environmental Justice Community Intern Program, 71
Environmental Protection Agency (EPA), 53, 70–71
environmental racism, 48–53
　communities of color and, 49–50
　criticism of, 50
　criticisms of, 53
　distribution of risks of environmental harm, 51–52
　early cases of, 50–51
　factors in, 49
　initial framing and naming of, 48–49
　intentional discrimination in, 53
Environmental Small Grant Program, 71
Erie Railroad v. Tompkin, 113, 114
European Court of Human Rights (ECtHR), 104, 121
excessive fines clause, 85

Fairman, Charles, 83, 91
Federal Interagency Working Group on Environmental Justice, 71, 72–75
federalism, 19–20
　human rights theory and, 97–99
　incorporation doctrine and, 78–79
　selective incorporation and, 94–99
Fifth Amendment, 80, 81, 82, 84, 86
Filártiga v. Peña-Irala, 112
First Amendment, 80
Flint, Michigan, 52
Fourteenth Amendment, 10, 34, 77, 78, 79, 87, 90, 93
Fourth Amendment, 76, 80
Francis, Pope, 29

Gabčíkovo-Nagymaros case, 56
Geneva Conventions, 116, 118
Genocide Convention, 4
Gideon v. Wainwright, 85, 86, 91–92
globalization, 5
Governor's Commission on Youth, Public Safety, and Justice (New York), 40–41
Graham v. Florida, 34, 120, 129
grand jury clause, 84, 86
Grotius, Hugo, 134
Growing Up Locked Down, 25–26, 37
Guantánamo Bay, 115

Index

Hague Declaration on the Environment (1989), 9, 55–56
Hamdan, Salem Ahmed, 117–18
Hamdan v. Rumsfeld, 116–19, 123
Hanes, Melodee, 38
Horowitz, Morton, 3
human rights
    incorporation doctrine and, 78–79
    instrumental, 131–37
    selective incorporation and, 94–99
human rights advocacy, 14–20
    factors in, 15–17
    federalism and, 19–20
    government levels and, 19–20
    role of activists in, 17–19
human rights claims, 15
Human Rights Council (HRC), 58–59
human rights theory, 83–94
    comparison with precedents, 86–88
    definition of, 80
    federalism and, 97–99
    overview, 10
    selective incorporation and, 84–85, 96
Human Rights Watch, 25, 37

immutable principles of justice test, 96
In re Oliver, 86
incorporation doctrine, 76–99
    consequences of, 77
    federalism and, 78–79
    human rights and, 78–79
    human rights theory and, 83–94
    precursors before 1948, 80–83
    principled rationale for, 94–97
    selective incorporation, 79
    Supreme Court's development of, 77
Independent Expert on Human Rights and the Environment, 58–59, 67
instrumental human rights, 131–37
Inter-American Commission on Human Rights, 37, 57, 74
International Bill of Rights, 54, 77–78, 83, 86, 89, 91, 92, 96–97
International Court of Justice, 110, 111, 126
International Covenant on Civil and Political Rights (ICCPR), 9, 23, 26, 28, 35–36, 38, 54, 65, 77, 101
International Covenant on Economic, Social, and Cultural Rights (ICESCR), 54, 78, 101
international environmental human rights, 54–60
international human rights, 100–29
    Alien Tort Statute, 111–15
    core rights and, 103–05
    Court's jurisprudence, 121–29

    internationalist, 125–29
    sovereigntist, 121–29
    domestic force of treaties, 107–11, 123–24
    domestic law and, 101, 102–03
    domestic role of, 105–06
    foreign law in constitutional interpretation, 119–21
    military commissions and, 115–19
    overview, 100–01
    selective incorporation and, 88–94
international humanitarian law, 116
internationalists, 11, 125–29
Irvin v. Dowd, 85, 86

Kennedy, John F., administration of, 120
Kiobel v. Royal Dutch Petroleum, 113, 114–15, 123, 127
Klopfer v. North Carolina, 85, 86
Knox, John, 58
Ksentini, Fatma Zohra, 57

Lau v. Nichols, 63
law of war, 116
Lawrence v. Texas, 120–21, 127
Leff, Arthur, 134, 135
local governments, 19–20
Lochner era, 81
Los Angeles County, 50
Loving v. Virginia, 90

Malloy v. Hogan, 85, 86, 87
Mandela Rules, 24, 27
Mapp v. Ohio, 85, 87, 97
Marshall, Thurgood, 93
Marxism, 4–5
McDonald v. City of Chicago, 95–96, 97
Medellín v. Texas, 107, 110, 123, 126–27
Mendez, Juan, 23, 24, 27–29, 30, 31
Merry, Sally, 15–16
military commissions, 115–19
Miller, Alice, 17
Miller v. Alabama, 34
Mossville, Louisiana, 74
Mossville Environmental Action Now, 74

National Association for the Advancement of Colored People (NAACP), 6
National Association of Social Workers, 40
National Center for Homelessness and Poverty, 18
National Environmental Justice Advisory Council, 71
National Environmental Policy Act (NEPA), 63, 71–72

National Task Force on Children Exposed to Violence, 38
New York, raising age as human rights issue in, 39–42
New York City Bar Association, 30
New York Civil Liberties Union (NYCLU), 25, 31
Nuremberg Tribunals, 101, 103

Obama, Barack, 1, 8, 29, 72
O'Donnell, Danny, 31
Office of Juvenile Justice and Delinquency Prevention, 15, 38

Palko v. Connecticut, 81, 88–89, 91
Partnership for Sustainable Communities, 72
Pelican Bay State Prison, 28
Pointer v. Texas, 85, 86
Powell v. Alabama, 81
Prison Rape Elimination Act (PREA), 38, 39
Prisoners Legal Services, 31
Protection of the Juvenile Deprived of Their Liberty (1990), 36

racial discrimination, 66–67
racism, environmental, 48–53
 communities of color and, 49–50
 criticism of, 50
 criticisms of, 53
 distribution of risks of environmental harm, 51–52
 early cases of, 50–51
 factors in, 49
 initial framing and naming of, 48–49
 intentional discrimination in, 53
Raise the Age Campaign, 14, 18, 38, 41
Rehnquist, William, 121
Rikers Island, 40, 41
Ring v. Arizona, 98
RISE Inc. v. Kay, 62–63, 71
Roberts, John, 11, 108–09, 111, 115, 123
Robinson v. California, 85, 87, 90
Roosevelt, Franklin, administration of, 117
Roper v. Simmons, 34, 120, 121, 128

San Salvador Protocol, 57
Sanchez-Lllamas v. Oregon, 11, 107, 108–09, 110, 123, 125
Scalia, Antonin, 2, 118, 121, 123
Schilb v. Kuebel, 85
Schmidt, Hans Peter, 15
Second Amendment, 80
selective incorporation, 79, 84–85. *See also* incorporation doctrine
 federalism and, 94–99
 human rights and, 94–99
 international human rights and, 88–94
Senate Subcommittee on the Constitution, Civil Rights and Human Rights, 28
Senville v. Peters, 72
September 11 attacks (2001), 4
Seventh Amendment, 84
Sierra Club, 74
Sikkink, Kathryn, 15, 17
Sixth Amendment, 76, 80, 81
slavery, 6
social movements, 6–7
solitary confinement, 20–32
 children in, 23–24
 history of, 20–22
 as a human rights issue, 25–28
  advocacy before international human rights bodies/experts, 26–28
  federal acceptance of, 28–29
  in New York, 29–32
  reports, 25–26
 international human rights standards on, 22–25
  civil society's involvement in, 24
  government officials' involvement in, 24
  persons with mental disabilities in, 23–24
Sosa v. Alvarez-Machain, 113–14, 123
South Bronx Coalition for Clean Air Inc. v. Conroy, 63
South Camden Citizens in Action v. New Jersey Department of Environmental Protection, 64
sovereigntists, 11, 122–25, 134–35
Special Rapporteur on Human Rights and the Environment, 9, 57
Special Rapporteur on Torture, 23, 24
Standing Rock Sioux, 52
state governments, 19–20
Stevens, John Paul, 118
Stockholm Declaration on the Human Environment (1972), 9, 54–55
 preamble, 54–55
 Principle 1, 55
Subra, Wilma, 48
Supreme Court decision making, 10

Third Amendment, 80, 84, 85
Thomas, Clarence, 118, 121, 123
Thomas Aquinas, 136
Thompson v. Oklahoma, 120, 121
torture, 17, 22, 36
Trop v. Dulles, 119, 128
Truman, Harry, administration of, 3
Trump, Donald, 76
Twining v. New Jersey, 82

Index

UN Charter, 111
UN Commission on Human Rights, 6
UN Committee Against Torture, 27, 31, 38
UN Committee on the Rights of the Child, 22
UN Human Rights Committee, 22
UN Rules for the Protection of Juveniles Deprived of Their Liberty, 22
UN Standard Minimum Rules for the Treatment of Prisoners, 24, 27
Uniform Code of Military Justice (UCMJ), 117
United Church of Christ, 48–49
United Church of Christ Commission for Racial Justice, 48
Universal Church of Christ, 8
Universal Declaration of Human Rights, 5, 10, 54, 76–77, 83, 101, 105
US Commission on Civil Rights, 30
US Human Rights Network, 18

Vienna Convention on Consular Relations (VCCR), 11, 108, 110, 125
Village of Arlington Heights v. Metropolitan Housing Development Corp., 61

Warren, Earl, 119
Warren County, North Carolina, 50
Warren Court, 79
Washington County v. Department of Navy, 71, 72
Washington v. Davis, 9, 60–61
Washington v. Texas, 85, 86
Weeramantry, C. G., 56
Wilson, Richard, 4
Wolf v. Colorado, 85, 86
women's rights, 17
World Summit on Sustainable Development, 68

youth justice, 32–42
    age as human rights issue in, 37–38
    federal involvement in, 38–39
    human rights bodies/experts, 37–38
    in New York, 39–42
    reports, 37
history of, 33–35
international human rights standards on, 35–37
prevention of torture and CIDT, 36
prosecution in adult court, 37